MAHA BHARATA

Relevance and Application in Contemporary Thought

Bharat Thakker

गरुड

Published by
Garuda Prakashan Private Limited
Gurugram, Bharat

www.garudabooks.com

First published in India 2023

ISBN: 979-8-8857-5055-4

Printed in India

To my wife, Smita, for her tireless patience and constant support.

Intent of this Book

MAHABHARATA can be different things to different people and many things to some people. As a child, it was a story of kings, princes and princesses, demons, wars, opulent palaces etc. that made fascinating reading. TV serials on the Epic showed humans interacting with monkeys, snakes, firing off multi-headed arrows more powerful than any missile known to man from a single bow and other visualisations. The diverse efforts, of so many, have kept alive the interest in the Epic. It is the longest poem ever known to man.

Creation of our Universe is credited to unexplained phenomena. For human civilisation to survive and prosper, several different social orders continue to be created. Every order has a Personal Code for creation of the Universe to co-exist. Such a Personal Code created under the leadership of its social order needs adherence and a concept of reward and punishment was introduced mainly in the form of Heaven and Hell. Believers of all faith suggest that the ultimate goal of life is Moksha or Salvation. Help in the form of guidance from others in achieving this goal is like taking tuitions. Each of us has to travel this path alone and we need to do so based on introspection and analysis.

Humans not only need a role model; we need guidance, acknowledgement, appreciation, recognition, motivation and deterrence. The concept of heaven and hell and punishment by law all focus on what not to do.

The events and surrounding circumstances in the Mahabharata provide us with guidance relevant to our personal conduct, business, social and political lives and focus on what to do. Life stops when we stop. The Epic deals with Dharma, which is an obligation to self, family, society, country, occupation, era and time. It also deals with important aspects of life like Itihas, Kula, Parampara and Sanskar. Several fundamental principles of modern law are embedded in the Epic with the events providing the substance for the principles involved. Many of us have been to discourses on Dharma, Karma, Salvation, Redemption, God, Hell, Heaven, and the need to achieve Moksha or Salvation; essentially we are seeking peace of mind. This book will provoke your mind to provide an impetus for action based on realisation. When we believe in what we do, we overcome conflict and achieve peace of mind.

CONTENTS

PART-B
Mahabharata: The Great Epic

Part-A

Introduction

CHAPTER 1

Introduction to the MAHABHARATA

Krishna Dvaipayana, also known as Ved Vyas, composed the Mahabharata about 5,000 years ago in verses. Often referred to as the fifth Veda, it is recited either as a poem or played on the stage. Vedas are the oldest scriptures that deal with the Sanatan way of life. The story revolves around two groups of cousins of a royal household, involved in a bitter dispute of succession. Scholars date the Mahabharata to about 3,200 BCE.

The Epic is based around a pan-India settlement, focusing on the so-called Indo-Aryans, their culture and society. It details how kings govern their subjects and how they influence culture. It acknowledges the diversity of race, colour and cultures and their inter-action with other communities, often referred to as serpents or nagas, demons or rakshas or as vanars.

Every event in the Epic comes with a comprehensive background. The characterization is detailed, often originating in a past life. The story of an individual may begin from his previous birth and may end upon this death or may continue even beyond. Some episodes involve many characters in a single event, adding to its complexity, together with a narrative of their pain, love, suffering and attachment. It unravels their financial conditions, upbringing and social background and how these influence their behaviour.

The purpose of the Epic is to help us follow the rules of Dharma, a set of moral and social laws by which a person is bound. The author wrote the Mahabharata to bring out the significance of the Vedas, necessitating their dramatization, projecting larger-than-life characters, to convey its wisdom in the form of plays or folklore.

The Epic aimed to educate even those who could not study the Vedas, basing Dharma on examples. This has helped sustain interest in the Mahabharata until the present day. The authors dramatized the core message with the sudden materialization of a god or a celestial being. The divine intervention facilitated the move between acts.

Characters may have a divine or an undivine aura to help convey the teachings of the Vedas and of Dharma. Together they create a single reference book of what is right or wrong in the individual context and situation. Good guys are not always good, nor are the bad guys always bad. This is often perplexing as it introduces us to grey shades.

In the Indic Way of Life, we do not judge an individual; we judge his actions, because he is not always regarded as evil. His actions may be right or wrong, depending on several factors. The authors of the Mahabharata have conveyed this reality through several episodes. They have described the motivations and the circumstances of characters which predispose them to act in certain ways, through which they explain the concept of Dharma.

The Epic initially comprised 8,400 verses, but expanded to 100,000 verses, resulting from later additions. Many individuals memorized the epic down the ages, adding their own interpretations of events and episodes, which helped reinforce or elaborate its central theme to connect with the listener/reader. These nuances also reflect the social customs, culture and folklore specific to a region. These also represent the prevailing views of society when the additions were made during successive phases ever since the Epic was first composed centuries ago. Although several versions exist, the basic story remained unchanged.

There are several versions of the Mahabharata. One version does not include the *Bhagwad Gita*. Bards carried these versions orally over many centuries, but now they are available in written form. The Pune-based Bhandarkar Oriental Research Institute undertook an examination of the different versions and published a unified narrative, known as the critical edition. Their study showed that reciters/enactors added many local nuances to existing versions to help preserve the interest in the Epic. Lately, the Epic has also been appropriated by the entertainment channels. A number of authors have narrated the story in their own style, highlighting certain perspectives to connect with the readers.

The Epic incorporates the Bhagwad Gita comprising some 700 verses, rich in meaning and content with multiple layers. The discourses of thinkers and preachers have mesmerised listeners. Fathom then the power that must be there in the 100,000 verses that make up the entire Mahabharata.

CHAPTER 2

Hindu Way of Life, Modern Religion and Rituals

The principles of Dharma guide Hindus in their way of living. But when viewed in the modern context, it is difficult to understand. Modern society follows a binary principle. A Rule is or not followed, a person is right or wrong; truthful or deceitful. A jury can make a judgement looking at the grey, but we mostly look at things as either black or white.

Dharma in the Hindu way of Life depends on the context. It deals with our obligations, responsibilities, or duties. We owe this to ourselves and to our families, friends, society, country and occupation. We need to fulfil our Dharma in order to support evolution and all living beings. Hindus must pursue Dharma without exception as it keeps the wheels of civilisation moving. Adharma arises when an individual does not fulfil his obligations. The world will function in the intended way only when every person fulfills his Dharma. This idea radically differs from the concept of sin or sacrifice, both of which require a person to act.

Abrahamic religions have dominated civilisation for many centuries, influencing modern thinking and society. These religious systems believe there is only one life and that the soul does not leave the body to take another, whereas the Hindus believe in re-incarnation. An individual is right or wrong, unlike the *Sanatan Dharma,* where right or wrong is never absolute. Hindus leave the interpretation of Dharma to the individual and consider the world as a big family, unlike Abrahamic religions which promote exclusivity and postulate that only those of their ilk will ascend to Heaven. Others are destined to suffer in Hell. For Hindus, soul is immortal, which takes successive births after death, each birth being a process of wiping out past or accumulated karmas until it attains liberation or *moksha,* a state when the soul unites with Paramatma or God.

We can credit the success of Abrahamic religions with bringing clarity to help the simple and the unlettered. They took over the responsibility of distinguishing between right and wrong, and these monotheistic systems made morality a part of religion. Only trained priests could preach and promote the teachings and conduct prayer meetings. They taught that there was only one God who should be worshipped.

Abrahamic faiths believed in exclusivity that theirs was the only way to salvation. The Indic way of life co-existed with other faiths. Although Buddhists and Jains challenged Hinduism, their ideas were not suppressed but allowed to flourish. In Indic thought, Yuga Dharma recognizes the need to change with the times. Change is a challenge; it can surprise and shock. Yuga Dharma promotes innovations and also protects the lives of the innovators. This is because tolerance and mutual coexistence are the requirements of

Manav Dharma. This is our obligation towards all living beings. Association of Hindu Gods with animals cements their coexistence as part of Manav Dharma.

Rituals form an integral part of the Indic way of life and all modern religions must fit into four categories, according to Emily Schultz and Robert Lavenda. There are four rituals common to most societies, as for instance, ancestor-worship as Shraddh or Pitru Puja in India. It is performed in other ways in different parts of the world, Pilgrimage to a holy site, like Hajj in Islam or visiting the Vatican for Roman Catholics. Sacrifice is a common feature among all faiths, such as offerings to a deity at a temple, church or mosque, invoking cosmic forces to gain merit or some benefit. Public celebrations like Navaratri, Durga Puja, Ganesh Puja, Carnivals, etc. People of all faiths, social status and castes inter-mingle, partake of food, worship or party.

Rituals in **Hinduism** may vary from region to region. For instance, *Shraddh* is performed after the death of a person. In some parts, it is customary to invite many people to a feast. Others may feed some Brahmins. The ritual of marriage also differs by region, some perform it before sunrise, some after sunset and others during the day. These differences are in form and maybe even in substance, but their intent is common. Rituals serve a dual purpose. It educates and keeps us connected with our roots. At a ritual puja, a priest will ask for our *gotra*, besides the names of our parents, grandparents and great grandparents, the place of our ancestral origin. In many temples, only a priest associated with our community and region can perform a ceremony. They call him a *'kula pundit.'* These priests document the visits, including the names of persons with dates.

CHAPTER 3

Gods and the Hindu Way of Life

Hindu gods often intrigue the followers of their faith. They are unable to understand why there should be so many of them, when a belief in one God is prevalent. Gods belonging to the Puranic period differ from that of the Vedic period. The Vedic era is estimated from 1500 BC to 500 BC, when the Indo-Aryans settled in northern India and brought with them their religious practices, followed by the Puranic period.

In the Vedic Period, humans regarded forces of nature as gods. Critical for their survival, no god was superior to another. Agni was the god of fire based on earth. Vayu or Indra resided in the air, and Surya or the Sun roamed the sky. Thinkers surmised that as water could extinguish fire and fire could vaporise water, they were equal. Similarly, air could create a fire and send down rain to extinguish it. Living creatures needed the sun, water and air. They regarded these three powerful forces of nature as equals.

Worshippers gave these Gods a human profile. These visualisations soon became their settled individual profiles. This made it easy for us to recognise them.

In the Vedas, more hymns are devoted to Agni, than to Indra. A puja requires the lighting of a fire. Hindus worship Agni because it is pure and is a witness to all our worship, vows, prayers and ceremonies performed. We also invite and seek the blessings of all the planets, including the Sun, whose own Agni provides human life with light and warmth.

As Hindu thought expanded, it recognised that all these forces of nature must have a creator. Once created there must be someone to sustain these creations. Creatures will continue to evolve and so there must be a force that helps them evolve. Thus at some point would have come into our belief system, the Trinity of Gods called Brahma, Vishnu and Shiva.

Brahma is credited with creation of the Universe; Vishnu sustains it and often descends on the earth to restore Dharma. This category includes great religious leaders like Jesus, Buddha, Mohammed.They are referred to as an avatar of Vishnu or Son of God or a Prophet. Shiva is the last of the Trinity who regulates and balances created orders, with varying life cycles. Some will outpace or outgrow others, some may go extinct and others may mutate.

These ideas of creation, the need for its sustenance and its evolution may have contributed to this early thinking. Hindus attribute unexplained phenomena of nature and life to the Trinity. This idea fits well with the concept of Birth, Death and Re-birth. Scriptures provide the reasons for not worshipping Brahma. No major religion claims its founder to be a Creator. Today, Hindus worship an avatar of Vishnu or Shiva, or even both, which is not unusual. Worshippers of Shiva and Vishnu coexist peacefully.

The Ramayana and Mahabharata detail the lives of Ram and Krishna, who are regarded as Vishnu Avatars. A closer examination of that time point to the worship of Shiva.

Early religious thinkers would have realised that many questions surrounding creation will remain unanswered, attributing it to the Creator. Someone in his quest for knowledge may discover answers to many of these questions, but will it ever demystify the Creator? Every religion allows us to worship one of their leaders as a mentor or a guide. But they have never claimed their founders are the Creators themselves. They do not have complete knowledge of the Creator or the Creation.

Hindus also worshipped goddesses, unlike male-centric Abrahamic schools. Foreigners, who had subjugated India politically and militarily were followers of Islam or Christianity. They undermined and suppressed Hinduism, stigmatizing the worship of female deities and whose followers were suspected of conducting human sacrifices. No such evidence exists. Hindus continue to worship the Devi as Durga, Kali, Sarasvati, Lakshmi, etc. Male Gods handled the universe, goddesses helped sustain life.

3Ms of Life: Life can only be sustained with the help of means, methods and motivation. Means represent material needs such as food. Methods represent the process of eating, digesting and removal of wastes, while the more abstract Motivation is the wish to live.

In Hindu philosophy, Lakshmi stands for Means, she is the goddess of wealth and Vishnu's consort. Sarasvati provides us Methods as the goddess of knowledge and consort of Brahma. Durga stands for Motivation. She is the goddess of power described as Shakti and Shiva's consort.

Power of Prayer: In Vedic times, preceptors called gurus or rishis set-up their own ashrams to guide devotees and students. These Ashrams received support from the royals, becoming important centres of learning. The Gurus imparted knowledge to their pupils, who helped sustain life at the ashram with activities like hunting, farming, etc. Priests like Dhaumya performed fire sacrifices. He maintained the ceremonial fire for the Pandavas. Many Hindus keep an oil lamp, called the *Akhand diya*, lit round the clock at home. Others light an oil lamp in the morning and evening, as required by rituals. Hindus regard fire for its purity, positive energy, the ability to sustain life. As light, it could be seen from afar besides warding off predators. In the ages gone by, wayfarers would be drawn to light or smoke, where they could find food and security.

A typical puja involves chanting of *shlokas* in praise of God, beating of drums, ringing of bells, the smell of *homa*, incense, rounded off with distribution of prasad.

The involvement in rituals detaches the mind from worldly concerns and is as therapeutic as swimming or playing. Similarly, invoking God helps us focus better on our problems.

In Vedic times people worshipped life-giving forces such as Agni, Vayu and Surya and also Shiva, symbolized by the union of a phallic symbol with its feminine counterpart, representing procreation. We hold in awe the yet unknown force that transforms a seed into a fruit-bearing tree. The underlying process is an act of nature, which has been identified with Shiva.

Religions are like branches of a Banyan Tree: As each human has the 3Ms, we need the Rules of Conduct to uphold and sustain the Universe. These Rules of Conduct cover our duties to self, family, society, work, country, universe and our lives as it evolves from birth to death.

These religions offer us a path; these paths are like trunks of a banyan tree which we can pursue to reach the canopy. It is unimportant whether the trunk is the main root as each root leads us to the same canopy. This canopy is our Atma uniting with the Paramatma or Moksha.

The Trinity, their Consorts, non-believers: Shiva symbolises procreation. It is the union of the male phallic symbol with its female counterpart. Indic thought advises us to revere our procreators, namely Shiva. However, deeper interpretations provide more detailed and nuanced meaning of the *Shivalinga*.

Vishnu is our Guru and mentor. In our lives, we will learn from someone or aspire to be like someone. We can place them on a pedestal and follow that goal or wish. It conveys this idea through Eklavya. He uses Guru Dronacharya's statue as a surrogate and learns the craft.

Brahma, or infinity, inspires us to search for knowledge. They associate him with Saraswati and we can represent her as Methods.

For procreation to be successful, a fertilised seed must be nurtured and transformed into a living entity. Once born, our mother protects us and prepares us to face the world. We are the outcome of a mother's selfless perseverance and effort. This is her Motivation to bring us into this world and prepare us for our lives. We associate Shiva with Shakti. Our birth is our gift from our procreators, thereafter, every input requires an output, every result needs an effort, to exhale air we need to inhale. We therefore associate Vishnu with Laxmi.

Atheists will also find relevance in the Hindu Trinity and their female consorts, based on their interdependence, represented by the 3Ms. Every faith creates its own Vishnu, its own structure and rituals. But the search for *moksha* or *nirvana* in our mortal state is common to all, although, the exact meaning of the same and the ways to achieve it vary. Indic thinkers developed the concept of the Trinity and its female equivalent, based on their interdependence, besides permitting other religions to coexist and recognizing the presence of non-believers too.

CHAPTER 4

Dharma and the Hindu Way of Life

Originally, Hinduism was not formalized as a religion, but as a way of life. It offered precepts and norms to follow a righteous path, embracing the totality of life. The word Dharma has neither literal nor equivalent translation in English. It is derived from *'Dhar'* which stands for 'hold.' So Dharma literally means "that which holds." In the Indic context, it refers to the principles or actions that holds or allows life to run in the intended way. Adharma suggests its very negation, which would only disrupt life.

A Hindu would define Dharma as the righteous way, the responsibility of every individual. One may face extraordinary circumstances during one's lifetime. Depending on these factors, the seemingly right way may not always be so. The only condition being that such behaviour must fulfil a higher goal. When a person risks his life to defend his country, he is fulfilling a higher goal. But normally, a person cannot risk his life.

The rules of Dharma covers a person's life in all its aspects. The first is the responsibility an individual bears towards himself. They call this *Vyakti* or Personal Dharma, comprising observance of moral and ethical principles to ensure an individual's mental and physical health, besides control over anger, being honest in our dealings, acting selflessly, avoiding temptation, exercising self restraint in matters of sexual desires and passions, etc. Most importantly, *ahimsa* or not causing injury to all life forms.

Parivarik Dharma is the responsibility of a person towards his immediate family, which he must support, maintain and protect. The larger family also includes our siblings, their children and spouse. This definition is open to inclusion of more persons and depends on the structure of the family. *Samaj* Dharma implies duty towards society. Individuals must observe a code of conduct to support a well-integrated society. He must practice non-violence, integrity and honesty. He should avoid speaking ill of others. It comprises people who share the same Jati, Varna, religion and language. They may even live in the same city or state. Such city-based people identify themselves as a community. Samaj can now mean people who inhabit the same housing society or town.

Rashtra Dharma is an obligation towards the nation. One is required to follow the code of conduct in the service of the country, pay taxes regularly, follow the law in letter and spirit and ensure the security and honour of the country.

Manav Dharma, as distinct from *Samaj* Dharma, refers to our obligation to mankind and to ensure that we do everything in our power to protect the environment; besides doing our bit to improve the quality of life on the planet.

Varna Dharma refers to our professional obligations, enjoining us to act with honesty and integrity. For instance, a doctor asking a patient to have a medical test done because it earns him a commission is an example of misconduct.

Apad-Dharma is doing one's duty in exceptional or abnormal situations. The *Mahabharata* provides several examples. It is best understood when actions are viewed in their totality. A person might fulfil one Dharma, yet violate another, wittingly or unwittingly. It is a matter of relativity, when a seemingly wrong deed might not be so wrong after all.

Yug Dharma is about transformative changes, unique to the Hindu way of life, the importance of changing with times and adapting our traditional practices to reflect the present.

Ashram Dharma is about an individual's role at different stages of life. In our initial years, we are students and our duty and responsibility is clear. We then grow up, marry, raise a family and take up new responsibilities. This process is crucial for our well-being. We face new challenges when we age and our families expand. Our priorities also change as we grow older.

Dharma is explained through events in the lives of the characters in the Epic. In most cases, an individual's choice in any situation is between the right and the wrong. Circumstances may compel characters to make difficult choices. An individual may also have to choose between an oath and a duty that fulfils a larger end.

Dharma brings us to a conflicting third option called *Apad*-Dharma. The individual has to choose between two wrongs, or when circumstances may compel him to commit a wrong in the interest of a larger good. Our laws also recognise this possibility. Then, in such cases, a jury will examine the cause of a crime and only then pass judgement. A person may have to choose between his duty to his family or country or between loyalty to his employer or society, especially when a company resorts to unfair practices. In the Epic, sometimes a person carries out his duties, oblivious of the abnormal conditions, thinking he is right, he may yet be in the wrong. It is a warning to people who commit *Adharma* when they act out of ego, love or loyalty.

We must credit the Epic for the depth of characterization, together with the background. It demonstrates how and why individuals following Dharma make their choices and their justification for the acts. It delves deep into the life of its characters, sometimes going into a previous birth and how their actions then influences the present one.

This elaborate report card based on an individual's actions is called Karma or the fruits of action (as you sow, so shall you reap). There are many examples of this concept. The Mahabharata deals with the past life of some characters and explains how their Karmas shaped their present lives.

The Epic shows the impact of Karma, from which there is no getting away, with many examples. For instance, no grief could be more traumatic than that of parents haplessly watching their only child die. But as Mahabharata would explain, unknown to them, it was caused by their negative karma in a past life.

Karma refers to our actions in our lives, past or present, and their outcomes. The consequences are inescapable, lasts over successive births, until the score is settled.

CHAPTER 5

Hinduism and the Caste System

The word 'caste' has no root or reference in Vedic texts, but is of Portuguese origin. The stratification of Indic Society based on birth occurs much later, especially after Islamic invasions and British rule. Yet, some understanding of the principles and practice of the society of that time is necessary and helps explain the behaviour of the two clans in the Epic.

In Vedic Society, social stratification was based on two factors. Occupation; they called it the Varna, which excluded tribals. It comprised four categories. Brahmins specialised as priests, teachers and keepers of the faith. Kshatriyas protected society and ensured security as warriors and rulers. Vaishyas cultivated land, reared cattle, and conducted trade. Shudras served the people of these three classes.

Jatis loosely means community. The classification of an individual would be based on a combination of their Jati and Varna. In Vedic society, they based a person's Varna on his profession and aptitude. Birth would not determine his Varna. As usual, there were exceptions. A child born to a couple from two different Jatis or Varna would adopt that of its Father. The other exception was that if a child was born to a Kshatriya father, but the mother was not Kshatriya, they called such a child a Suta. Suta served the Kshatriyas and were discriminated by birth. Suta women could marry a king, their children would not be a Suta. They often occupied high positions of responsibility. Discrimination did not lead to exclusion or exploitation.

Vedic Astrology also uses the term Varna to describe a person's caste (as in aptitude) based on his birth chart. As per Vedic Astrology, a person's caste was not pre-determined based on his parents but determined through his birth chart.

Children would get their lineage from their father. This was devised to preserve Gotra. So essentially, they considered the daughter of a Kshatriya father, a Kshatriya. In the Epic, they considered an abandoned Kshatriya child adopted by a Suta couple as a Suta.

Gotra in Hinduism and Science of Genetics: The gotra system rules that the male child alone can preserve the bloodline or family lineage.

This idea stands validated when tested with the chromosomal makeup of humans. In humans, each cell has 23 pairs of chromosomes. Twenty-two of these pairs, called autosomes, look the same in both males and females. The 23rd pair, the sex chromosomes, differ between the two genders. Women have two copies of the X chromosome while males have one X and one Y chromosome. So in effect, a girl child will inherit "X" chromosomes from both parents, but only a male child can inherit the "Y" chromosome from the father.

Accordingly, a man and woman belonging to the same gotra may be siblings and therefore cannot marry. The son always inherited the gotra of his father, while the wife would adopt the gotra of her husband. This is consistent with the unique way the "Y" chromosome flows.

Childless couples preferred to adopt a sister's child because when the child gets married, the gotra of the male child would stay referenced. But, someone may lose over time the knowledge of this real Gotra and so adopting a male child from the same paternal lineage may have gained preference. This change of preference found greater support with the rise of Buddhism and Abrahamic Schools.

A couple adopting a male child born to a male sibling of the husband would affect the adopted child. They would bring up the child in the same household under the care of the natural mother and the foster mother. He could suffer conflicts of emotional attachment and engagement. The later distribution of wealth would also be uneven. The family line of the natural parents would receive an extra share over others. In the Hindu way of life, the paternal uncle and aunt are like parents. Therefore adoption did not add any value to the relationship.

There has been a recent research on the legacy of DNA of people of Indian origin. Indians have a legacy of mixed inter-racial and inter-regional marriage. This, they believe, could go back to several thousand years before the Mahabharata. Hindu Society may have desired to contain marriages within their ethnic group. They intended it to keep the trace of their bloodline. The advances achieved in genetic science are of more recent origin. Indians rely on gotra to establish marital alliances. Some countries have laws that need couples to give proof of their bloodline. As per their laws, no sibling or bloodline relationship can exist between a couple or between persons in their three preceding generations. Research has also shown that consanguineous marriages increase the risk of birth defects.

CHAPTER 6

Mahabharata and the Bhagwad Gita

The Bhagwad Gita has inspired countless studies. Many have come up with elaborate commentaries, offering their own interpretation and understanding. The content has a wide and universal appeal and is one of the most thought provoking compositions known to mankind. The Bhagwad Gita focuses on the Creator and addresses our concerns about Karma and shows a way out of human predicament.

The Bhagwad Gita comprises 700 verses and would take over four hours to recite. So, under normal circumstances, it is doubtful whether this narration ever took place as two battle ready armies faced each other. Authors of the Epic would have surely understood this 'insertion,' placed centre-stage to reveal the purpose of life.

In simple terms, the recitation and appreciation of the 700 verses of the Gita will add to our resolve to follow the path of Dharma.

Gita in the Mahabharata is like the pinnacle of a circular pyramid. Inverted, it would appear as the centre or an omnipotent Lighthouse. The Mahabharata is that map of the universe from which the Captain can find his co-ordinates. Inspired by the guiding light of the Omnipotent Lighthouse, the fixed constant, he can map his path to the harbour. This harbour is moksha or the destination of our soul. It is believed that what is in the Mahabharata is somewhere and what is not is nowhere. The Epic maybe an aggregation of experiences of humans in their lifetime.

Events and characters in the Mahabharata are referred to as Time - the position when an event occurs in our life. However, its value and relevance are inestimable.

Episodes and incidents from the Mahabharata still bear relevance today. Such as when Eklavya absorbs Dronacharya's knowledge without his consent, or when Karna obtains Parshuram's insights by deception. Both Eklavya and Karna are punished by their preceptors, in the same way that violators are fined or jailed today. This is also similar to how we sentence offenders based on the degree of their crime. A study of the Mahabharata and its application to our contemporary lives would be extremely rewarding.

CHAPTER 7

The Mahabharata's Unique Construct and Characters

The Relevance of Number 18

Mahabharata has 18 sections. Bhagavad Gita has 18 chapters. Mahabharata war lasted for 18 days and involved 18 armies, 11 fought on behalf of the Kauravas and 7 on behalf of the Pandavas.

There are 18 Puranas (1+8=9) and 108 Upanishads (1+0+8=9). Numbers 1+8 add up to 9. It is a multiple of a prime number 3. Shiva is associated with this number. It also points to other important aspects of Vedic philosophy such as Triguna, Tribhuvan, and also stands for Me, Mine and That which is not mine. There are 9 planets called Navagrahas that represent the Universe. They associate adulthood with 18.

The compound number 108 has also very significant relevance in Hindu thought. Our mantra beads make up 108 pieces as we recite our mantra 108 times. There are 9 planets and can each form 12 definitive patterns based on constellations and this total 108. Distance between the earth and the moon is 108 times the diameter of the Moon, the Sun is 108 times the diameter of the Earth. Also, the distance between the Earth and the Sun is 108 times the diameter of the Sun.

Numbers 9, 18 and 108 as numbers have many associations with Indic Thought and with the Cosmos. In Vedic Astrology, there are 27 Nakshatras or Stars and every Star has 4 Padas, so there are 108 star signs in Vedic Astrology. The 108 Mantras would therefore aim to secure the well-being of every human being. As per Quantum Physics, creations are the outcome of energies that vibrate at different frequencies. Atoms and Protons believed to be a solid matter are nothing but space and energy. Mantras are sound vibrations. We recite these 108 times. When this is done, in some random order it would align with the unique frequency of the chanter. The mantra would then benefit the chanter.

The authors have associated the number 18 with the Mahabharata. This is to signify the deep connection between the Epic and the Cosmos. Hindus have a special regard for the nine planets or *navagrahas*. When an individual recites a mantra, he connects with the Cosmos. They intended the guidance in the Mahabharata so that the Cosmic Order can function in the intended way. They believe humans are all connected with the Earth, moon and the Sun along with its planets. They make this connection through sound, which is energy. They believe there is a strong relation between the Cosmos (Number 9) and the Cosmic Soul Number represented by any of the 108.

There are 144 characters in the Mahabharata. In the Epic, 18 characters have a key role, another 18 characters have significant roles and 18 had minor roles.

The Mahabharata is a composition that explains the principles of Sanatan Dharma. The characterisations of individuals, their background, including their past lives, the details of the present lives and circumstances all play an important part in the story. Authors would have used heroes and anti-heroes so that Dharma and Adharma could be explained. They depict Krishna as the Hero with foresight and vision who fought on behalf of Dharma. Shakuni is the anti-hero who also had foresight and vision but could have fought on behalf of Adharma. They could also split a character to highlight their virtues or faults. Whilst in most stories the Good would always win over Evil, in this Epic, Dharma would win and prevail over Adharma.

Key Characters:

1. **Bhishma (alias Devavrata, Ganga Putra Bhishma):** The son of King Shantanu and Ganga. The regent of Hastinapur, who remained celibate, received a boon that entitled him to life at will. Well versed in statecraft, he taught Yudhisthir the principles of Good Governance for a King.

2. **Ved Vyas:** The son of Satyawati and wandering Sage Parashara. He is credited with organising the Vedas into its current known structure and for authoring the Mahabharata. He is the biological father of Dhritarashtra, Pandu, Vidura and Suka.

3. **Dhritarashtra:** The blind eldest son of King Vichitravirya and Queen Ambika. Initially, he was passed over from being appointed King in favour of his more eligible younger brother Pandu. They credit him with 101 sons i.e. 100 sons from Gandhari and one from his Slave Queen and a daughter from Gandhari.

4. **Karna:** The first-born child of Queen Kunti born in a union

with Demi-God Surya. Abandoned by Kunti, he grew up under the guardianship of foster parents. His father was a charioteer to the King Dhritarashtra and hence a Suta. Karna was referred to as Suta-Putra.

5. **Krishna:** The son of Devaki and Vasudeva brought up as a cowherd by his foster parents, Yashoda and Nanda. He was a nephew of Kunti (sister of Vasudeva) and a prince of the Yadav dynasty. Also called Ranchhod for running away from battle. Hindus worship him as a re-incarnation of Vishnu and he is granted God-like status similar to Ram.

6. **Shakuni:** The younger brother of Queen Gandhari, he lived in Hastinapur. His sole motive was to avenge the humiliation of his sister who was compelled to marry a blind Dhritarashtra. A character with great vision and foresight, but fought for Adharma. In our story, he is an anti-hero cast opposite Krishna.

7. **Draupadi:** The beautiful and enchanting daughter of King Drupad and wife of the five Pandavas. Her humiliation in the court of Hastinapur caused the Mahabharata War, or was it because she insulted Duryodhana that resulted in the Mahabharata War?

   An interesting characterisation of a woman, of her plight and resolve. Was her marriage to five men intended as a study of the virtues of an ideal Man and a study of the complex feminine mind?

8. **Kunti:** Adopted daughter of Kunti-bhoj, wife of King Pandu, mother of three Pandava princes and Karna. In the entire Epic, she marries by her choice, lives life on her terms and has the resolve to lead her minor children in their fight to re-claim the rights of her deceased husband. Kunti was already living in forest with Pandu. And when she returned with her sons, she was allowed to be part of the palace.

9. **Gandhari:** She is the wife of Dhritarashtra and mother of 100 sons and one daughter. After her marriage, she led her life blindfolded so she could understand and empathise with her husband.

   Or a woman of resolve forced into a marriage against her wishes and so refused to favour her husband with the benefit of her vision that could offset his blindness (real or personified).

   Or of a woman forced into a marriage who decided not to stand by her husband and guide him as an equal partner in conducting his life based on Dharma. Marriage without mutual affection can be a union of two bodies where the two minds stay apart.

   Or was her blindfold a reference to her parenting of her children, who despite access to the best tutors and presence of Bhishma all ended up following the path of Adharma?

   This is relevant when Dhritarashtra's son Yuyutsu (dashi putra) born to his dashi/servant, who also grew up as a prince and received the same education, but followed Dharma.

10. **Yudhisthir:** The eldest son of King Pandu also known as Dharma.

11. **Bhima:** The second son of Kunti, he was the first to marry. He married Hidimbi and his son Ghatotkacha, who would have been the first in line to ascend the throne after Pandavas, but was killed in the war. There are temples where people worship him. He killed all the 100 Kuru Princes and thus paved the way for Yudhisthir to be King.

12. **Arjun:** The great archer and third son of Kunti. He won Draupadi in her Swayamwar, married his cousin Subhadra. Apart from his skills of archery, and his role in the war, he received the great message of Gita but could not recall it after the war; he requested Krishna to repeat the message. This revised message is a new message called the Anugita.

13. **Ashwatthama:** The son of Dronacharya and loyal friend of Duryodhana. Brahmin by birth, he was crowned king of Southern Panchal. A great warrior who sided with Duryodhana. He felt that Arjun was receiving his father's attention that belonged to him. Yet his father's love for him was unmatched and exploited by the Pandavas in the war.

14. **Duryodhana:** The eldest son of Dhritarashtra and the Crown Prince of Hastinapur. History may have sided with the winner. Duryodhana was born two years after conception, this seeded enough confusion as to whom amongst him and Yudhisthir was the eldest and entitled to be Crown Prince. Controversies surround his name and some believe his name was Suryodhan meaning 'great warrior' but was twisted with the term DUR signifying negativity. However the name Duryodhana also means 'the unconquerable one.'

15. **Satyawati:** The daughter of a fisherman and wife of King Shantanu, the ordeal of a divided house of Hastinapur starts with her. King Shantanu committed that the son born to her after her marriage with King Shantanu would be the Crown Prince and future king of Hastinapur.

16. **Dronacharya:** The impoverished Brahmin related to the Head priest in Court of Hastinapur. Bhishma appointed him as the tutor to the Royal Princes. A school/ashram was set up for the Royals under his stewardship.

17. **Vidura:** Vidura was the half-brother of Dhritarashtra and Pandu of Hastinapur. Son of the sage Ved Vyas and Parishrami, the maid to the queens Ambika and Ambalika.

    He was Prime Minister and despite remaining loyal to King Dhritarashtra was always known to side with Dharma.

18. **Drupad:** The king of Panchal, and father of Shikhandi, Draupadi and Dhrishtadyumna. Panchal was partitioned and a half of it was annexed after King Drupad was brought captive to Hastinapur. He conceived a great plan

to avenge this humiliation and was a major source of strength to the Pandavas in the battle that brought down the Kauravas.

Characters with Significant Roles though not Major:

1. **Ghatotkacha:** Son of Bhima and Hidimbi, a dreaded warrior who wrecked havoc on the Kaurava army forcing Karna to use his 'Divine Weapon' he had reserved to kill Arjun.

2. **Nakul:** The twin son born to King Pandu and Madri. The most handsome person of his time, known for his undying loyalty and affection towards his siblings. He could calm an aggressive Bhima. The name Nakul means full of love and the male characteristics implied by the name are: Intelligence, Focus, Hard Work, Handsomeness, Health, Attractiveness, Success, Popularity, Respect and Love.

3. **Sahadev:** The twin of Nakul, a great devotee of Krishna, he was blessed with tremendous foresight. According to some accounts, once Krishna asked Sahadev, what should be done to stop the war? Sahadev told him that Krishna must be tied down and imprisoned, the Pandavas along with Duryodhana must be sent to forest and Karna must be made the king. When Krishna challenged him to tie him down, he meditated and envisioned Krishna as a small baby and tied him down. Unable to move out of his bondage created by Sahadev in his meditative trance, Krishna blessed him with a divine vision for his release from bondage.

4. **Balarama:** He is the elder brother of Krishna. The guru of Bhima and Duryodhana in art of fighting with the mace. He often opposed Krishna, but always gave in to Krishna's arguments based on Apad-Dharma. Balarama refused to side with the Pandavas. He proceeded on a pilgrimage at the time of the Battle.

5. **Subhadra:** Sister of Krishna and Balarama. She was to marry Duryodhana, but Krishna manipulated the events and encouraged Arjun to abduct her and marry her. The marriage between Subhadra and Arjun strengthened the alliance between Pandavas and Yadavas.

6. **Shikhandi:** The eldest son of King Drupad. Bhishma refused to fight with him as he was a transsexual. He was Amba in his previous life.

7. **Dhrishtadyumna:** The second son of King Drupad. Born through a sacrificial fire. Drupad raised him with a mission to avenge his humiliation by Dronacharya. He was the Commander-in-Chief of the combined Army of the Pandavas and their Allies. He killed Dronacharya in the epic Battle.

8. **Dushasan:** The second son of King Dhritarashtra. His name means 'tough ruler' although some believe his original name may have been Susashan meaning 'just ruler.' He was singled out by Bhima and killed most brutally for dragging Draupadi into the court and trying to disrobe her.

9. **Pandu:** The son of Vichitravirya and Ambalika sired by Ved Vyas. He was crowned King of Hastinapur in preference to his blind elder brother. A gallant warrior and married to Kunti and Madri. Pandu withdrew from his Kingly duties for penance after being cursed by a Rishi couple, who were killed by him in a case of mistaken identity during a hunt in the forest, in favour of his blind brother Dhritarashtra and went into exile and met his end there.

10. **Jarasandha:** The king of Magadha and an alliance partner of Hastinapur; was a fearless warrior. His daughter was married to Kans (maternal uncle of Krishna). Krishna killed Kans, widowing Jarasandha's daughter, an infuriated Jarasandha attacked the Yadavas 17 times compelling them to shift their capital from Mathura to Dwarka.

11. **Hidimbi:** The demon wife of Bhima and the mother of Ghatotkacha, the eldest grandson of Kunti. Hidimbi was attracted to Bhima and preferred to marry him. Bhima killed her brother who opposed his demon sister marrying somebody from outside the community.

12. **Ganga:** Wife of King Shantanu and mother of Bhishma, she walked out of her marriage with King Shantanu, who broke his vow to her. Ganga married King Shantanu on the condition he would never question her or prevent her from any action.

13. **Shantanu:** The King of Hastinapur initially married Ganga and then Satyawati. He was the father of Bhishma, Chitrangada and Vichitravirya. He agreed to replace his son and Crown Prince Bhishma in favour of a yet to be born son from his marriage with Satyawati.

14. **Virata:** The King of Virata, the nation where the Pandavas in disguise spent their final year of exile. The Kauravas attacked his kingdom to flush out the Pandavas. Virata's daughter Uttara was married to Arjun's son, Abhimanyu.

15. **Uttara:** Daughter of King Virata was the wife of Abhimanyu—the son of Arjun and Subhadra. Married just before the Epic Battle started, her son, Parikshit, ultimately succeeded Yudhisthir as King.

16. **Shalya:** Brother of Madri and uncle of Nakul and Sahadev, he was deceived by Duryodhana and committed to his word, fought against the Pandavas. He was Karna's charioteer and in the battle was killed by Yudhisthir.

17. **Eklavya:** A tribal who regarded Dronacharya as his guru but was refused training by Dronacharya. At the request of Dronacharya, he offered his right thumb as his guru Dakshina (tuition fees).

18. **Abhimanyu:** Son of Arjun and Subhadra, who grew up under the guidance of his uncle Krishna. An accomplished

and brave warrior martyred whilst surrounded in unfair combat by the best of warriors.

Minor Characters:

1. **Amba:** She was abducted from her Swayamwar for marriage with Vichitravirya. She wanted to marry someone else, but he refused to marry her. She returned to Hastinapur and demanded that Bhishma marry her. When Bhishma refused, she committed suicide vowing to kill him in her next life.

2. **Ambalika:** Abducted by Bhishma and married to Vichitravirya, she was widowed and then bore a son fathered by Ved Vyas. Her son was Pandu.

3. **Ambika:** Also abducted along with her sisters, she was, widow of King Vichitravirya and mother of Dhritarashtra.

4. **Bakasura:** A cannibal feared by the Kings. Bhima killed him and relieved the locals from his oppression.

5. **Dushala:** The only daughter of King Dhritarashtra and Queen Gandhari sister to not only all the Kuru Princes but also the Pandava Princes. She was married to King Jayadratha.

6. **Jayadratha:** King of Sindhu-desh and husband of Dushala. He was caught trying to abduct Draupadi. Bhima wanted to kill him but was spared because his death would have widowed Dushala.

7. **Kichaka:** Head of the army of King Virata, he was enamoured by Draupadi who was living in disguise in the Royal Court of Virata. At Draupadi's behest, Bhima killed him for making sexual advances at Draupadi.

8. **Kripacharya:** Adopted by King Shantanu, he was the chief priest and also tutor to the sons of Pandu and Dhritarashtra. His sister Kripi married Dronacharya, who was appointed as the Royal Tutor.

9. **Sanjay:** Charioteer of Dhritarashtra, with the distance/ divine vision granted to him by Ved Vyas, he narrated to Dhritarashtra the events of the Epic Battle. He and Arjun heard Krishna narrate the Bhagvad Gita.

10. **Vikarna:** The third son of Dhritarashtra, who objected to Draupadi's humiliation in the Royal Court. Was killed by Bhima in the Epic Battle.

11. **Takshaka:** A Naga tribal chief who lived in the Forest of Khandavprastha. He and his tribe were uprooted and their forest dwellings were burnt down by the Pandavas to make way for their capital Indraprastha.

12. **Vasudeva:** The father of Krishna and brother of Kunti. He and his wife were imprisoned by King Kans (his wife's brother). He was the first to experience the divine powers of Krishna.

13. **Parashuram:** A great rishi who hated the Kshatriyas as a race, was the guru of Karna and Bhishma.

14. **Yuyutsu:** Son of Dhritarashtra and his maid wife. He did not support Duryodhana's ways, in the battle sided with the Pandavas.

15. **Sage Durvasa:** The angry sage who was revered by most and dreaded by all for his curses. Visited the Pandavas in exile at the behest of Duryodhana.

16. **Madri:** The second wife of King Pandu, sister of King Shalya and mother of Nakul and Sahadev. She self-immolated herself in the funeral pyre of King Pandu.

17. **Mayasura:** Asura Renowned for his skills of architecture, built the capital of Indraprastha for the Pandavas.

18. **Purochana:** Chief Architect for the kingdom of Hastinapur and a trusted aide of Duryodhana, assigned the duty to construct the lac palace in Varanavat, where the Pandavas were supposed to be burnt as per Duryodhana's conspiracy.

Part-B

Mahabharata

The Great Epic

CHAPTER 1

Early History of the Kuru Dynasty

Synopsis: Perfection is a continuing journey. Even the intent of molestation deserves punishment. The rules of succession; how reward and punishment shape our lives.

Our story of the Epic begins from the early history of the Kuru Dynasty. In Sanskrit, they refer to history as *Itihas*, and family as *Kula*. It is also important to know why the Epic is called Mahabharata. They often refer to India as Bharat. We derive this from Bharata, a clan of the Purus. Their descendants are the Kuru. They were so-called Aryans and Hastinapur was their Capital.

The story starts with an incident in heaven. Ganga was an exquisite and enchanting maiden. At a prayer session in heaven, a strong wind blew away some of Ganga's clothes. It distracted people at the prayer. Shantanu continued to stare at her whilst the others returned to the prayer. This upset Brahma and he punished him. Brahma also punished Ganga for her misdemeanour. His curse returned Shantanu and Ganga to earth as humans. In their mortal state,

Shantanu would marry Ganga and suffer emotional pain at her hands.

The story then focuses on King Pratipa of Hastinapur. Shantanu was born as his third son. Over time, the King had to decide on his successor. The eldest son was unfit to be King and so passed over. The eldest apparently suffered from leprosy and was unfit. He consented to his being passed over. Pratipa gave his second son away in adoption and so the youngest, Shantanu succeeded him. This will help us understand if the later succession decisions were influenced by settled or inherited practices called Parampara.

Commentary

It is fascinating how Mahabharata delivers, from the very beginning, important lessons on principles of Righteousness, Karma and Dharma.

Succession: King Pratipa chose his youngest son to be the King. As a ruler, it was his responsibility to ensure proper succession. He must ensure that the one who succeeds him is fit enough to deliver stability and peace to his citizens. He took the consent of his eldest son before appointing the one next in line. This avoided any future challenges to the succession. The person being passed over must be taken into confidence. In corporate succession, the one being superseded is left in the cold. After the announcement, such a person leaves. With his departure, the organisation loses a valuable resource. If such a person lacked ability or competence, he should not have been there. They based Shantanu's appointment on his fitness. In our times too, they base succession in a business on merit and not seniority; although, the consent of the one being superseded may not always be taken.

Adoption: *There are many instances of children being given in adoption. Often this is between close relatives to ensure succession. In such instances, they give the adopted child the paternal lineage of the foster family. The childless couple by adopting the child of a close relative can preserve the history of the child's bloodline. After marriage, they accept the bride and the groom as a part of each other's family. Their children belong to both the families. Any adoption within this larger family brings with it a sense of care that can grow with nurture. A building is as strong as its foundation. Adoption in business is the appointment of an external candidate as CEO. It is the case when there is no suitable internal candidate to run the business.*

Perfection is a Continuing Journey: *Shantanu's atma had achieved Moksha. Overcome by temptation, he continued to stare at a half-naked Ganga. She had also distracted the other celestial beings present. They tried and succeeded in not letting their minds stray. Brahma perceived Shantanu's craving for the human form. As punishment, he returned him to earth to the life of a mortal. Ganga may dress and groom as she pleased. Brahma should not punish the victim. In death, a soul leaves the body. When Ganga dresses herself, it means that she still craves for worldly pleasures. A soul that has achieved Moksha would not have emotional or material attachment or aspirations. The souls of both Ganga and Shantanu craved for earthly pleasures and had to return to earth so they could fulfil their desires. Once satisfied, they could strive and achieve Moksha. In this journey the end may appear near, but it never ends. Perfection achieved is an illusion, like the mirage in the distance merging with the sky. Shantanu as a celestial being let his guard down. Temptation can overwhelm even the strongest. In our contemporary world, this is the process of re-learning and the need to improve ourselves on a continuing basis.*

We find Heaven and Hell as an idea across most religions. This helps either as a temptation (to seek heaven) or frighten us (that we will go to hell), so that we live according to rules. The Mahabharata conveys a message to all classes of people. Heaven with its vision of eternal bliss in Paradise and Hell as a furnace of unbearable suffering is a perfect model. It is the carrot and stick for the simple and uneducated. The educated know that following Dharma will allow the world to run in the intended way and they are a part of this process and must do their bit. In the Epic, the rules of Dharma apply to human beings, celestial beings and even Demi-gods. The idea being that every human being can aspire to be a celestial being. If they have to rise to that status, they must follow Dharma. They suggest that the rules of Dharma also apply to celestial beings. They promote Dharma as the means to success. It motivates individuals to follow Dharma as it is the highest form of knowledge that will get them to achieve success and be successful.

Protection of Modesty of Women: *Every act of molestation starts in the mind and then in the action. The Epic suggests that even the thought is punishable. But in the present times, only the act of molestation is a punishable offence.*

CHAPTER 2

King Shantanu's Marriage and Bhishma's Birth

Synopsis: *Promises and trust in marriages; breakdown of trust and divorce; child custody and rights of children; concept of re-birth and karma. Contracts, breach of contract and non-waiver in disputes.*

The story of Ganga's return to earth begins with a sage catching a group of eight Vasus (demi-gods) red-handed while stealing his divine cow. Upset, he ordered them to return to earth as humans, where the Vasus would have to repeat an indeterminate cycle of births to attain moksha. Given the severity of punishment, they begged for mercy. They could return as Vasus, he said, only on the condition that they were killed upon birth. However, he withheld his mercy from the eighth Vasu for masterminding the crime.

The accursed Vasus immediately approached Ganga, urging her to be their mother on earth and end their lives upon birth, so that they could regain their past status. Ganga agreed to help them out.

As expected, Shantanu met Ganga and proposed to her. She set a precondition that Shantanu shall never question or stop her from doing as she pleased. He should trust her judgement implicitly. A besotted Shantanu agreed immediately.

In due course, a son was born to them. Ganga took the newborn to the river and drowned him. A shattered Shantanu looked on helplessly, but kept quiet because of his promise. Ganga repeated her shocking act with every new birth. On the birth of their eighth son, Shantanu could not restrain himself and pleaded with Ganga to spare the child. They needed a son to ensure the continuity of the family and for the succession as a Kuru king.

Ganga immediately reminded Shantanu of their promise. She told him that his intervention meant he no longer trusted her. She then explained to him her reasons. However, at the end of their conversation, she ended their marriage. They agreed that Ganga would keep the child, educate him and when he was grown-up, she would hand over the custody of the child to Shantanu. Several years later she returned this child, named Devavrata, to her former husband.

These eight demi-gods were Sun, Moon, Stars, Wind, Fire, Water, Earth and Sky. Ganga released the first seven from the punishment. However, Sky took birth as the eighth son and had to spend time on earth.

Commentary

Marriage, trust, divorce and child custody: A marriage between two consenting adults depends on trust. Ganga asked for a promise, Shantanu gave her his word. Ganga trusted him and agreed to marry him. Trust is not just about adultery; it is central to a marriage and in all aspects of a relationship. Couples base a relationship of marriage on trust. When Shantanu questioned Ganga, he conveyed his lack of trust. He suspected her, and she had to explain her conduct. Suspicion enters a relationship when trust is broken. She recognised that suspicion meant their relationship was broken. She ended the relationship.

Shantanu married Ganga because he was attracted to her. He wanted her and, motivated by his temptation, made an unconditional promise. We all want something that attracts us. When our temptation gets the better of us, we make commitments we regret later.

In a marriage, both partners must share a common vision to succeed. Ganga married Shantanu because he promised to let her do as she pleased. Her actions did not contribute to the success of the marriage. Her husband needed a successor; she would give birth to their son and then drown him. It was like showing food to the hungry and then throwing it away. This was torture. Ganga had an agenda different from that of her husband. Both wanted a child, but for different reasons. They did not share a common vision and agenda. Shantanu married her because of his infatuation, he was not in love. Ganga married because Shantanu agreed to let her do what she wanted. She wanted to fulfil a prior promise. The two had nothing in common, their marriage failed. Ganga ended her marriage with Shantanu.

There is another perspective to Ganga's decision to end the marriage. Shantanu knew his marriage would end if he questioned Ganga. This showed he no longer valued his relationship. He sacrificed his relationship to satisfy his new need. He showed he wanted the baby more than her. We have often seen a man marry another woman because he feels his first wife cannot bear a child. We have instances when couples have to choose between a child or the mother. They all point to another human weakness. We do not value what we have, but ascribe a higher value to that which we do not have.

*When they separated, Ganga kept custody of the child. She
promised to bring him up, see him through his education. She
promised to send him to his father once he was ready to take up
responsibilities. A mother is best placed to take care of a child. Courts
prefer to give the mother custody of a minor child in a divorce. It
entitles a child of divorced parents to the care and nurture of his
mother and to the assets of the father. This ensures both emotional
and material security to a child of divorced parents. The mother
represents the soft side like love, care, education, etc., and the father
denotes the material side of wealth, inheritance, occupation, etc.*

Karma and Dharma: *Re-birth as a concept is introduced and
reiterated in different settings. We are all tied to our obligations of
Dharma and our Karma can influence our current and future lives.
Ganga fulfils her duties inherited from an earlier life. Shantanu
broke his vow never to question or prevent his wife from doing what
she was destined to do. Breaking his promise as a husband, he ended
his marriage. However, by saving his son, he secured the succession.
We have to make choices between competing obligations. We need to
choose that which fulfils our greater and larger responsibilities, even
if that choice comes at a great personal cost.*

*Dharma and Karma apply to all human beings, whether in life or
in the afterlife. Our past Karma can influence our present life. As
human beings, we cannot ordinarily recall events from our past lives.
The story of the past lives and their influence on the lives of Ganga,
Shantanu and Bhishma border on the unreal. However, advances
made on Past Life Regression give us a new perspective. Psychiatrists
believe it has immense therapeutic value. They believe our earlier lives
can influence our behaviour in our current life. Past life analysis is
used to identify this and re-engineer our minds. Karma influences our
lives and not just our mind. Vedic astrologers believe the adverse
experiences of our ancestors will influence our current lives. They
refer to this as Pitru Dosh. This is an example of how even our
relationships from our earlier lives can influence our present lives.*

Our own actions can be shocking. Drowning babies is shocking, but then we know of the cause and intent from her past life. This subtle message will aid us in understanding inconsistencies in behaviour in ourselves or people around us. This is to clarify and not justify.

Shantanu had to choose between his marriage and his child. He could honour his vow or fulfil his Dharma. He had an obligation to his wife and as a King he had a larger obligation to his country in ensuring stability by offering a clear path of succession. Dharma comes before vows.

Rules of Contract: *When Shantanu stopped Ganga from drowning their eighth child, she was not obliged to explain herself. She explained and also did not drown Bhishma. Their conduct contradicted the terms they agreed upon. Her decision not to enforce her rights did not take away her right to end the marriage. Ganga applied the principles of non-waiver and exercised her right of breach and ended her marriage. Shantanu had promised not to stop Ganga or question her actions, but ending the life of a child is adharma. Shantanu was not obliged to support Ganga's acts. He, therefore, prevented her from drowning his eighth child. A contract can unconditionally bind a party, but it cannot create an obligation that compels another to act against dharma. Shantanu was bound by Dharma as a Kshatriya and King to protect lives. This obligation was greater than his promise to his wife and his Dharma as a husband.*

CHAPTER 3

King Shantanu Marries Satyawati

Synopsis: Pre-nuptial agreements and rights of women. Why do contracts cover rights of successor and assignees? Paternal right of children.

King Shantanu's marriage with Ganga had ended. Their son Devavrata had grown up under the care and guidance of his mother. After completion of his education, she handed over his custody to Shantanu. The King was very pleased with his son's education and training. He appointed him as his Crown Prince.

Once on a hunting trip, Shantanu accosted Satyawati, a fisherwoman and the daughter of a tribal chief, who also ferried people across the river. Satyawati often helped him on the boat. Enchanted by her beauty, he wanted to marry her. Satyawati already had a son out of wedlock named Krishna Dvaipayana, known as Ved Vyas, who wrote the Mahabharata.

But when Satyawati did not consent to the marriage, Shantanu's son, Devavrata, approached her father with his marriage proposal. The tribal chief insisted that children born to Satyawati and Shantanu must succeed him as King. Devavrata would also have to remain celibate to avoid any challenge to the succession. He happily accepted those conditions for the sake of his father.

Overjoyed, Shantanu granted his son the boon of *ichcha mrityu*, so that he could live as long as he wished. He exhorted his son to serve and protect the Crown and would be known the world over as Bhishma.

Commentary

Understanding Human Indiscretion: An unwed mother married a King. There was no social stigma attached to her having a child before her marriage. The father of that child took responsibility for the child. He trained him and that child grew up to be the author of this Epic. The father gave this son his lineage. The King married a woman of unknown background. Caste and social status did not affect the Royal's wedding. Interestingly, his weakness for women plays out again. He marries another. Incidentally, in this case too, it is a promise that helps him get married; although, it was not him, but his son, who made that promise. In the first instance, he gave up his marriage for his son and now he wants another woman even at the cost of that son's personal future and well being. As a King, he put his dynasty at risk with no clear sight of succession. Humans do not appear to value what they have.

Women, unlike men, show greater clarity of vision. They are neither emotionally driven nor intellectually weak. Satyawati knew beauty was this man's weakness. He had gone back on his commitment before and could do so again. Yet he was King, and the most a woman could aspire to be was to be a Queen. She wanted to not only be

Queen but also the future Queen mother. She demanded, and got from an enchanted King, all she needed to ensure lifelong security for herself and her children. Like her, Ganga had also shown she could stand equal to her husband. We would expect a commoner to fear a King because they are dominating or revered. Yet these women could stand equal. Even if the husband was King, he could not demand subservience as it allowed them to stand as an equal.

In Vedic times, men and women had equal rights. A woman could decide for herself. The Epic highlights this aspect of a woman's status. She had the ability to stand equal to men irrespective of the circumstances. Under the Abrahamic Schools, women suffered, as they were given a lower status and had to give in to the demands of a male-dominated society. The concept of male dominance had entered social life under their influence. In Vedic era, they identified a son with the mother. They called the Pandavas, Kunti-Putra, Karna was Radheya and Bhishma was called Ganga Putra. Society always associated a child with both the parents. If his father was a Brahmin, they considered the child a Brahmin too; irrespective of the mother's varna. It entitled a child to inherit the father's lineage. However, the father had the absolute discretion on the grants of any rights arising from his estate. In the modern patriarchal system, they have enshrined the concept of a legacy as a right of birth. In the Epic, the father must give such rights. It does not entitle a child to the rights and legacy of his step-father as it limits the child's right to the assets of his biological father. The owner has absolute right to assign his rights, title and interest. There are many claims in our times based on birth-right; this dispossesses the owner of their absolute discretion in dealing with their property.

Actions of Father and Son Explained: *The father had saved the life of his son; a grateful son showed his love for his father and gave up his right and agreed to remain celibate. In appreciation of his sacrifice, his father rewards him a boon. This is touching and emotional, but the father compromised his country and family. He disregarded the rules* *of succession. These rules were based on fitting precedents and could not be demanded as a legacy. The King had the absolute right to decide on his successor, the eldest son may not be the successor. This autonomy in succession is clear in this Epic and also in Ramayana, another Epic. The crown Prince has to walk in the shadow of the King. He must serve the King. Every Citizen must be loyal to the crown. Even Bhishma, a powerful person, bows to authority. Bhishma had no right to give up a duty to himself and the state. Both Bhishma and Shantanu disregarded the principles of succession based on Dharma and Parampara of their Kula. Both Bhishma and Shantanu gratified each other with actions that violated Dharma.*

Mahabharata and Contracts: *Bhishma surrendered his right to the crown in favour of a future son of Satyawati. Bhishma waived his right to all benefits of succession. His actions amount to a voluntary waiver of rights. By promising to stay celibate, Bhishma ensured that his waiver also covered his successors. This is like agreements where parties to a contract include and commit their successors and assignees. By covering his successors, Bhishma ensured that there would never arise a conflict of claims from any of his descendants. The conflict in the Mahabharata arises because of a dispute in succession. When lawyers prepare a contract, they seek to bind the party to the contract and their successors and assignees. In the Mahabharata, Bhishma and his father have to agree to the conditions before the contract of marriage. This legal term is referred to as conditions precedent to the contract. The marriage of Shantanu and Ganga ended in divorce. A pre-nuptial agreement preceded the marriage of Shantanu and Satyawati. It did not limit a bride's right, but provided for her.*

CHAPTER 4

Succession Vacuum in Hastinapur

Synopsis: The choice between duty and promise; the choice between substance over form. One can escape the law, but none can escape Karma; Importance of dialogue and arbitration in a dispute.

Shantanu married Satyawati. They had two sons: Chitrangada and Vichitravirya. After Shantanu's death, as agreed, they passed over Bhishma and Chitrangada was made King. Bhishma served as the Regent. He had the responsibility to protect the kingdom and remain in service of the Crown. On the untimely death of Chitrangada, they made his younger brother Vichitravirya, the King. The Kuru had now treated succession as a legacy and applied the rule of seniority. The newly appointed king was physically weak. In normal circumstances, he would not be eligible to be the King. It concerned Satyawati as he had not found a bride. It was common for a royal family to host a Swayamwar. This was an event where a young princess would choose, from amongst the invited kings, princes and noblemen, the one she would marry. Vichitravirya could not find a bride at such events. A worried queen wanted her son to marry and provide a successor to the Kuru Dynasty. Out of desperation, she asked Bhishma to find a bride for his half-brother.

As directed, Bhishma set out to find a bride. He went to the kingdom of Kashi, where a Swayamwar was being held for three princesses — Amba, Ambika and Ambalika. Bhishma invaded the event and kidnapped the three princesses. He wanted to take them to Hastinapur for marriage to Vichitravirya. The kidnapping was difficult; the royals put up a fight. The King of Shalwa relentlessly pursued Bhishma, fought with him, but could not get the princesses released.

Bhishma returned to Hastinapur with the three princesses. Of the three princesses, the eldest was Amba. She declined to marry as she had sworn to marry the King of Shalwa, the love of her life. They sent her to King Shalwa, but he refused to marry her. He had lost the fight with Bhishma over her, so following conventions it entitled Bhishma to marry her. Rejected, she returned to Hastinapur and demanded that Bhishma marry her. Bhishma refused because of his vow of celibacy. Amba felt humiliated and abandoned; she accused Bhishma of ruining her life. She approached Bhishma's Guru, Parashuram, to persuade Bhishma, but failed. Isolated, she committed suicide. In some accounts, she went for penance and got a boon that, in her next life, she would become the reason behind Bhishma's death. She was re-born as Shikhandi, who became the reason for Bhishma's death in the Mahabharata war.

Ambika and Ambalika, the two other princess of Kashi, were married to Vichitravirya. Soon after their marriage, the King died. They ended up as widows before they could give birth to a child. The King had died and had left no successor. The Kuru dynasty would end naturally, as there was no successor. Satyawati asked Bhishma to give up his vow of celibacy, perform Niyoga on the widows of his brother and ensure that Kuru Dynasty had a successor. But he refused to comply and remained celibate.

Niyoga was an ancient practice, permitting a wedded woman to cohabit with a man other than her husband to beget a child. A husband would permit his wife to do so, if he was unable to father one himself. The child thus born would be theirs by right, not belong to the biological father.

Commentary

Rights of Women Re-enforced: A Swayamwar allowed a girl to choose her marriage partner. Amba is an evidence that a girl could make a prior choice. Also, no girl could be forced to marry. This added another dimension to her rights and independence. They protected the rights of a woman. The violator of a women's dignity had to marry her. It required him to restore in society her self-respect. When Bhishma refused to marry her, she sought the intervention of Bhishma's guru to compel him to change his mind. When this failed, she fought for justice. When she failed, she committed suicide but warned Bhishma that he would pay with his life for destroying her life. In later events, Amba was re-born as Shikhandi and caused Bhishma's death in the battle.

In Hindu thought, Karma will make sure we face the consequences of our action even if all other attempts to seek a remedy fail.

Karma and Rebirth: These events reiterate the concept of Karma and of how our actions/choices and decision affect our current life and of their influence in our next life. Bhishma ruined Amba's life and drove her to suicide, so the concept of Karma was reiterated but in a different dimension. Bhishma suffered the consequences of his Karma in this life itself; he did not have to wait for his next life. Amba in her next life avenged the violation of her right. This is not Karma but the effect of how events of our past life can influence our actions in our subsequent life.

Bhishma's Actions- A Perspective: *How should an individual respond when an action can, on the one hand, be Adharma and, on the other, be his Dharma. The Epic gives guidance in these very unusual and conflicting circumstances.*

The queen directed Bhishma to get a princess for marriage to his half-brother. He attacked the Swayamwar for three princesses and abducted them. Abducting a girl for marriage is one of the eight marriages acceptable as per Hindu Custom, though it is not considered of high righteous value. The marriage must be between an abductor and the abducted. Bhishma abducted the princesses for marriage to his brother. Amba demanded that Bhishma should take responsibility for his action and marry her. He refused as this violated his vow of celibacy. He could not fulfil his responsibilities as a husband because of that vow. At a later date, Satyawati asked Bhishma to give up his celibacy. Satyawati wanted him to perform Niyoga on his brother's widows.

In each of the two events, Bhishma had to deal with a conflict of duty or responsibility. He had to get a bride for his brother as he could not do so on his own. He needed to fulfil his responsibility of service to the crown. He had to get the king a wife and when their baby was born, the country would have a successor. In performing this duty, he violated a woman's right to choose her groom. He fulfilled his responsibility to the family and country. When choosing between Vyakti Dharma and Raj Dharma, he sided in favour of Raj Dharma as it did the larger good. The story of Amba reflects his violation of a woman's right. The punishment for that violation was his death. The Epic has warned that in our choice between two obligations, we must choose the one that fulfils a larger obligation. Such a choice must not affect or harm anyone. The price for every wrong deed is punishable irrespective of whether it is unintended, accidental or incidental.

Satyawati asked him to perform Niyoga on the widows of his half-brother. Bhishma, duty-bound to the state, refused to do Niyoga, even though it would have provided a successor to the kingdom of Hastinapur. He refused to marry Amba because his vow of celibacy would not let him fulfil his obligations as a husband. He had refused to do Niyoga on the widowed Queens because this would have broken his vow of celibacy. He had taken the vow so that neither he nor his children would ascend the throne. Niyoga was his duty to family and country. If he did, it would have violated his promise. Bhishma had surrendered his right and that of his successors to the throne of Hastinapur. So if Bhishma had performed Niyoga, he would have given the right to the child born from his seed in a union with the widowed Queens. He did not want such a child to be King. One must fulfil a promise, duty, obligation or Dharma not just in form but in substance.

Bhishma established the principles of substance over form. They do not consider the children born in Niyoga to belong to the man who donates his seed. But Bhishma realised that the children born would have been his in substance. Given that there were alternatives, can we question Bhishma's intentions or decisions?

Dealing with a Dispute: *When Amba was being abducted, her beloved, King of Shalwa, challenged Bhishma to a duel. Instead of engaging in dialogue and trying to resolve the matter, they engaged in a duel. Bhishma won the duel and the right to take Amba with him as a bride. When Amba returned to King Shalwa, he refused to marry her as now only Bhishma had the right to marry her. Amba now wanted Bhishma to marry her, but when she could not persuade him, she approached his guru Parashuram for help. When Bhishma declined the advice of his guru, a battle broke out between him and the guru which ended inconclusively. This narrative describes the concept of arbitration. Parashuram as an arbitrator was acceptable to both the parties. As one party did not agree with the award of the arbitrator, they tried to enforce the award, but failed. Thereafter, a still aggrieved Amba took the dispute public, which is like our idea of suing in a court. When she again could not get justice, she took her case to the supreme court of Karma.*

CHAPTER 5

Ved Vyas Invited to Perform Niyoga

Synopsis: The overbearing mother-in-law; when Itihas and Parampara are not followed; social customs are abused.

Hastinapur was now without a King or successor. Tempted by the power vacuum, rival kings wanted to subjugate the kingdom. Bhishma refused to perform Niyoga on his widowed sister-in-laws. In desperation, Satyawati ordered Ved Vyas, her son from Sage Parashara, to perform the act. Ved Vyas had just returned from penance in the forest and looked repulsive. He wanted some time to make himself presentable before the ceremony. But Satyawati insisted that he consummate the act immediately.

As expected, the widowed queens were reluctant to cohabit with Ved Vyas. They initially tricked him into impregnating a maid of their late husband. However, they were forced to submit to Niyoga. Their experience was shocking. Ved Vyas's appearance terrified Ambika. She shut her eyes in fear and disgust as he performed Niyoga on her. The experience of Ambalika was no different, she was in such a shock that she turned pale. The dasi queen or maid did not react negatively. She was welcoming, as she thought a Kuru royal was performing Niyoga and it would entitle the baby thus born to life as a royal.

Ambika gave birth to a son, Dhritarashtra, who was born blind. Ambalika birthed Pandu, and he was born an albino. Ved Vyas's son with a palace maid of Vichitravirya was born normal and called Vidura. The kingdom of Hastinapur now had two Princes of whom Dhritarashtra was the eldest and they ordained Pandu next in line. Vidura being born of a maid had a lower status and was not eligible to be a King.

Commentary

Niyoga has its Application in a Childless Marriage: The King was dead, without a successor. Satyawati wanted her widowed daughter-in-laws to have a child from a stranger. She misused the rules of Niyoga for her convenience. It reflects the plight of the abused widows at the insistence of their mother-in-laws. Satyawati as a woman demanded and got her terms before agreeing to marry Shantanu. She did not care about the rights and dignity of her sisters. They married these young women to a weak man, against their wish. Both the wives did not have a child from their husband. Imposing Niyoga on them fulfilled the personal agenda of a royal.

Bhishma refused because of his vow. However, the demand made on him was not appropriate. In Hindu custom, they expect a man to treat his younger brother's wife as his daughter. Likewise, the woman must accord to the elder brother of her husband the status of a father. Ved Vyas was also in a way the elder brother, but he was not a Kuru.

All the Kuru widows kept their status. Satyawati directed the conduct of the affairs of the state and her family. This was very different to the plight of widows in our current times, when often their rights and authority are taken away. This continues even today.

CHAPTER 6

Young Princes Grow up

Synopsis: Eligibility must not lead to discrimination. Childbirth has a sticky emotional connect. Risk of emotional attachment in surrogacy and Niyoga are similar.

Hastinapur now had three princes. The focus was on bringing them up. Dhritarashtra was born blind. He trained himself to overcome his physical disability. He grew up to be a strong, well-built young man. Pandu was born an albino. He trained himself as a great warrior. As Vidura's mother was not a Kshatriya, they treated him as a Suta. This in no way affected his education and training. They regarded him for his mastery of Dharma.

In a version of the Mahabharata, Vidura was the eldest by age, while others point to Dhritarashtra. Vidura must have been the firstborn, the widowed queens had tricked Ved Vyas into believing the woman was a royal. His lineage being weaker than that of the sons of Ambika and Ambalika, they never considered him to be in line for the crown. As Dhritarashtra was born blind, he was not suitable to be king. They appointed Pandu, who was next in line as king.

Dhritarashtra resented this appointment. He was neither consulted nor given an opportunity to prove himself. He had worked hard to overcome his disability and believed his strengths more than made up for his disability.

Commentary

Importance and Role of Women in Society: Queens had an equal and important role in the conduct of the affairs of the state and could alter the course of history of the family. It recognised a woman's role in sustaining the lineage of the family and where her husband was unable or didn't father a child, they could seek to have a child born into the family from another man. The Mahabharata points to a time when men and women shared equal rights, duties and status.

Succession and Eligibility: Children born to non-Kshatriya mothers were brought up as royals. But only those born to a Kshatriya queen were eligible for succession. In the absence of a king, it vested accession to the throne in the hands of the Council of Ministers. However, it restricted their choice to the eligible lineage of the princes. Only patriarchal lineage got from a father or a male child got through Niyoga could be considered. They also expected competence, physical fitness and virtues in a king. They exercised judgement and fulfilled their obligation towards the nation by appointing Pandu, instead of Dhritarashtra. King Pratipa followed this rule and passed over the immediate next in line. He based it on the principle of competence when he appointed his youngest son Shantanu as King. Parampara and Itihas of Kuru Kula was a good guide in fulfilment of their Rashtra Dharma. Pratipa consulted his eldest son and got his consent. But Dhritarashtra was not consulted, which should be seen as a mistake. Rules that were black or white did not govern succession as these could be grey. This is again an example of the Hindu way of life where there is no one truth, no one right or wrong, but right is what is correct as per time and circumstances, and, ultimately, Dharma. A king must be good for his country, its people, and society. They did not adopt a rule-based approach and automatically appoint Dhritarashtra as king, because of his biological age. They looked at his appropriateness and disabilities.

Niyoga and Surrogacy: In a Niyoga, a man must donate his seed so that a woman can bear a child. The child so born belongs to the woman and her husband. The child inherits the lineage of his mother's husband. As a concept, a woman is the field, the man performing the Niyoga is the farm worker who provides his seed for benefit of the landowner. The landowner is the husband who will reap and enjoy the benefit of the harvest. As per the rules, the donor of the seed must not associate himself with the child. Ved Vyas was married and had a son called Suka. He performed Niyoga on women or engaged in sex with women other than his wife. Ved Vyas had no obligation to the children born, nor did the children regard him as their father or his son Suka as their half-brother. Yet, the children sired by Ved Vyas received his paternal support and guidance several times in course of the Epic.

In modern thought, in place of Niyoga, they get a seed from an unknown donor from a sperm bank. This takes away the risk of human attachment between a donor and the child. However, with a surrogate mother, the risk of sticky human attachment between the woman and child remain. Mahabharata uses the father instead of the mother to highlight this attachment. It points out that, if it happens between father and child, fathom then its extent between a mother and child.

CHAPTER 7

Marriage of Dhritarashtra

Synopsis: A successful marriage needs mutual respect, consent and understanding. We may have problems, under different circumstances, yet we are duty-bound.

Marriage of Dhritarashtra was conducted after Bhishma went to Gandhar and sought Gandhari's hand for him. Gandhari's father agreed. However, the fact that Dhritarashtra was blind weighed heavily on Gandhari, who decided to remain blindfolded all through her life.

Commentary

Marriage, Consent, Respect and Emotional Connect: Satyawati asked Bhishma to find a bride for her blind grandson. The family had to help him get married, so he could fulfil his obligations of Ashram Dharma. He again forced a woman to marry without regard to her right of choice. Being a celibate, an unmarried Bhishma probably did not understand the importance of consent in marital relationships. After his rather high-handed ways with the princesses of Kashi, he should have realised that a marriage needs mutual consent of the partners. He ignored this and again used fear and compulsion. In fact, mutual consent must prevail throughout the relationship, the separation of Ganga and Shantanu sets out this basis. In some versions, Bhishma forced Gandhari to marry a blind person, when her family objected, they were imprisoned. These were enough indicators that no attraction, respect or consent existed in this relationship.

There are instances of princesses being abducted by suitors in a Swayamwar. The abductors would marry the princesses and their unions would be based on respect and attraction for the abductor.

The Epic dramatised the importance of emotional connect between husband and wife. They dramatised this need for emotional connect to great effect by blindfolding Gandhari for life. She could not take part with her husband or support him. It was too idealistic to suggest that the blindfold allowed her to empathise with her husband and feel the world as he would. Dhritarashtra may have been blind or blind, as in, lacking judgement. Gandhari as his wife and queen could have provided wise counsel, but preferred to stay blindfolded after her marriage. In the epic, they present her as one who chose not to or would not give wise counsel to her husband in the fulfilment of her duties.

Hindu scriptures describe eight forms of marriage. These forms are not as wide as the choice available to a royal princess at a Swayamwar. However, consent is a prerequisite in all circumstances. Relationships in a marriage can only be formed by mutual consent. Where sustained, it can survive widowhood and where violated end in spirit at least. The epic provides this guidance through various events.

The presentation of Dhritarashtra as blind and Gandhari in a blindfold is a dramatic play on their Dharma and relationship. They call a person blind if they lack discretion or sense of justice or ability to see reason. When someone pretends or shows indifference, then such behaviour is often referred to as one who has worn a blindfold. A blindfolded Gandhari was a woman who refused in spirit to be the wife of a man they forced her to marry. She refused to be by her Husband's side as an equal partner, to aid and help her 'blind' (wayward) husband to follow the Path of Dharma. Marriages *between man and woman is not a partnership that can be thrust upon either, but requires mutual consent and respect on both sides. They dramatise Gandhari's refusal to accept Dhritarashtra, as she spends the rest of her life blindfolded. They could not force on her the obligations of a wife. The Epic here provides us with a very subtle guidance on Dharma. Our obligation of Dharma must be fulfilled as they arise through our life phases.*

Some believe Gandhari blindfolded herself so she could understand the disability of her husband. This is appealing at an emotional level. However, such an emotional bond may not have existed or developed in the time between her marriage and meeting her husband. We may have missed the possibility of love at first sight or the idea that only a differently abled person can understand the predicament and suffering of another.

There is a Dhritarashtra in Each of Us: *Ambika shut her eyes as Dhritarashtra was being conceived, and did she turn a blind eye to her obligations to him as a mother? The Council of Ministers turned a blind eye to his right to be King, despite being the eldest born. Gandhari refused to accept him, turning a blind eye towards him once again. The authors have so scripted the character of Dhritarashtra as one in whose life nothing appears to go right. There is an element of Dhritarashtra in some form or another in each one of us. It is that something that has not gone right in our lives, like a denial or failure or a weakness.*

No one Escapes from Dharma and Karma: *Through Dhritarashtra, the Epic introduces a differently abled person, and a person who has been served a bad hand in the game of destiny. Nothing appeared to go right in his life, and yet his obligations of Dharma remained equal. The Mahabharata does not provide a Karma-based back story to explain Dhritarashtra's life, this prop is no longer required and also not available to us in the normal course. The message is: no one can escape Karma and Dharma.*

CHAPTER 8

Pandu Crowned King Marries Kunti and Madri

Synopsis: Mahabharata accords great importance to a woman's consent in marriage and examines the effect of consent.

They crowned Pandu as the king, and the Kuru Dynasty was now under the stewardship of an accomplished archer. He re-established the supremacy of Hastinapur. With this success his fame spread far and wide.

Pandu married Kunti at her Swayamwar and another princess by the name Madri. Bhishma got her on payment of a bride price. The future of Hastinapur now appeared to be bright and glorious with a brave king who had brought wealth from his several victories in battles.

Commentary

Marriages and Outcomes: Pandu's marriage to Kunti, a princess of the Yadav community, was based on mutual attraction and consent akin to a 'love marriage.' His marriage to Madri was akin to an 'arranged marriage,' consent existed, though they started the union through payment of a customary bride price.

Thus woven in this story are the principles pre-requisite for a successful union between a man and a woman. Marriages based on attraction and conditions fulfilled, as between an enchanted Shantanu and Satyawati. Swayamwar between Pandu and Kunti based on mutual consent. A marriage between Pandu and Madri arranged on payment of a bride price.

Contrast the above with the marriage imposed on the abducted sisters Ambika and Ambalika with Vichitravirya. There is also the forced marriage of Gandhari to Dhritarashtra. There is, however, a subtle distinction between the two imposed marriages, Vichitravirya's marriage was not consummated. Marriage did not give the husband the right to force himself on his wife. Only after Ved Vyas brought about a rapprochement between Gandhari and Dhritarashtra, their children were born. This suggests that one could force a woman to marry, but not compel her into a physical union.

In an earlier Epic, the Ramayana, Ravana kidnapped Sita; he imprisoned her, threatened her with death unless she agreed to marry him, but did not force her. Hindu custom was not just opposed to rape, but also to marital rape. It is heartening to note that some High Courts in India are now supporting the campaign to recognise marital rape.

Kunti was the only woman in the entire Epic to have exercised her choice in seeking her husband. They forced all other ladies in the Epic to marry with a view to forming alliances.

The marriage between King Shantanu and Ganga fell apart because of mutual needs not being fulfilled and because of the selfishness of the partners who betrayed each other. Ganga married Shantanu to fulfill her own desires and Shantanu failed to keep his promise.

The marriage between King Shantanu and Satyawati was based on the infatuation of the male towards the female. Satyawati gave her consent after she extracted some very difficult promises.

The depth of characterisation and events deal with a marriage between a man and a woman, and the basis of their relationship.

CHAPTER 9

Pandu along with his Wives Goes into Exile

Synopsis: It explains Ashram Dharma. It sets Indic thought apart. A celibate Bhishma lacks experience of relationships; role of trustees and caretakers in protecting a minor's rights.

Pandu had married two beautiful queens, but he had no children. Disheartened, he gave up his throne. He abdicated the crown and moved with his queens to live in the forest. The Epic has dramatised the reasons for his abdication, this is unacceptable to the modern mind. He was either removed or surrendered his rights as king and exiled himself to the forest along with his two queens.

Hastinapur had to fall back on Dhritarashtra; he now acted as the King. In the forest, Kunti and Madri used a mantra given to Kunti and gave birth to five sons. The user of the mantra could summon any demi-god or celestial being. They would give to the invoker a child with his qualities. These children were growing up in happy surroundings until Pandu's sudden death.

In the Epic, Pandu would die if he ever engaged in sexual intercourse. One day, enamoured by Madri's beauty, he could not restrain himself and engaged in sexual intercourse with her. He died as the curse took effect. Madri blamed herself for the death of Pandu and self immolated herself on her husband's funeral pyre. This now left Kunti with the responsibility of looking after the five sons born to her and Madri.

Commentary

King and his Responsibility of Dharma: Kings in Indic Dharma had a god-like stature. He was the protector of Dharma and of the Brahmins who were the preachers of Dharma. As an upholder of Dharma, he must enforce it, if required, through fear of punishment and other forms of compulsion. Dharma are the rules that govern society. If the king was unable to fulfil his Dharma towards himself or his family or Society, he had no moral authority to continue. He had to lead by example.

Ashram Dharma in the Hindu Way of Life: The rules of Dharma include the rules of Ashram. This requires every human being to divide his life into four stages. The first stage is that of a student, they call it the Brahmacharya stage, in which a young male lives under the care and guidance of his Guru. He gains knowledge and education that prepares him for the next stages of his life. During this stage, he has no attachment to material wealth and relationships. He prepares for his profession, his family, social and religious life ahead. He learns the principles of Dharma which he must adopt for the rest of his life. In the next stage, he becomes a householder or a Grihastha. As an adult, he now returns home, marries and takes up the responsibility of supporting his family. Hinduism supports the pursuit of wealth or Artha as a necessity. It approves sexual pleasure or Kama under defined social norms. Often humans are so much in love with this stage that it lasts a lifetime. Then comes the Vanprashta or the Hermit stage. By this time, the man has become a grandfather, his children would have reached the Grihasta stage. They do not expect him and his wife to leave home or live in a forest hut. They must allow the transition of responsibility to the next generation and be available for advice and guidance. The person takes on the role of an advisor instead of being the centre of action. He must hand the reins of control over to the next generation. This would allow the next generation to pursue an identity of its own. They can bring more wealth, name and fame to the family. A consistent application of this principle would ensure that human endeavours would be amongst near equals. It would allow both man and society to evolve. The person focuses on spirituality. The last stage is when he takes Sanyas or renouncement. At this stage, he should have no emotional or material attachments, and would have renounced his duties and responsibilities. His worldly ties are ending and he devotes his time to God. His children would have entered the third stage, many of his friends and maybe even his partner may have passed away. He limits his life and thoughts to his concern of attaining moksha, or release from the circle of birth and death.

Abrahamic Schools, Buddhists and other modern religions require their monks and priests to live their lives as a Brahmachari. Hindus must live their lives governed by the rules of Ashram. The Mahabharata uses Bhishma to prove this point. After Bhishma completed his Brahmacharya stage, his mother Ganga returned him to King Shantanu. He had started life as a Crown Prince, however, because of his vows, he renounced the grihastha phase of his life.

A man will experience relationships with a woman in several forms. Bhishma was a celibate. He had no emotional engagement with a woman as a lover, husband or father. He could not realise the sufferings of Amba a woman in love when he kidnapped her. Her lover rejected her when she returned to him. As a celibate, he did not understand the mind and heart of a lover. He also did not understand *the emotional and sexual violation that Ambika and Ambalika suffered. As women, they were being forced to have children in the act of Niyoga. He forced Gandhari to marry a blind Dhritarashtra. His limited range of relationships with women caused his insensitive behaviour. Had he experienced life as a grihastha, he would have understood and respected the right of choice of women. They suffered because of his behaviour. His heartless behaviour is clear in his inability to understand the love of Amba. He then does not protect two widows from being violated. They forced the widows to engage in a physical union reserved between a man and his wife. He then forced Gandhari to marry a man unsuited to her. Later on, he sits through the humiliation of Draupadi. Some of them were both young enough to be his daughter and granddaughter.*

According to Sanatan thought, a person who lives through all stages of life according to Ashram Dharma will be enriched. A male will have experienced a relationship with a female in all its many dimensions, and so would a female. This will add maturity to their thoughts and actions. A man who has never been a father cannot understand the real emotions between parent and child. If a person does not marry, he cannot understand the love between a couple.

Following Ashram Dharma, Pandu needed to marry, have children and live life as a grihastha. But being childless, he would not have lived a life in keeping with the rules of Ashram. Unable to fulfil his dharma, he had to abdicate his role as a king and go into exile. However, this is inconsistent with the conduct of other kings. Childless kings would adopt a male child and thus provide for succession. Why did Pandu not do that? The authors wanted us to understand the difference between form and substance. Adopting the child would have met the requirement in form, Pandu moved to the forests hoping he would concentrate on his family. This is the other message intended. We often get busy with our material goals and postpone our obligations as a family. Pandu was guilty of that, and he had to make that good. He had failed to strike a balance and therefore had to resort to a drastic re-focus.

Succession, Modern Law and Hindus: In the Mahabharata, the right of succession was craftily positioned in the grey area. Dhritarashtra was differently abled and passed over as king. They made Pandu the king, but he then discovered he was sexually incapable of providing a successor. They pitted a blind brother against an impotent brother. Pandu was King and an upholder of Dharma. He realised that both he and his brother suffered from a physical disability. Once a disability is discovered, one must give it due consideration. He could not remain king. As we delve further, Pandu handed over reign to his elder brother Dhritarashtra, who could only be a caretaker. Both Pandu and Dhritarashtra could only be custodians awaiting a king. Dharma required that only the ablest amongst their progeny to be the King. This would explain the race between Pandu and Dhritarashtra to get a son. Seniority was of consequence only because it would advantage the eldest in capability by his age and earlier growth. The rules of succession did not entitle the firstborn to be crowned the king. It made the firstborn the first contender. If there were no grounds for his rejection, he would be eligible to be king. This is also the reason Bhishma had to swear himself to a life of celibacy so he could never have children who could later stake a claim to the throne based on any unforeseen contingency.

Hindus live in a joint family. The eldest male member has the responsibility for all the members within the family. He is obligated to all as it entitles them to an undivided interest in the family. This concept extends beyond adulthood and extends to all aspects of life and livelihood. The challenge arises when the 'karta' dies, Mahabharata deals with this succession. It deals with the claim to the assets of the joint family between the male inheritors and the conflicts that arise.

The eldest progeny need not be the king. They may rule him out for lack of competence, ill health, or inability to fulfil the principles of Dharma. The children of the one passed over cannot stake a claim to the throne. This should have been the settled principle, because the children of King Shantanu's siblings did not stake a claim. However,

Bhishma had to take a vow of celibacy to avoid this possible claim by his children. This brings us to the complex rules of the Hindu joint family, where the eldest in line is the head of the family. On passing of a generation, the eldest amongst them becomes the new head. It thus introduces us to the principles of a trusteeship in a joint family.

They made Pandu the King and upholder of Dharma. He realised that he suffered as much as his brother did from physical disability. Once a disability is discovered, they must take it into consideration. When he discovered he would be childless, he no longer had the right to remain King. He abdicated and went into exile. As we delve further, Pandu handed over reign to his elder brother Dhritarashtra, who could only be a caretaker. Whilst in exile, he had children. Whilst still in exile, Pandu died and this should have ended his claim to the throne and that of his progeny. This is re-enforced by the lack of a claim made by Pandu during his lifetime, and so no claim was subsisting at the time of his death. Could then the children of Pandu have a claim to the throne?

Succession is an obligation of every leader. A leader must ensure that he secures and provides for a clear plan of succession. This risk first arose when Bhishma stepped down as crown prince in favour of a yet-to-be-born. Then Vichitravirya died, leaving no successor. They abused the concept of Niyoga to provide for a successor. The symbolic message in the Niyoga on Ambika and Ambalika is when there is no available successor we must consider an external candidate. As with Pandu and Dhritarashtra, where there is no successor, caretakers or interim managers must take charge.

Status of Widows: Queen Madri's self-immolation might suggest this was a tradition. Widows of slain warriors would commit self-immolation to avoid being taken by other men against their wishes. There is a greater meaning behind it. A married couple not only share an emotional and physical bond, but also share a legacy and obligation. *When Pandu dies, the emotional and physical bond ends and this is symbolised by Madri and her self-immolation. Kunti, the widow, had to take responsibility for her husband's legacy and the obligations they created as a couple. She fulfils this obligation by parenting their young children and guiding them, so that when they grow up, they could stake a claim to their father's legacy.*

Laws of Contract: *As per the law on contracts, an agreement is void and ineffective ab initio if parties have based a contract on information that was incorrect. They did not appoint Dhritarashtra as a King for his clear disability. Instead, they appointed Pandu, but when he discovered his disability, his appointment was void ab initio because his disability had pre-existed his appointment. Unable to fulfil his Dharma, he would have ended his appointment because of impossibility of performance.*

Pandu's Abdication is an Everyday Guidance: *There are times when we may find ourselves unable to deliver on a responsibility. If we are not able to do so, we must forthwith stand down. This message applies equally to the head of a family or society. The message is not about giving up, but about giving way. Often in a home, the eldest lady in the house is no longer able to shoulder her responsibility but refuses to give up her authority. Pandu could not fulfil his responsibility of providing a successor, he, therefore, also gave up his authority.*

CHAPTER 10

Dhritarashtra, the Blind King and his 100 Sons

Synopsis: The 100 sons represent the large number of human traits. Idea of incubation and test-tube babies visualised then are now realised.

Dhritarashtra was now the caretaker of Hastinapur. Neither Pandu nor he was eligible to be King. Pandu was childless, and so was Dhritarashtra. Kuru dynasty once again lacked a successor. In the forced marriage between Dhritarashtra and Gandhari, there was no emotional connection between the couple. Ved Vyas had to intervene, and with his efforts the couple agreed to come together. Gandhari became pregnant, and the Kuru Dynasty was looking forward to the birth of a successor.

Her pregnancy was not normal, necessitating Ved Vyas' intervention again. He split the fertilised ovum and then incubated it in artificial wombs. As the story has it, a 100 sons and one daughter were born through this process. This sounds impossible, but it serves a purpose. The relationship between the couple was not normal, it was a compromise. Gandhari submitted to the physical relationship only once. Another son was also born to Dhritarashtra through his Dasi Queen. This point was introduced to bring relevance to several issues, the first of which was, such a child was not eligible to succeed as king. The later issues will focus on upbringing.

Dhritarashtra was believed to have the strength of 10,000 elephants. As a father to 102 children, it would have been impossible for him to fulfil his responsibilities as a husband, a father and a king. He may have been called blind to mean blind to responsibilities. The ruling family's concern of a claim for return of the kingdom by Pandu or his progeny is dramatized by the race to bring to life the eldest successor amongst them all. Little is said of how and to whom most of the 102 children of Dhritarashtra were born. But medically and practically it could not have been to Gandhari. Out of the 101 sons of Dhritarashtra, Duryodhana, Dushashan and Vikarna have important roles. Dushala was the name of his daughter.

Both Pandu and Dhritarashtra had to give up their claim to the throne, but they both knew their next generation had a right to the throne. Dhritarashtra was the eldest but passed over for king, he was now acting king. His younger brother Pandu was king but had to give up his throne. So it entitled the children of both to the throne. There was a race between them to be the first to have a male child. Not all was clear; the children of both the siblings were not born in normal circumstances. There would be a controversy, and this enabled the authors to give us a story, rich in content which covered the lives of several characters comprehensively.

Commentary

Ideas are Often Ahead of their Times: The authors provide a foundation to the events and characters involved. Did he really have 101 sons? Incubation of a fertilised ovum in a test tube-like environment was much ahead of its time. An ovary releases one or more eggs but the maximum number of babies born in a single pregnancy is eight, based on record. Similarly, splitting a single ovum into 101 units each growing into a baby has not been achieved. Test-tube babies and their cloning were visualized thousands of years ago, they appear to be possible today. Human progress is only possible when we dream of evolution. Only if we dream can we pursue its realisation. Every couple has a dream for the child they plan. They want their child to have the best; they want them to have that which they could not or did not have.

Relationship between Couples: The Epic deals with the relationship between couples. A couple must accept their relationship before they have a child. Families are advised not to impose social pressure on a newly-married couple to have a baby until they have a settled relationship. The birth of a child can introduce a common agenda for the couple. It cannot bring them together. Gandhari continued to wear her blindfold even after the birth of her children. They forced Gandhari to marry, like her mother-in-law. When the latter did not provide for a successor, they forced Niyoga upon her. She knew the Kuru dynasty was facing a challenge of succession again. Pandu had failed to produce a child and had abdicated. No one knew what had happened to them. Under the circumstances, she could be in the same situation as her mother-in-law. She submitted to the unacceptable because of her fear of the unknown. In a marriage, couples often consider and accept a compromise rather than risk the unknown.

CHAPTER 11

Kunti Returns with the Five Pandava Sons

Synopsis: Lies and deceit will be discovered. People are not bad, but they have strength or weaknesses.

On the death of Pandu and his wife Madri, Queen Kunti returned to Hastinapur with five young children in tow. She claimed three as her own, given to her by the boon granted by the demi-gods. Their names were Yudhisthir, Bhima and Arjun. Demi-gods gave the remaining two children to Madri, namely Nakul and Sahadev, because Kunti had transferred the boon to Madri. Kunti claimed that, before her marriage, she had been blessed with a boon by Durvasa Rishi. It was a mantra that could invoke any god, demi-god or celestial being to bless her with a child with their attributes.

Kunti claimed that the children born out of a boon possessed the attributes of demi-gods. This aura of Divinity reinforced their legitimacy beyond question. Kunti felt apprehensive, even as the Gruhyakas informed the gathering. Bhishma stepped in and gracefully accepted the children as those of Pandu.

There is an interesting anecdote attached to the boon. Kunti wanted to ascertain whether it worked and how. Out of curiosity, she invoked Surya, resulting in Karna's birth but she cloaked the event in secrecy. Even after marriage with Pandu, Kunti used her boon three more times. She transferred her boon to Pandu's other wife Madri, who gave birth to twins, twins Nakul and Sahadev.

Commentary

Incredible Story of Birth of Pandavas and Kauravas: *Kunti's story of the birth of her children is improbable as it did not require pregnancy or a physical union. This was as impossible as Gandhari's single fertilised ovum being split into 101 units. Each of which was then incubated in an artificial womb and 101 children were born. However, these ideas serve a purpose. They allowed the authors of the epic to explain the rules of Dharma. Some believe the five Pandavas represent the attributes we seek in a human. The 100 Kauravas represent the innumerable traits found in humans. This is no suggestion we humans can have only five good attributes and the bad traits are innumerable. In the course of the Epic, we would discover the story of Pandavas vs Kauravas is not about good vs bad. Their story is about the impact of human strength and weaknesses on the outcome of their lives. We will realise they gave the Pandavas the attributes to deliver a message. People expected them to be good, and so their weaknesses became all the more apparent. The Kauravas appear steadfast in their mission; they appear to plan and respond to the Pandavas. They saw the Pandavas as a threat to their right to the Kingdom. It is normal to develop a soft corner for the underdog. The Pandavas would receive our emotional support as they had to fight for their claim and unseat the rich and powerful Kauravas. The idea of creating this classic rich vs poor or strong vs weak has a purpose. The Epic wants us to focus on Dharma and not our emotions. In the events that follow, Dharma was abused by both sides. In our lives we must align our emotions with our Dharma.*

The Pandavas, Boon, Divine Linkage and Claim: *They could not* adopt Niyoga more than once. In the Epic, Madri submits only once, and she gets twins. The idea is to avoid creating controversy around multiple characters. Every character and its role carried a message. These messages become obvious in course of the Epic. They introduced divine intervention to side-step potential controversy. Pandu needed only one son to succeed him, and not so many. Divine Linkage for each child enhanced their acceptability for royal duties. Ambika and Ambalika, the childless widows both bore children. This would suggest it entitled every wife to take part in Niyoga. There could be a reason for this. They expected a woman to submit to Niyoga only once. It was not possible to determine the sex of the child before their birth, so they would ask all the queens to submit to Niyoga. Married couples have a responsibility to provide for the evolution of life. Each couple has a responsibility towards Ashram Dharma. Every person must experience in their life all the relationships possible. A childless couple cannot experience parenthood and beyond. This also explains why each of the wives submitted to Niyoga.

Kunti's marriage with Pandu may not have been consummated. Her sexual relationship was limited to having offsprings from the four celestial beings. In the public eyes, she had children from three celestial beings and Pandu was her fourth relationship. Her relationship that resulted in the birth of Karna was kept a secret. As per traditions, had Kunti acknowledged that Karna was her child then Pandu could have consented to be his foster father. He could have adopted Karna. However, she did not know if her abandoned child was still alive. The issues and challenges of succession would never have arisen. But it was not until much later that she found out that her first child had, in fact, survived.

No Escape from the Consequences of Karma and Lies: Karna's birth was as an act of indiscretion. It would haunt and torment Kunti. It helps us to understand how her karma affected her life and of those around her. It will also bring to bear how one lie leads to another. The Epic shows how, at the end, despite cover-ups, truth will surface. Owning up to truth is difficult, but once acknowledged, life becomes easy. Hiding a truth or lying is easy, but living with it can torment us and destroy our soul.

CHAPTER 12

The Young Princes Growing Up

Synopsis: Successive invasions of India and foreign rule changed Indic thinking on worship. Dignity and plight of widows; why grandfather cannot be like a father?

In Hastinapur, they referred to the sons of Pandu and Dhritarashtra as Pandavas and Kauravas. The Pandavas had now settled into life as young princes. Dhritarashtra made Kunti and her five wards part of his royal household. This accorded them a royal status. He involved family elders and gurus like Bhishma, Vidura and Kripacharya in training of the princes for their future royal duties. Yudhisthir excelled in matters of Dharma. Bhima stood out for his physical prowess. Arjun showed his sharp focus and resolve.

Behind the scenes, there was an intense rivalry between the cousins. The Kauravas were not happy with their new-found cousins. This pushed them into rival groups. The race for the claim to ascend the throne had also begun.

The Pandavas did not feel secure. The Palace did not feel like home; they did not feel they belonged there. In their effort to gain acceptance, they kept their best behaviour. People would talk about them in admiration, this upset the Kauravas. Arjun was the favourite of Bhishma, they would often see him playing with his grandfather. The Pandavas were missing their father. One day, a young Arjun addressed Bhishma as a father. Bhishma corrected him and told him he was his grandfather and not the father.

The young princes now needed further education. They could not provide this education at home. They needed a guru who could train them for their duties as a Kshatriya.

Commentary

Women and Widowhood: *Why did Kunti return to Hastinapur and not to her father's home? This is the most important message for widows. The death of the husband is the death of the emotional union. It does not end her rights; she inherits the rights that belong to her husband. It binds the family of the deceased husband to allow her this right.*

In the Epic, we learn how women in the Kuru household dealt with their widowhood. Satyawati as a widow carried forward the legacy of her husband. She took the responsibility for the family. She asked the widows of her sons to provide for succession. She would direct the Regent on matters of state. Kunti followed in her footsteps. Ambika and Ambalika as widows surrendered themselves for the benefit of their family. Madri preferred to die on her husband's funeral pyre. We must not view her death as an escape. Kunti and Madri symbolise the two sides of a marriage. These two sides are the emotional side and the responsibility that comes with marriage. Madri's death represents the death of the emotional side of the union. Madri and Pandu died because of their sexual attraction, symbolic of the death of their emotional union too. The responsibilities of the surviving partner did not end upon widowhood. Kunti did not return to her father's home, but went to her husband's family home. Widows must continue to fulfil their obligations to their families, society and country as did the Kurus widows. A widow does not have to jump into the funeral pyre, she can even marry again.

Kunti, the sole surviving adult within the Pandu household, took charge as the mother and guardian of all of Pandu's children. She returned to Hastinapur so that, once grown up, the Pandavas could stake their claim to succession. She continued to guide and influence them in the fight for their rights. The Kuru widows continued to fulfil their responsibility after the demise of their husbands.

Gender Inequality: *Gender inequality must have crept into Hinduism after the Puranic Phase. They also reflect it in the dominant male focus of Buddhism and the Abrahamic Schools. In this male-dominated environment, women in their childhood were under the control of her father, then as a wife under her husband and upon his death under the control of her male children. It would appear that the status of women was reduced to that of an inferior being. The will of a male dominated her will.*

They considered women weak and inferior. Until almost 50 years ago and possibly in some parts of India, they still expect a widow to shun jewellery or wear only white cloth. They often force her out of her home and she lives a life of penury in some dharamshala or ashram, barred from festivities and family functions.

Devi Worship Ostracised: *Over the past centuries, they have conditioned us to recognise God as male. However, the reality is different. Hindus also worship Devi, the female version of God as Durga, Kali, Laxmi, Sarasvati, etc. For several centuries European and Islamic powers ruled India, according a lower status to women. Even indigenous religions became male-centric.*

In India, worshippers of Devi were suspected of conducting human sacrifices. It influenced Hindu thinkers to come up with the concept of Ardhanarishwara, or a half-male, half-female God. Although goddesses were attributed with life-giving power, women were still treated as inferiors.

The bias against women was not limited to India. After the death of Christ, his apostles and his mother Mary wanted to spread his preaching around the world. The apostles knew their lives were at risk. They sent Mary to the third largest town of the Roman Empire called Ephesus in Turkey, where they passed no legislation without the approval of a women's council. The apostles felt that Mother Mary could live there and promote Christianity in its secure environment. Her home is now a place of pilgrimage for members of the Christian faith.

Grandfather is not a Father: *This is an important message. The Pandavas were young when they moved from their home in the forests to the family home. It was reasonable for them to feel out of place. They wanted to gain acceptance and put on their best behaviour. Arjun displays this insecurity as he is looking for a father in Bhishma. A father is a protector to his child, he is the provider of safety. We often refer to children brought up by a divorced parent as coming from a broken home. This feeling of insecurity and desire to gain acceptance becomes a weakness in their personality. Later, this weakness was exploited by Narada to convince them to perform a Rajsuya Yagna.*

A child can have a foster mother. Kunti was a mother to the children of Madri. Krishna and Karna both had foster mothers; both loved each other dearly. If a woman can be a mother to a child not her own, why could not Bhishma be a father to Arjun? The answer lies in how each views a relationship and the responsibility that comes with it. Bhishma had subordinated himself to the service of the crown. They would expect a father to give priority to his children.

Bhishma had many grandchildren; he could give someone extra attention, but he did not want to choose one over the other. This is a valuable piece of advice on parenting. We must not play favourites. Another advice is that whilst both parents love their child, they have a specific role in his or her upbringing. They point to a God being responsible for creation and goddesses being accountable for their sustenance. These responsibilities shared between couples will transfer to the surviving partner as it did on Kunti. Bhishma instinctively knew Arjun was a child and vulnerable; he would not understand the subtle difference between the Dharma of a father and grandfather. A grandfather under the principles of Ashram Dharma has taken up the role of an advisor. He is no longer pursuing life as a householder. He did not want Arjun to think he could be to him what Dhritarashtra was to Duryodhana. In Hindu thought, the elder brother of a father is also regarded as a father. Dhritarashtra however makes a very interesting and subtle distinction. He acknowledges the sons of his brother Pandu as his own, but attaches greater importance to his offsprings as they are his own flesh and blood.

CHAPTER 13

Dronacharya, the Royal Tutor

Synopsis: Avoid the trap of Blind Faith. Respect and learn from your guru or teacher, but be cautious of his agenda. Tutors may choose and develop the skills of their pupil.

The Epic now introduces Dronacharya, a Brahmin. He was an expert in weaponry and warfare, the brother-in-law of the royal guru, Kripacharya. He was trained by his father at the ashram, along with the royals, who included Drupad. The two became fast friends. After their training, Drupad ascended the throne of Panchal, but an out of work Dronacharya found himself in dire straits. He could not even afford milk for his young child Ashwatthama. Recalling Drupad's promise to share half his kingdom with him, Dronacharya travelled to Panchal. Face to face with Drupad, Dronacharya reminded him of his friendship and promise. Drupad angrily asked, how could a poor Brahmin ever think of being friends with a king? Drupad curtly told him their association had ended after they left the Ashram. He could offer him some alms but refused to do so because of his impertinence and turned him out. Dronacharya swore to avenge his humiliation.

Dronacharya then approached his brother-in-law in Hastinapur for employment. Bhishma knew of the background of Dronacharya and his father's work as a Royal Tutor. He asked him to teach and train the royal princes. An ashram was set up for this purpose, where he also trained his son Ashwatthama. An accomplished archer, he had the knowledge of and access to celestial weapons. Dronacharya carried very strong moral and social views. His exposure to poverty influenced his behaviour. He was insecure and would go to any means to protect his newly found status. Dronacharya was spoiling the environment of the Gurukul. He wanted to build a team of loyal royals. In time, he wanted them to avenge his humiliation by Drupad.

Dronacharya segregated his students based on their aptitude. Instead of paying more attention to weaker students, he would give more time to those who could learn more. He focussed on building and developing their strengths rather than paying extra attention to the weaker princes. As per Duryodhana and his brothers, the Pandavas were being given extra attention. Even his son Ashwatthama accused his father of imparting additional knowledge to Arjun. Arjun also felt that his guru paid more attention to his son. Arjun was an eager student and wanted to acquire additional skills.

In the town, a royal charioteer and his wife lived with their adopted son Karna. This boy was being brought up as a Suta, but he showed no interest in being a charioteer. He would practise all day to gain the skills of an archer. On his insistence, his father got a Royal Decree that would gain his son admission into Dronacharya's ashram. Karna joined the Ashram, but to his dismay, Dronacharya refused to train him. He would only train royal princes and not a Suta. The role of a Suta was to serve the Kshatriyas, they were not required to learn weaponry. Karna felt it was unfair, and he left the ashram. Karna was not the only one to suffer Dronacharya's bias.

In the jungle, there also lived a tribal community. The young prince of that community also wanted Dronacharya to teach him archery. Dronacharya refused him too. In his view, being royal was not enough, the young prince was not an Aryan. The young tribal prince's name was Eklavya, he was also upset with the decision of Dronacharya. He would watch the Guru train the Royals from a distance. He would then try to replicate the training, practise hard and soon master it. Eklavya was very motivated, he replicated the entire training to teach himself.

One day whilst the students were on a royal hunt to practice their skills of archery. They spotted a target, but before they could launch their arrows, an arrow hit the target. This shocked the group. Dronacharya and his students branched out to locate this archer. This search led to Eklavya.

Eklavya was pleased to see his guru and confessed that he had gained these skills watching Dronacharya train his pupils. Eklavya acknowledged him as his guru and then led the group to his hut. In his hut, he had erected a statue of his guru; he used it as a surrogate of his guru to get his inspiration. Dronacharya was flattered to see his statue and proud to see how a student could learn his skills with no help. At the same time, he was upset as he realised that Eklavya had, through subterfuge, gained his knowledge and mastered archery. He feared for his reputation and failure. His job was to show he had trained the princes into being the best, but here was someone better. He needed to keep his job, and he wanted glory as the best teacher with the best students at any cost. He did not want Hastinapur to take a view that he had not given his best to the princes.

Dronacharya tricked Eklavya. He congratulated him and told him his training was complete. Eklavya wanted his blessing. Dronacharya asked for his Guru Dakshina on completion of the training. Eklavya was overwhelmed that the man who had refused to train him had now accepted him. He gracefully offered to meet any demand of his Guru. In a flash, Dronacharya asked him for his right thumb. He knew without the right thumb, Eklavya could not release an arrow. He would be disabled as an archer. Eklavya with no hesitation, took out his knife, axed his thumb and offered it to his Guru.

Commentary

Dronacharya's Bias and Weakness: Was Dronacharya right in refusing Karna and Eklavya? He used Varna to exclude Karna, and he refused to train Eklavya because he was not an Aryan. He refused a royal decree; this showed the weakness of the state. They could not control the ministers and employees. Later, he would use this knowledge to get his way. Taking away Eklavya's right thumb showed the depravity of his persona. He might also have done this to show that he was the best trainer, and he was doing his assigned work. He refused Karna to avoid the chance that someone other than the princes was his best student. His own son saw this in his behaviour. It was his insecurity; he was not just doing his job; he wanted to secure his job. He wanted to be indispensable by showing that only through his tuitions could one get the foremost warriors of his time. Dronacharya exploited the rivalry between the cousins. He used the opportunity to build his influence with the Pandavas who were the underdogs but painted with a Divine Lineage. He was single-minded; he wanted control over a group of powerful, loyal royals for his planned revenge against Drupad.

Beware of the Opportunist: *Opportunists can exploit our agenda to seek benefits and to fulfil their own agendas. The most learned can also have faults. We need to exercise judgement and discretion at all times. We must respect and trust our teachers, but we cannot follow them blindly. A teacher has a responsibility towards all his students, both the weak and the meritorious.*

CHAPTER 14

Karna Seeks out Parashuram as his Guru

Synopsis: Lying in a relationship? Can you hide your true self in a relationship? Rules relating to Intellectual property rights.

Even though Karna possessed a royal decree, Dronacharya refused to train him personally, because he was not of a royal lineage. Humiliated, Karna quit the ashram and approached another powerful warrior Parashuram, Bhishma's guru and a Brahmin himself like Dronacharya, for training. The guru only accepted Brahmins as pupils but loathed Kshatriyas, many of whom he had killed. Karna hid the fact of his being a Suta. The Mahabharata narrows the divide between Brahmins and Kshatriyas. Dronacharya and Parashuram are Brahmins by varna and but both are regarded for their combat skills, the calling of the Kshatriyas. One trains royal princes and the other trains the trainers. So Brahmins served not only as priests but also tutored royals in the art of warfare, among other things. Karna showed great potential. He learnt the rules of war, the art of using lethal weapons. Recognizing his potential, an immensely pleased Parashuram taught him arcane secrets of launching deadly arrows, sharing every bit of his esoteric skills.

One day, Parashuram slept with his head on Karna's lap when a scorpion stung the latter. Karna stayed still despite excruciating pain and all the bleeding so that his guru's sleep remained undisturbed. But when Parashuram woke up, he noticed Karna's agony. Only a Kshatriya could withstand so much pain. He questioned Karna about his origins, who then confessed to being the son of a Suta. A furious and upset Parashuram banished his favourite pupil and decreed that he would forget this knowledge when he needed it most.

Commentary

Principles of Intellectual Property: Parashuram refused to teach the Kshatriyas. Dronacharya would only train Royal students. The owner of an intellectual property cannot be forced to handover or transfer their intellectual property. Eklavya's action amounted to duplication. We could consider Karna's act being theft. In both instances, the owners punished them. The owners prevented both from using the Intellectual Property as they had gained it dishonestly or without consent. We can call Eklavya's actions copying or plagiarising, and that of Karna was theft. They varied the punishments as would a judge today. They punished both; it disabled Eklavya from using the knowledge. Karna's punishment was harsher; they gave him a death sentence.

In a later event, after the Princes had completed their training, their guru required them to pay his fees. This deals with an important aspect of law. No transfer is complete without payment of consideration. The transferor must agree to such consideration as adequate. A transferee can gain absolute Right of Use only after the payment of the required consideration. Until they make such payment, the right of use is under the absolute discretion and control of the owner. Any fruits from such use will continue to belong to the owner. In our times today, software developers working on Product Development within a company cannot claim intellectual right to the development.

Knowledge Discrimination: *Whilst a wrong is a wrong, yet we realise that both the wrong doers were themselves wronged. Dronacharya denied Eklavya an education because he was not a Kshatriya. When he gained it, Dronacharya denied him the right to use it. Dronacharya also denied Karna training as he was not a royal. When he used dishonest means, his guru denied him the right to use it. One cannot right a wrong with a wrong. The Epic did not provide the victim the option to right a wrong. They provide this message through Amba; she fights for her rights, does all she can to remedy the wrong done to her. The Epic wants us to understand that even if our choices are limited, we cannot right a wrong by using wrongful means.*

It appears, the authors also wanted to draw our attention to how the system can oppress individuals. It highlights the need for access to education and skills. It must be granted without discrimination based on class or community.

Honesty in Human Relationships: *Often, in our desire to gain acceptance in a relationship, we use subterfuge; we put on a pretence; we act as the one that the other would want us to be. Thus, we embark on a relationship putting up an act that may often mask our true selves.*

Karna enters Parshuram's Gurukul pretending to be a Brahmin. He could carry on with this for a while but could not change his true character. Whilst this relationship with his guru lasted, it grew so deep he granted him access to all his knowledge. A deep bond and trust developed between him and his guru, just as we would like to achieve in a relationship we desire.

However, if, like Karna, we are faking the act, we cannot be our true selves. When this fake act is discovered or our true character is unmasked, we will bring upon ourselves unknown misery. Such behaviour is disappointing and can lead to a vicious response that can often lead to the end of the relationship. Karna pleaded, cried and tried to justify his behaviour. A disappointed and violated guru ended the relationship with a curse that would play out as a death sentence.

This might bring back memories of some experiences in our own life. We may have made false promises, our behaviour would have been discovered and the relationships would have ended. The outcome of Karna's behaviour once again brings out the relevance of the Epic to our lives.

CHAPTER 15

Passing Out Parade and Entry of Karna

Synopsis: A mother and her unwanted child. Humility is important. No test in life is final. There is always someone somewhere who can better the best. Money cannot buy loyalty.

At the end of the training of the Princes, they held an event called the Passing Out Parade. Dronacharya required the Princes to show off their acquired skills to the King, with the royals and local people attending it. They intended these demonstrations to convey the prowess of the princes to the Kings of nearby kingdoms.

Arjun showed his excellence as an archer. From the crowd emerged Karna. He showed that as an archer; he was as proficient as Arjun. Karna offered to duel with Arjun. This would allow people to decide who amongst them was better. Dronacharya did not want the demonstration of his pupil's skills to turn into a competition. At his behest, his brother-in-law Kripacharya asked Karna to identify himself. When Karna said he was the son of a charioteer, Kripacharya mocked him. He told him to go away as this was an event for Kshatriya Royals. A son of a charioteer, i.e. a Suta Karna was not entitled to take part. The Pandavas joined this humiliation. Bhima and Arjun were insulting towards Karna. They had planted the seeds of hatred that Karna would never forget in his lifetime.

Duryodhana was watching the humiliation of Karna from the side-lines. He saw this as an opportunity to get Karna to his side. Duryodhana appointed Karna as the King of Anga. As Karna was now king, he could challenge Arjun for a duel. However, they could not hold the duel because of want of time. By handing over a small kingdom to Karna, Duryodhana could win Karna's loyalty for a lifetime. The Passing Out Parade finished without a conclusive duel. The title of the Mightiest Prince of all eluded the Pandavas.

In the royal gallery, Kunti recognised that the young archer was her unwanted child she had abandoned at birth. She had always thought her child was no longer living. Finding him alive and in front of a crowd, she fainted out of shock. She could not bear the humiliation they subjected Karna to. Only if she could have run across and acknowledged him as her son, but she could not. She had abandoned him at birth to save the reputation of her family. Now she could not acknowledge him for the fear of putting her reputation in jeopardy. People would doubt her integrity, her story of the birth of the Pandavas and much worse. This would mean she had relationships with five men. Even if she wanted to accept all the risks, she could not bear to think of the emotional turmoil it would cause the young Pandavas.

Commentary

Caste was not Based on Birth or Lineage: The Epic wanted us to realise how soul destroying any form of discrimination based on birth can be. They will play the story of the Karna and his background as a Suta several times in the Epic. They gave us a warning, which we ignored. This abuse inflicted on people based on birth has caused concern to humanity ever since.

Circumstances Surround and Contribute to Success: Even the best has a match somewhere. Mahabharata in its unique way teaches us the need to be humble. Insults meted out on that day were remembered and the enmity it caused influenced the course of future events. It led to a rivalry between Karna and Arjun which influenced their future behaviour. Dronacharya adopted subterfuge to show that Arjun as an archer was unmatched. Arjun was successful because of his circumstances, both Eklavya and Karna were not Kshatriya Royals. Competitions are limited by time and contestants. There may be those who are better but did not participate. There are others whose time will come soon. We are winners only for the moment.

Duryodhana's vision and presence of mind on that day enabled him to find in Karna a loyal friend. As an archer, he could match the power and capability of Arjun. He showed his skills as a leader by being able to spot and recruit challengers to the Pandavas. He analysed the strength of each Pandava and ensured he had a friend who could challenge and equal the Pandavas. He had thus executed a plan for meeting future challenges to his succession as the King of Hastinapur.

Mother's Love and Commitment to her Children: We all know of the undying love a mother has for her child. What then happened to Kunti? Why did this love not show up for Karna? In our Epics, we have many stories of a mother's love. Krishna had two mothers, one who gave him birth and the other who nurtured him. Kunti was also the mother of Madri's children; her love for them even surpassed her love for her own children. She fainted when she saw Karna after several years, this showed her intimate connection with her first born. Kunti preferred to remain quiet as she did not want to inflict unknown emotional harm on her young sons. They were young and could not understand her predicament or her actions. It could also jeopardise their future. This raises the question that is a mother's love for her child always unqualified? It would suggest that the relationship between mother and child is not just based on birth but develops based on nurture. Krishna had two mothers, Devaki who gave him birth and Yashoda who brought him up. Krishna is as often referred to as Devaki Nandan as he is also called Yashoda Nandan. This illustrates the association based on nurture. Kunti's affection for Madri's children or Karna's affection for his foster mother Radhe are also examples.

In the Epic, Ganga drowns her newborn sons, and Kunti also gives up her son on birth. These are two subtle takes on modern day behaviour. These are akin to abortion and abandoning an unwanted newborn. Karna is adopted by a childless couple who provide him a home, love and care. Yet, he never grew up in his foster parent's home with a sense of belonging. The physical connection that bonds a mother with her child can snap but remains at the emotional level.

Parents often discover common traits and behaviour between them and their children. These inherited traits appear without effort and training. Karna grew up in a Suta household. He was never comfortable with a future as a Suta because of his Kshatriya traits and aspirations. It made him feel at odds with the Suta background of his foster parents. In our times, we commend inter-ethnic adoption. This is fashionable and shows the liberal views of the foster parents. It could make a child feel at odds because of the obvious differences. Whilst we all must give a home to an orphaned or unwanted child, we must be mindful of his emotional well-being too.

Dharma between Parties are not Dependent: *Every relationship gives rise to an obligation. We cannot base relationships on give and take. Every party must fulfil their obligation without exception or expectation. Failure by one party to discharge their obligation does not release the other party from theirs. The duty of a child towards their parents remains an obligation, even if the parent did not fulfil their obligation. Ved Vyas and Karna grew up without receiving the care and attention of their mother. Their mothers called upon them in later life and the sons responded. Our parents are our Creators. They are like our Shiva and Shakti on Earth. This bond with our Creators is selfless and does not require nurture. This urge to know and connect with our creators has its effect on adopted children too. They often launch a search for their biological parents. This desire to search them out is evidence of an intimate and deep connection. In the Epic, this connection shows up often, Ved Vyas tries his best to avert war. He guides his grandchildren to safety. Kunti tries to save her son Karna. Karna knows he cannot do what his mother expects of him, but he does his best to reduce her pain.*

In a relationship, we should not base our response on whether the other side has fulfilled its obligations. Our response is our obligation and is not subject to any condition. The obligation of each party is independent of the other. This advice does not apply to obligations arising out of a service. In a service, we describe it as counter party obligation. In a service, the obligations of a party depend on each other. An obligation to pay a fee or Guru Dakshina arises when a Guru provides training. When a mother gives birth, it gives rise to her duty. When the child grows up, it gives rise to their duty towards their parents. The duty of the child is not conditional upon whether the parents fulfilled their duty. The obligation of each is independent. Each owes it to the other a duty. An ability to differentiate between rights and entitlement on the one hand and duty and obligation on the other is important. The ability to understand their difference helps avoid negativity and despair. We often fail in our duty in a relationship because we feel that the other had not done enough. We often despair because they have failed to do their duty. The cause of this stress is down to two important aspects. We cannot treat the duty to be performed by the other as our entitlement. We must not put a value to the duty performed by another. We must not limit our own performance with a mental measure that works as a balance on a weighing scale. We must not think, when we have done so much, why was their response so poor? We must not think why should we do so much when they do not? A gift of a silver coin from a poor man maybe a much bigger deal from his perspective than a gift of a gold coin from a millionaire.

Both Kunti and Satyawati did not fulfil their duty as mothers. Yet, both their sons responded when approached. They based their responses on their duty. Bhima left his first born on birth and several years later asked this son to join him in battle. This was his right, his son joined as his duty. Shantanu saved his son from infanticide; that was his duty. His son gave up his position as Crown Prince, that position was his right. The Pandavas fought to recover their kingdom, this was their right. Dronacharya and Parashuram had a right to choose their students. It did not entitle Dhritarashtra to establish a conjugal relationship just because he had married Gandhari. She had the right to decide. Recovering Pandu's legacy was the obligation of Kunti. Looking after Madri's children and her own children were her duty. When Dhritarashtra accepted a widowed Kunti and Pandu's children in his household, it was his duty. Refusing to honour a childhood promise was not Drupad's obligation. It did not give Dronacharya any right. This misunderstood perspective of obligation and right caused a destructive battle in the years ahead.

Marriage does not give the husband a right to have sex with his wife but being faithful is a duty. A couple may share responsibilities in a house. This sharing of responsibility differs from their duty to provide food for their children. A demand for a car from a parent maybe justified because of need or circumstances. It does not give rise to a right or an obligation.

Dharma of a Wife and a Mother: *Kunti on that day had to choose between her Dharma as a wife and as a mother. As a duty to her deceased husband, she was trying to recover his throne. She also had her duty as a mother to acknowledge, protect and confer upon Karna his lineage. It was this conflict that caused her to faint. If Kunti had acknowledged Karna was her eldest born son, it could have jeopardised her effort to position the Pandavas as successors to the throne of Hastinapur. People would doubt her character and reject her claim as unreliable. In a marriage, a couple's duty towards each other is paramount. We may, for some years, give precedence to our duty to the children. If we have to choose between one's duty towards one's family, our first obligation is to our partner. Shantanu suffered in agony seeing Ganga drowning their children until it became unbearable. Their separation was of their bond, with all things that are joined, there will always be a breakpoint. Whilst our children are growing up it is our Dharma to care for them. This is a collective responsibility of the parents. Hindu thought defines a marriage as a relationship that survives many lifetimes but the responsibility of parenting ends once the child enters the Grihastha phase.*

Dharma and Dronacharya: *Dronacharya refused to teach Karna. His cruel demands on Eklavya and his partiality towards Arjun make him appear as a villain. However, we need to analyse his actions from his perspective. The Royal Family hired him to train the Princes, and he was duty-bound to give his best to them. In doing so, he also neglected his son, Ashwatthama. He punishes Eklavya for his misconduct. The cutting of the thumb is more drama than real as it implies that Eklavya could not use his ill-gotten knowledge. He pays special attention to Arjun, who shows a greater commitment and application to his training. As a tutor he gave to all, and those who had the ability to learn and absorb more, he gave more.*

CHAPTER 16

Dronacharya Seeks
Dhrupad's Humiliation

Synopsis: Ancient wisdom, credit for which was denied to us, others stole it. Five thousand years ago, we had rules for intellectual property, relating to minors, promises, gifts, etc.

The Passing Out Parade formally marked the end of their education. Tradition required the Princes to pay their preceptors *guru dakshina*. Dronacharya asked the princes to invade the kingdom of Panchal and bring back its ruler Drupad bound in chains.

Accordingly, the Kaurava princes launched an attack but failed to subdue Panchal. But then the Pandavas succeeded and brought back Drupad as a captive. Dronacharya reminded him of his childhood promise about sharing his kingdom. He annexed half of Panchal and appointed his son Ashwatthama as its ruler. Dronacharya taunted Drupad that they were equals now, avenging his humiliation.

Commentary

Human Frailty and our Inability to Give up Power:
Dronacharya's story did not end with his settling scores with
Drupad. His assignment as a tutor had ended, he had now been
paid. Instead of settling down in the new kingdom, half of which his
son ruled, Dronacharya continued as a royal tutor.

Intellectual Rights and Rules of Consideration: The princes
were not free to use the skills taught by their tutor until they paid
him. A transfer is not complete until a consideration is paid. Until
the buyer makes such payment, the seller of the property will
continue to own the right to his property.

We must have the prior consent of the owner of the intellectual
property before its use. Until they transfer it for consideration, we
must use the knowledge solely for the benefit of the owner. The
princes could not use their knowledge without the prior consent of
their Guru until the Guru Dakshina was paid.

A contract requires the exchange of consideration. The promise
of a gift is not a contract. Drupad, a minor in Gurukul, could neither
gift nor promise to share half his Kingdom with Dronacharya. He
had no ability to commit to give away what he did not own at the
time of promise. The principles of Raj Dharma impose upon a King
the responsibility of a trustee and an obligation to protect the interest
of his subjects. A king could not give away or share his kingdom, it
was not his to give away. A commitment or a promise to fulfil an act
of Adharma cannot be an enforceable promise.

This brought up many legal principles: A minor's right to
contract, contract and promise of a gift. Rights of owner vs
obligations of a trustee.

Dronacharya misused his right to Guru Dakshina. He used the
power of Hastinapur to settle a personal grudge. He then abused his
rights further; he annexed half of Panchal. Dharma did not permit

Kshatriyas to annex the territory of a defeated King. They required him to submit to the supremacy of the winning King. The court of Hastinapur may have justified their behaviour as Apad-Dharma. The state of Panchal saw this as an act of war. In judging an action, the perception of the other party is as important as the intention of the first party.

CHAPTER 17

Outcomes from the Passing Out Parade

Synopsis: Bad decisions have a cost to pay for. Recognise and limit the cost of bad decisions. Are you a victim of open-ended promises? We get Sanskar and Parampara from our parents, not from tutors.

After annexing half his kingdom, they set Drupad free. It was against Kshatriya code to annex the kingdom of a defeated King. Dhritarashtra should not have allowed this; it was his duty to intervene. Drupad returned to Panchal and vowed to avenge his personal humiliation. He wanted to remove the Kurus from Hastinapur as he held them responsible for his loss. On his return, he undertook a severe penance. The Gods were pleased and from the sacrificial fire, emerged Draupadi and Dhrishtadyumna. He trained these two children along with his first-born child to achieve his aim of destroying Hastinapur.

In Hastinapur, Dronacharya crowned his son Ashwatthama to be King of the annexed half of Panchal. Despite being made King, he continued to live in Hastinapur. Dronacharya's role as a tutor had ended, but he also held on to his position as a member of the Royal Court. Duryodhana had cemented his friendship with both Karna and Ashwatthama. His own allies could take on the Pandavas. Destiny endowed Ashwatthama with a gem on his forehead. According to Bhishma, no one could ever defeat or kill Ashwatthama. Hatred united the three against the Pandavas. Ashwatthama resented the special favour his father had granted to Arjun. Karna hated Bhima for his rude behavior and resented Arjun's claim of being the foremost archer. Karna wanted to prove he was better than Arjun. Duryodhana hated the Pandavas; in his view, they were not entitled to the throne. He wanted them out of the race for succession. This apart, Dronacharya as a member of the Royal Court had a duty to serve Hastinapur. Duryodhana knew he could use Ashwatthama to influence him.

The Pandavas had captured Drupad. They got no political mileage or royal favours. They proved themselves to be great warriors. Drupad saw them as an instrument of the state. Unlike Duryodhana, they had no ability to influence the state. They had no kingdom, treasury or alliances. The Pandavas were just close relatives of the King. Contrast this with Duryodhana, he was building allies; he made Karna King. The Pandavas were left to themselves.

Commentary

Strategic Failure: We can accuse the Court of Hastinapur of taking a short-term view. The defeat of Panchal may have shown their strength, but it threatened long-term peace. They used the assets and public interests of the state to pay for a personal obligation of the rulers. The rulers should have refused Dronacharya's demand as

Adharma. The attack and the annexation of one half of the territory was against Kshatriya Code and would lead to future conflicts. Action could also have been taken against Dronacharya; they could have ended his office. Drupad would then have targeted Ashwatthama to regain his territory. The Kurus would have avoided the Epic War.

Open-Ended Promises and Commitments: *Dronacharya had a right to his fees which should have been agreed upfront. It entitled him to his fees, but his demand was not legitimate. It was against the interest of the State. They could have corrected their failure at several stages, but they continued to allow a decision to take its own course. They should have stopped him from annexing half of Panchal, this was against the Kshatriya Code. The attack itself was against the Kshatriya Code because a Kshatriya must go to war only as a last resort. Dhritarashtra could have asked Dronacharya to reconsider his demand as it violated Dharma. They could have ended Dronacharya's office and it would have avoided the threat to the Kuru State.*

Mahabharata cautions us against the risks of open-ended promises and obligations. It gives us two instances of such promises; first by Shantanu to Ganga and then Dronacharya's obligation. Whether in contract or commitment, we must not take the risk of making an open-ended promise. We can make bad choices or decisions. We must, in such cases, take immediate corrective actions. We must avoid the mistake of letting one mistake lead us to another. The example above highlights how, at each stage, the cost of that incorrect choice can escalate but can still be limited. Another important guidance is that even if the promise is open-ended, it must not violate any Dharma.

Influence of Sanskar, Kula and Parampara: *Dronacharya could provide knowledge of weaponry and warfare to the Princes. He did not have the exposure of a Kshatriya. He lacked the knowledge of Sanskar and Parampara associated with a Kshatriya Kula.*

Dronacharya got the Kuru Princes to wage war. He then annexed a part of the vanquished King's territory. A Kshatriya's primary responsibility is to avoid war, loss of life and misery to people. When he is compelled to wage a war and is victorious, he can demand that the vanquished King pays him a tribute, but he cannot annex territory. A tutor can train us, teach us skills, but he cannot provide us with Sanskar. Sanskar can only come from the family, as does Parampara.

CHAPTER 18

Power Struggle and the Assassination Attempt

Synopsis: Assassination as a tool of statecraft. Why Dissidents are not criminals? How to respond to state persecution?

The power struggle for Yudhisthir to be made Crown Prince was ongoing. The court needed to decide who should be the next King of Hastinapur. In this power struggle, Hastinapur was a divided house. The Pandavas appeared to have the support of Bhishma and Vidura. Kunti was also trying to lobby support by attending to Brahmins. Pleased with her hospitality, they would in return extend their support to the appointment of Yudhisthir. Dhritarashtra was cornered and forced to appoint Yudhisthir as the Crown Prince.

Yudhisthir was humble. People admired him for his knowledge of Dharma. His popularity and influence spread around in the Kingdom. The Kauravas were unhappy with the growing popularity of their Pandava cousin. They needed a plan to get back into the race.

Dhritarashtra sent Yudhisthir away to Varnavat. He thought this would limit their popularity and give his sons a chance to come back into the race. He knew how it felt to be ignored for succession. He did not want his son to have the same experience.

The Pandavas were now preparing to leave for Varnavat. Everyone knew they were being sent on exile. Duryodhana felt this was not enough because they could come back. Yudhisthir as a Crown Prince still had the right to be the next King. Duryodhana realised that only if someone killed them, would he become entitled to be Crown Prince. He and his confidantes planned their assassination.

They commissioned the Chief Architect of Hastinapur to build a palace made of wax in the town of Varnavat. This would be the new home of the Pandavas. They planned to drug the Pandavas and Kunti, and then they would set their abode on fire and kill them. They planned this as an accident. A divided court of Royals on coming to know of this plan, forewarned the Pandavas. Vidura sent one of his trusted aides and they built a secret tunnel to escape from this wax palace. On the day of departure, Kunti and the Pandavas took the blessings of the family elders and left. At Varnavat, they were housed in this newly built wax palace under the watchful eyes of the guards of Hastinapur.

At their abode, the Pandavas would often house and feed several visitors. One day, a woman with five sons arrived and were hosted at this abode. That night, when they went to sleep in the palace apparently intoxicated, the Pandavas, unaware of the six persons sleeping in that palace, burnt it down and escaped. After setting the palace ablaze, the Pandavas went into hiding in the adjoining

Forest. The locals found charred bodies the next day, also the fire had burnt to death the Architect of the palace. They assumed the bodies as that of the Pandavas and their mother.

Commentary

Under Pressure: The Pandavas did not know of the conspiracy behind their relocation. Their supporters informed them of the threat to their lives. They were living under the watchful eyes of a state that was planning their assassination. They had no means to confront or accuse them of any agenda. The Pandavas needed to hide their real feeling; they maintained a cordial relationship. On the day of their departure, they took the blessing of Dhritarashtra. They had planned their future escape. Had they escaped from Hastinapur, the onus of proof would be on them which the Kauravas would deny. The Pandavas would have no evidence. The Kauravas would use the unproven allegation to sever their relationship with the Pandavas. It would isolate the Pandavas with no resources or alliances to support their claim. They moved to Varnavat, away from the watchful eyes of the Kauravas and their spies. At Varnavat, there was circumstantial evidence, and they could escape.

Dissidents and Assassination in State Craft: The Pandavas were trapped; they needed to escape and find another way to realise their plan. They killed a widow and her sons to save themselves. On the face of it, both sides were pursuing their selfish agenda. But there was one subtle difference, the Kauravas did not want their dispute to escalate into a public crisis and cause unrest. They wanted to avoid internal divisions that would lead to a fight and loss of lives and property. The Pandavas murdered people to protect their own lives. The fight between the cousins had now caused the death of innocent people.

Mahabharata warns that citizens of a Country will have divided loyalties.

Response under State Persecution: *The Pandavas, cornered, expelled and aware that their lives were at risk maintained a dignified calm. As underdogs, they planned their response. A lesson on how opponents, dissidents or individuals must respond when being persecuted by the state.*

CHAPTER 19

Pandavas Escape and Bhima Marries Hidimbi

Synopsis: Love is blind; it disregards boundaries of religion, colour or other bias; the difference between love and infatuation.

The Pandavas fled the Wax Palace and took refuge in the forest. Kunti and her sons pretended to be a Brahmin widow with her five sons, after borrowing the identity of those they had drugged and burnt, in a bid to protect their identity. Bhima remained alert to protect the family from the Rakshas, a tribe of cannibals. Owing to their inexperience of forest life, they faced several hazards.

Hidimbi dwelt with her brother, a tribal chief, in the forest. She fell in love with Bhima and wanted to marry him. But her brother opposed it on the grounds of Bhima being an Aryan. In desperation, she approached Kunti, who consented to the alliance, as the Pandavas needed the *Rakshas* for their safety in the forest.

Hidimbi's brother died in the clash with Bhima, who then solemnized his marriage with Hidimbi and ensured their safety in the forest. In due course, a son was born to the couple. The Pandavas left the forest soon after, but Hidimbi and her son stayed back.

Commentary

Marriage of Convenience: The Pandavas were hiding from Kauravas to pre-empt any attempts on their lives. They were at risk from rakshas, a feared tribe of cannibals, who often exercised dominion over local kings. Rakshas and Aryans did not freely mingle with one another. Neither was their alliance well regarded. The Epic now deals with marriages of convenience. We might experience it ourselves or know of someone who does. There is a subtle difference in this marriage and the marriage between Ganga and Shantanu. The infatuation in the second case soon wore off. Ganga was fulfilling her promise in helping others realise moksha. In the first case, Bhima took advantage of Hidimbi's love, who discovered their real intent only when Pandavas quit the forest after their needs were fulfilled. A person might marry out of infatuation or love; his or her partner may breach the trust to fulfil their own agenda. So one must be aware.

Power of Love in a Relationship: In a tribal society, a woman would find a strong and virile man attractive, one who could be trusted and depended on to provide for her and her offsprings. Mahabharata provides a wealth of information on a woman's thoughts and expectations from a man. Hidimbi knew that her brother loved her. Even then, she rebelled because he would not permit her to marry outside the clan. She married the killer of her brother, disregarding family bonds. In our times too, people marry for love, overlooking their differences. We could co-relate these differences with caste, religion and community.

Inter-Racial Relationships: The local community of tribals and Aryans were a divided race. The rules of Dharma were not the same as the one applicable to Aryans. Her brother's objections were similar to the concerns a parent would raise. The objection is not about her love, it is about the differences in Sanskar and Kula. Religion and Parampara cause these differences. Hidimbi's brother wanted his sister's happiness and security. He was not willing to trust a family of unknown Aryans living outside their community. When Hidimbi gave birth to a son, her husband and his family deserted both of them. Many years later, Bhima returned to them because he wanted their son and the Rakshas to fight for the Pandavas.

Kunti consented to her son Bhima marrying before his elder brother. Obviously a marriage with the sister of a tribal chief would secure their safety in the forest. We can view her consent as selfish or as liberal. Guardians can also be like Kunti, learn from her. She allowed love to prevail over all differences. Love brings people together, independently of considerations such as religion, caste and ethnicity. It is a step towards integration of communities. Mutual attraction and need can have a binding influence on communities. Later in the Epic, the Rakshas joined the Pandavas and Kauravas in their war. The story of Hidimbi and Bhima has also been played out on a global platform. We know the challenges couples in inter-race and inter-faith marriages have to face. It is their love which keeps them together and helps them overcome the challenges they face. Often like Hidimbi they have to sever their ties with their families because of their opposition to the marriage. The killing of her brother symbolises not death but the death of ties with one's family.

Love and Infatuation Feel Similar, but are They? *The authors have brought out the difference between love and infatuation. Bhima risked his life to get Hidimbi as his wife. Being in love, she could go to any extent to be with the desired one. But he deserted her soon after the birth of their child; until he needed their help and received a warm welcome from them.*

Contrast this with Shantanu's one-sided infatuation for Ganga. He did everything he could to meet her expectations. Post the phase of infatuation, he sacrificed his relationship for the sake of what he wanted. Love has deep roots and does not wither with time. Infatuation is short-lived, the person will at some point wake up to reality.

CHAPTER 20

The Killing of Bakasura

Synopsis: Why is Kanya Daan the highest form of Dharma and not an escape from a burden? Why does India have so many charitable schools, hospitals, ashrams and societies that have been built and sustained for centuries? Beware of selfish people, for they are untrustworthy and will not change.

After the birth of Ghatotkacha to Bhima and Hidimbi, the Pandavas continued their journey through the forests, halting at a town called Ekachakra. The Pandavas maintained their disguise as Brahmins and lived in the house of a Brahmin family. As convention had it, they would go out in daytime to seek alms.

On the outskirts of the town, there lived a much-feared Rakshas called Bakasura. The King required every family to send one of its own as food to Bakasura. When it was the turn of their hosts, Kunti sent Bhima instead, who killed Bakasura, freeing the local community of the menace.

Commentary

Kunti's Second Master Stroke: *There were marked differences between the Aryans and Asura, regarding their appearance, style of living, dietary habits and Dharma. When Bhima married Hidimbi, the Pandavas had crossed a red line against the existing conventions. Kunti won back the Aryans. She sent Bhima to kill Bakasura, protecting a family of Brahmins. The Aryans were rescued from the threat of this man-eating monster.*

Pandavas and Breach of Trust: *They tricked a poor woman and her five children to death in Varnavat. They exploited Hidimbi's emotional attraction for Bhima. The Pandavas and Kunti now disguised as Brahmins took alms from the public. Kunti as a mother showed her selfish behaviour by abandoning her newborn child. She did not accept him despite recognising him at the passing out parade. Later in the Epic, when she wanted to protect the Pandavas, she offered to recognise him. There are many instances where Kunti's agenda overrides truth and trust, a pattern observed among the Pandavas too. A child's behaviour is influenced by its parents. We gain our Sanskar from our parents.*

In a human relationship, we often find that there runs a manipulative streak in the behaviour of a child which can be traced back to the parent. Often, negative traits like anger, impatience and the tendency to lie are influenced by a child's observation of adult behaviour. Children often learn to lie from their parents. They may ask their child to tell a visitor that they are not at home when in fact they are watching TV and do not want to be disturbed. Such events shape a child's Sanskar. As they grow up, they find lying is an easier option than speaking the truth. Lying becomes an integral part of their persona.

Concept of Charity and Hindu Thought: *Charity is of three types. Dakshina is a fee paid to a Guru, a teacher or a spiritual person out* *of gratitude and for services rendered. Hindus often invite Brahmins home on auspicious days. We serve them food, offer them money and presents as a token of gratitude for their visit. During the month of Shraddh, Hindus pray for the well-being of their ancestors. They offer Brahmins food and presents, believing this will please the soul of their late ancestors.*

Bhiksha is a Hindu concept. Brahmins and sages are people who have dedicated their life to religious activities, worship or meditation, without a regular source of income. But they depend on society for necessities. Pretending to be Brahmins, the Pandavas sought Bhiksha. They not only violated their Dharma but also abused the trust of their donors.

Daan is a donation for a cause. They give it to a temple, a school or a charity. Daan is used for building schools, old age homes or facilities for public use. It also refers to donations given to institutions engaged in service of society. A number of schools, colleges, hospitals, dispensaries and dharamshalas in India have been facilitated by Daan.

In each case, the donor is giving back to society what he owes to it; a payment for services to society or an individual. A discussion on Daan is not complete without a reference to the highest form of Daan in Hindu Thought. They call it 'Kanya Daan' or the act of giving away of a daughter to her groom in marriage.

Kanya Daan is an obligation to be fulfilled by a father with the consent of his daughter. Kanya Daan has been abused and misunderstood in recent times. The father is not getting rid of a burden. He does not adorn his daughter with jewellery and gives gifts to the groom and his family in consideration of accepting his daughter. The affluence, education and future financial prospects of the groom seem to determine the size of the gift. A gift differs from a demand, which is known as Dowry, and is often expected, if not demanded, by the Groom and or his family.

The Mahabharata acknowledges that Devi and the female form give us life and our life-sustaining 3Ms. It is only through their role and presence in our lives we can fulfil our Dharma. When a man gives his daughter in Daan to another man, he is transferring to the groom the same opportunity he got to fulfil his obligation of Ashram Dharma.

Kanya Daan is regarded as the highest form of Dharma. The father fulfils his own Dharma when he gets his daughter married. The couple will build their own home and family. This will allow society to evolve. Society and mankind will enjoy evolution and thus it will fulfil Manav Dharma and Yuga Dharma. Kanya Daan fulfils several Dharmas and, therefore, is regarded as the highest form of Daan.

Society and law recognise gifts or assets given to a bride at or even after her marriage are her exclusive property. Such property cannot be encumbered. They call such property "Stree Dhan". In Hindu families, they own jointly all property. It means that even a girl has a share. At a girl's marriage, it was customary for the family to carve out her share. They hand this over to her for her exclusive use and future security. In her marriage, whatever belonged to her then or thereafter became her Stree Dhan, in addition, she became an equal partner with her husband in his share.

According to the Mahabharata, Kanya Daan and Stree Dhan did not end the obligations of a girl's family to her. They continued to support her and her husband in times of need, often bringing up their children or joining them in war.

These ideas of charity differ from the act of giving money, food or other subsistence material to a person begging on the street, as it makes the receiver grateful to a donor.

CHAPTER 21

The Stage is Set for King Drupad's Revenge

Synopsis: Mahabharata will fascinate management students. It is a study on Strategy, Alliances and Partnerships. In the Epic, we see political strategies deployed today. Learn how to plan and execute Strategy.

At this stage, the epic introduces several new characters and prepares the stage for the future course of events.

King Drupad had vowed to unseat Dhritarashtra and avenge his humiliation, by killing Dronacharya and Bhishma, through the agency of his sons Dhristadumya and Shikhandi, respectively. He wanted his daughter Draupadi to marry Arjun and exploit the dispute between the Kauravas and Pandavas and destroy the Kuru Dynasty. Arjun could challenge Karna, a famed and accomplished warrior. A brutal Bhima could kill all the Kaurava princes. With this strategy in mind, King Drupad sought out Krishna, a Yadava Prince and a nephew of Kunti, the sister of Krishna's father. He believed Krishna could influence Kunti and the Pandavas. This would enable him to nail his strategy.

Krishna was a leader of the Yadava community. Kansa was a local king and his maternal uncle. Kansa placed Krishna's grandfather and parents in prison. Krishna killed Kansa and made his grandfather king again. Jarasandha was a powerful King. His daughters married to Kansa were now widowed. Krishna had angered Jarasandha. He attacked the Yadavas seventeen times and, in one battle, Krishna deserted the battlefield. Out of fear, they moved from Mathura to Dwarka. Jarasandha mocked Krishna and called him *Ranchhod* (one who fled the battle). Jarasandha, thereafter, refused to engage Krishna in a combat, who wanted to avenge his humiliation. He also wanted an alliance that would protect the Yadavas. The Kurus were an alliance partner of Jarasandha. The relationship between the Yadavas and the Kurus was not strong enough to stop Jarasandha. As Drupad was a powerful king, Krishna wanted his support. He agreed to join forces with King Drupad and the planned alignment with the Pandavas. They planned a Swayamwar for Drupad's daughter Draupadi. Kings and suitors from across the Aryan world were to be invited to this event. Draupadi was amongst the most enchanting beauties of her time. They also called her Krishna which means the 'dark one'.

Ved Vyas appeared in the story to give it a new direction and persuaded the Pandavas to attend this Swayamwar.

Commentary

Krishna and his Situation: Jarasandha had driven the Yadavas out of Mathura and into Dwarka. If Krishna married Draupadi, he could rely on the support of Drupad and prevent Jarasandha from attacking the Yadavas. But Krishna knew that an uneasy truce could not lead to an enduring peace. Krishna wanted to end the woes of his community without being dependent on Drupad. Krishna wanted to kill Jarasandha and avenge his humiliation. King Drupad was looking to pick a fight with Kurus.

King Drupad and his Situation: King Drupad had his two sons focussed on killing Bhishma and Dronacharya. However, this was not enough. He needed a cause to wage war and deploy capable warriors to combat the likes of Karna and the Kaurava princes. Arjun as an archer was a match against Karna, whilst Bhima was strong enough to take on the Kaurava Princes.

Pandavas and their Situation: Disguised as Brahmins, the Pandavas were living on alms. In Hastinapur, their supporters believed they had perished in the fire. Bhīma's marriage with Hidimbi from a tribal community was their first alliance, it got them safety in the jungle but no real power. They could look for support from the Yadavas, as their leaders Krishna and Balarama were their cousins. Drupad and Krishna were now implementing their strategy. The Pandavas were being used by men more powerful to fulfil the agenda. At the event, the participants were required to demonstrate their archery skills of a high order, present only in Arjun, Karna and Ashwatthama. The last was not considered because of the bad relations between his father and Drupad. The Pandavas had a good chance to win.

Alliances and Partnerships and the Key Players: Jarasandha had defeated many kings. He had an alliance with the Kurus and could draw on their army. As emperor, he received a royalty from other rulers. Krishna, a bitter enemy of Jarasandha, wanted to avenge his personal humiliation and earn the title of Vasudeva, besides securing the safety of the Yadavas.

Pandavas, living in disguise as Brahmins and surviving on bhiksha, had no real leverage, support or resources to enforce their claim over Hastinapur. They could be of use to Drupad, who had already experienced their valour and skills. He felt they could help him realise his key aim. A marriage between Arjun and Draupadi would improve the leverage of the Pandavas in Hastinapur and create disharmony within the ranks and the Kuru Family.

Krishna got the support of Drupad. He agreed to help him arrange Draupadi's marriage with a Pandava. This placed him in a position of influence far greater than the strength of the Yadavas. His alliance with Drupad would also stop Jarasandha from attacking the Yadavas. In his view, after a Pandava married Draupadi, they could regain their influence in Hastinapur. This would benefit the Yadavas and Drupad. Their new alliance would be born out of the marriage. This would isolate and weaken Jarasandha. A nation like Israel has used a similar strategy to make itself relevant despite its small size.

Pandavas were pawns in the larger game of the battling royals. They were in the hands of Krishna, a master strategist. Bringing back Pandavas from their exile, empowering them with resources to challenge the court of Hastinapur worked for both King Drupad and Krishna. In modern times, we have seen this "return from exile" strategy supported by strong nations and being used to extend influence or block the extension of influence of rivals. It is the strategy of the perfect ploy and the use of proxies to wear down or challenge competition.

Pandavas took the risk of coming out of hiding, this gave them the opportunity to once again stake their claim. There are many lessons to be learnt from their experiences. When fighting a bigger competitor, the strategy must focus on weakening the competition. One must have the resources to fight a sustainable battle.

Post World War II, we have examples of countries aligned with either the US or the USSR, which kept enmity alive but war at bay. Some countries realised owning nuclear weapons have acted as a deterrent, the risk and fear of mutual destruction enforced peace no matter how fragile. Yet another lesson, creating internal strife can weaken a strong enemy. It is like the strategy of a thousand cuts with which Pakistan is bleeding India.

CHAPTER 22

Draupadi's Swayamwar

Synopsis: Objectification of women. Align interests with the like-minded for success. Attacking a strong competitor, challenge his strength, not weakness.

Draupadi was exquisite. Kings and princes far and wide desired her. Many were invited to her *Swayamwar*. Duryodhana, his brothers and Karna also attended it. The Pandavas attended disguised as Brahmins.

The Swayamwar required the assembled suitors to show their archery skills. The bow had to be strung, and the contestant had to shoot an arrow to pierce the eye of a fish rotating on a disc installed at a height. They required contestants to aim at the target by looking at its reflection in a container of water placed on the floor.

It would entitle the winner of the contest to marry Draupadi. Draupadi would have to be won. The Swayamwar was open to the invited Royals and attending Brahmins.

Commentary

Lessons on Strategy to Management Students: Drupad's strategy is worth a study. By aligning with Krishna and giving him the responsibility to find a suitor for Draupadi, he excluded him from the Swayamwar. Draupadi's marriage to Arjun would create 'cause' to support the Pandavas. He would have to support them in their bid to take back power in Hastinapur. He converted a personal grudge into an obligation of dharma. Ashwatthama was not present, leaving only Karna and Arjun who could win the contest. They set the contest to get the desired result and not as a game of a fair chance. Contests are like the lottery; they benefit the initiator.

People with similar interests must work together, which will help facilitate success. When weak competitors join hands, they can challenge a mightier competitor. They must focus on their competitor's individual strengths. When taking on a giant competitor, they must focus on attacking the strength and not the weakness. A strong competitor has substantial resources. He will guard his weaknesses.

Advantages of Drupad and Krishna Combine: Drupad expected his son to kill Dronacharya. Shikhandi would kill Bhishma, an outcome of his karma for abducting Amba in her previous life. After his daughter's marriage to the Pandavas, he could use Bhima and Arjun to remove the Kauravas from their throne.

Krishna was close to his aunt Kunti, and this strengthened his influence over the Pandavas. Krishna knew Karna was Kunti's son, born before her marriage to Pandu. This would enable him to distract and divide Karna's loyalty to Duryodhana and weaken the Kauravas. He also knew Arjun could challenge Karna and of their bitter rivalry.

The management lesson is when up against a giant competitor, focus not on attacking his weakness but on how to challenge his strengths. A strong competitor has substantial resources to guard his weaknesses.

CHAPTER 23

Arjun Wins at the Swayamwar

Synopsis: Draupadi's Swayamwar is more about guidance than about skills of archery. Choosing a life partner or a groom? How important is Kula and Sanskar in a life partner? Marry not for money but a wealthy future.

The Swayamwar coordinated by Dhristadumya and Krishna was well attended. The royals present on the occasion could not string the bow. Duryodhana infatuated with Draupadi contested but failed. Karna then offered to win Draupadi for Duryodhana. He walked to the podium, strung the bow and took aim at the target. Draupadi intervened, asking him how could he as a Suta contest. Humiliated, Karna withdrew and left the venue.

There are different versions of the incident. In one version, Krishna prompted Draupadi to intervene. Another has it that Karna tried but missed the target, Draupadi did not object. In yet another version, as Karna had offered to act on behalf of Duryodhana, she refused him. As a Suta, he also could not participate.

When all the Kshatriya contestants failed, they invited the Brahmins to the contest. Arjun disguised as a Brahmin took up the challenge. As expected, Arjun won.

Commentary

Karna and the Kula and Sanskar Connection: *The Kingdom of Panchal accorded great importance to Kula and Sanskar than to their role in society. At a later stage, Karna confessed to Kunti that he had accepted life as a Suta. Karna had not trained as a Kshatriya, nor had he ever taken part in their rituals. He lacked their Sanskars. A Kshatriya would rather die a heroic death in battle, than submit to a lifetime of humiliation after being vanquished or as a deserter. The epic narrates the time when Karna fled from battle. As Karna had the genes of a Kshatriya, he could remain steady despite the pain from a scorpion's bite, but this reflects his inherent nature. Yet he could never gain the Sanskar of a Kshatriya as they brought him up in a Suta household.*

Practice at Swayamwar: *The humiliation of Karna as a guest was wrong. However, Draupadi was justified in questioning his credentials. As a Suta, Karna was expected to devote his life to the service of the Kshatriyas.*

It is unclear whether they refused Karna a chance on his own or to act on behalf of Duryodhana, not an unusual practice at a Swayamwar. Bhishma raided one to find brides for his half brothers. The competition required the winner to be a highly skilled archer. As Duryodhana's archery skills were not the best, Karna may have offered to act on his behalf. Draupadi may have found this objectionable.

People would marry within their Varna. A Brahmin could marry a Kshatriya, but this was exceptional. A Brahmin taking part at a Swayamwar was unusual. The Kshatriyas objected, and it was a source of conflict. Dronacharya was a Brahmin, who trained young princes in the use of weapons, after mastering their application. Kshatriya men had married Suta women, but a Suta could not marry a Kshatriya woman. Sutas served Kshatriyas and as a community married within.

Karna's Humiliation: Was there an Agenda? *Knowing of his ineligibility to marry Draupadi, Karna must have offered to act on Duryodhana's behalf. But his success would have upset Krishna and Drupad's plans. How would Drupad avenge his humiliation or Krishna fulfil his agenda?*

Draupadi's Swayamwar: Lessons for Girl and her Parents: *Each Pandava has one unique attribute or virtue. Yudhisthir was known for wisdom; Bhima for strength; Arjun remembered for his focus; Nakul embodied good looks, and Sahadev was known for foresight. These attributes are like the five fingers in a person's hand and so cannot be equal in measure. The epic narrates how Draupadi in her previous life wanted to marry a husband with the best of these attributes. The gods, pleased by her severe penance, granted her a boon. As full development of these attributes could not be embodied in a single person, she would have to marry five men. In arranged marriages, parents rely on these attributes to seek a groom.*

The Pandavas had the guidance of Kunti, Bhishma and Vidura in forging a good future. Conversely, Karna gained his education by deception and made a king by Duryodhana because of his mastery of archery. He often disregarded his foster-father's advice, dying out of obligation to Duryodhana. He knew he was Pandavas' step brother. Dharma demanded that he should have fought for restoration of rights of Pandavas. Good guidance comes from good parenting and the family. They are called 'Sanskar' and 'Kula.'

Significantly, Karna had all these five attributes. He was a king, had wealth, social status and was present at the Swayamwar. The

Pandavas were in hiding, lacked wealth and depended on charity of others for their daily needs. But Draupadi rejected Karna, because of his Kula and Sanskar. He lacked the education, and the upbringing needed to fulfil the role of king or kshatriya. Ved Vyas showed his immense depth of understanding of what a woman should look for in a man. The lack of Kula was enough to exclude Karna from a Swayamwar which he could have won.

The guidance suggests that we must look beyond the present. Marry not for money but for a wealthy future. This guidance does not end here. Towards the end, Draupadi, based on her life experience, reveals her choice from amongst the Pandavas. Krishna intervenes again to advice that Kula is essential, but Sanskar does not automatically flow. For Sanskar to flow, we need guidance from our parents. This lack of parental guidance can hurt our Sanskar. We have seen how children from broken homes suffer from insecurity and fear commitment. This is an example of how Kula and Sanskar can influence the emotional stability of a partner.

CHAPTER 24

Pandavas take Draupadi Home to Meet Kunti

Synopsis: Why is the eldest expected to marry first? Did Draupadi marry five men or one? The difference between consensus and agreement; how Draupadi's boon was realised by Pandu's desire and facilitated by Kunti's boon.

The Swayamwar ended when Arjun strung the bow and pierced the target successfully. Duryodhana, Shakuni, Karna, and others realised that the Pandavas were alive and had not perished in the fire at Varnavat. The Pandavas now took Draupadi away with them to their abode. They wanted her to meet their mother. Kunti had to fix a date for the marriage of Arjun with Draupadi.

Upon reaching their abode, Bhima asked Kunti to guess what they had brought today. Without looking up, she told them that they should share whatever they had brought back today. Her request cornered the Pandavas. To respect their mother's command, they all had to marry Draupadi. As a result, Draupadi ended up with five husbands.

According to one version, when a Brahmin won the Swayamwar, all hell broke loose. The Kshatriyas protested over the violation of the tradition. Another version says that as soon as Arjun won Draupadi, Yudhisthir, Nakul and Sahadev quit the venue and rushed back home to inform Kunti about the good news, thus avoiding the risk of discovery by the Kauravas at the venue. Bhima stayed back to protect and accompany Arjun and Draupadi. This version seems more credible because the Pandavas had attended the Swayamwar to win Draupadi, not to receive gifts and alms as Brahmins. Yet another version has it that Dhristadumya followed the couple after the Swayamwar. He informed his father Drupad that the bride had been won by a Pandava. He reported seeing all five of them with Kunti. There are divergent views on how Draupadi ended up with five husbands, though as a matter of fact only Arjun had the right to marry her.

Commentary

Did Draupadi Marry Five Men? Did Draupadi marry five men or was there only one Pandava born to Kunti to provide lineage to Pandu? The Pandavas represent the five attributes that a woman looks for in a Man. Karna had all the five attributes and was a King. But he lacked the Kula of a Kshatriya and therefore the Sanskar.

The Mahabharata is best understood when enacted as a Play. In plays on the Ramayana, Ravana is shown with ten heads. This symbolises his knowledge of the six Shastras and four Vedas. Whilst it would be possible to present Pandavas as one character having all five attributes, it would be impossible to highlight the individual contribution and shortcoming of each attribute. Another challenge was to depict and distinguish between a Pandava and Karna. Then there was the difficulty of an attribute interacting with another, or the response to an event influenced by the attribute. The authors resolved this by showing Pandavas as five instead of one.

Draupadi's Marriage to the Five Pandavas: Had Draupadi married Arjun, the third in line to the throne, she would have just been another Royal. However, if she married Yudhisthir, she would be the crowned queen. Yudhisthir without Arjun and Bhima could not wage war and win the throne. However, if Draupadi married all five Pandavas, she could unite them and drive them in the desired direction. King Drupad consented to the arrangement. His daughter would become the queen and he would have all five Pandavas on his side. He would be bound to support the Pandavas and their claim. In this way he could leverage the dispute between Pandavas and the Kauravas.

Kunti realised that her five sons were enchanted by the beauty of Draupadi. Whilst Arjun had won her, it was Bhima who had rescued them from the violence that followed. Bhima felt he had also played a role in winning her at the Swayamwar.

It would best serve Draupadi if she married them all. She could then be Queen and it would motivate her to ensure that she aligned all her five husbands to the interest of seeking the crown for the Pandavas. Also, if Draupadi married the future King of Hastinapur, then this would ensure that King Drupad and his army would join full forces in the power struggle. The most a woman could aspire, was to marry a king and become queen. We must allow the story to play out further to understand Draupadi's motivations. For the moment, let us assume that she accepted the situation and married the five Pandavas.

In Hindu custom, after the death of the father, the eldest son heads the family. Arjun could only marry with the approval of his mother and elder brother. Kunti wanted all her five sons to marry Draupadi. As both Bhima and Yudhisthir did not object, Arjun had no choice but to accept the situation.

The Eldest Son Must Marry First: *As per Hindu custom, the eldest son performs the last rites of his parents. Hindu customs require a couple to perform many of these rites. It is in this context they expect the eldest son to marry first. The concept of Sati was a much later development. A widow of the eldest brother can marry her husband's younger brother, whereas the wife of a younger brother is not available to the elder sibling. They expect the younger sister-in-law to extend the same respect and serve her husband's elder brother and his wife as her husband's parents. It is in this context that Kunti in the final phase of life joins Dhritarashtra and Gandhari when they renounce the world. She tells the Pandavas that she would find salvation by spending the rest of her life in service of her parent-like elders. It implies that a younger brother could perform Niyoga on his elder brother's wife.*

Consensus in a Group Working: *All involved had reached a consensus about Draupadi's marriage with the five Pandavas, but each of them had different reasons. Former British Prime Minister Margaret Thatcher described consensus as a process of abandoning all beliefs, principles, values and policies in search of something in which no one believes, but to which no one objects. The process avoided the issues that have to be solved, merely because no agreement is possible on the way ahead.*

CHAPTER 25

Draupadi Marries the Five Pandavas

Synopsis: Draupadi's boon was realised by Pandu's desire and facilitated by Kunti's boon. Mahabharata deals with Rape. We require prior and continuing consent for sex.

They solemnised the marriage of Draupadi with the Five Pandavas.

Commentary

Pandavas One or Five: *According to Bhil Mahabharata, Kunti gave three children to Pandu through Niyoga. When he asked her for a fourth child, she rejected it forthright being aware of her union before her marriage. The scriptures allow a woman to have a relationship with upto three males. When a woman enters a fourth relationship, she is a swairini i.e. a wanton woman, and if she does so a fifth time, she is a kulata i.e. a whore. This is not a judgment on the right of a woman to decide her life. Arjun is the sole exception amongst the Pandavas and had four wives. This subtle difference reflects on his character and is dealt with later. How could Kunti* *being aware of the scriptures allow Draupadi to live with five men? Again pointing to the possibility that there was only one Pandava, and he had the five virtues and they treated each virtue as a unique being. If he wanted Draupadi to be the chief queen, the Swayamwar could have been a competition on the principles of Dharma. Yudhisthir would have won.*

They forced Draupadi to submit to polyandry. This is not approved by religion. This is a clue that the authors created five Pandavas. Pandu needed Kunti to submit to Niyoga only once. She submitted to Niyoga three times. Then, his second wife Madri also submitted to Niyoga. This behaviour of Pandu is unexplainable. In the story, he justifies this to get sons with unique attributes. This is quite a coincidence because Draupadi's boon was realised by Pandu's desires and facilitated by Kunti's boon. Pandu and Draupadi both desire the same attributes in their sons and husband, respectively. This shows that parents desire attributes in their children that are the same as what a woman would desire from her spouse.

Polyandry was the consequence of a boon. The authors used divine intercession to deal with ideas which were unacceptable. They did not want to upset people. They gave Draupadi an aura of divinity. She was born out of sacrificial fire. This helped overcome any objections to her character. There was no objection to her being Queen or not being virtuous. The narrators could use these events to explain the intent behind the idea. Divine association, the appearance of Demi-gods or a celestial being all serve this purpose. Just as the appearance of Ved Vyas helped move the story forward.

Kunti did not own up to Karna as her son at or after the Passing Out Parade. Recognising him would have tarnished her reputation. It would have jeopardised her fight for the rights of the Pandavas. Acknowledging Karna meant that she had been in five relationships including with Pandu. This may be the reason behind the boon instead of Niyoga in her context.

Kunti refused to use her boon a fourth time. She transferred it to Madri. A woman must give her consent to Niyoga. Ambika and

Ambalika consented to Niyoga as their obligations to Rashtra Dharma. As per the rules of society, a husband's elder brother could not have them. To their shock, it was Ved Vyas. Ambika was not only disapproving but found Ved Vyas so revolting that she closed her eyes. It portrays her sense of violation, Dhritarashtra was born blind. Ambalika also felt violated but was so shocked that she could do nothing. Her feeling of violation is reflected by her cold shock and portrayed through Pandu who was born an albino. They tricked Ved Vyas into performing Niyoga with a maid or maybe a dasi Queen. As she had consented and facilitated the Niyoga on her, Vidura born to her was not only a normal child but also inherited his father's brilliance. Niyoga requires a woman's consent, and she must approve of the person who will perform it.

The authors showed their deep understanding of a woman's right over herself and her body. We define rape as lack of consent before and during sex. The queens may have consented to Niyoga, but they did not consent to the person sent to perform it. The Epic developed the concept of the need for consent. This consent is not just a prior need but must subsist during the act.

CHAPTER 26

Pandavas Return to Hastinapur

Synopsis: Should we stop talking when we have a dispute? In family disputes, should siblings stop communicating? See how Itihas and Parampara can decide our course of action?

The news of the wedding of Draupadi with the Pandavas meant the Pandavas had escaped from Varnavat. Their marriage had changed the balance of power too. With their marriage, the clout of the Pandavas had grown. Hastinapur realised the Pandavas had the support of Krishna and Drupad. They now changed their tack. They sent Vidura to bring them back to Hastinapur. Hastinapur wanted to squash any rumour of their hand in the failed assassination. They wanted to show that Pandavas were family too. A grand celebration awaited the Pandavas and Draupadi on their return.

Commentary

Strategy in a Dispute: The Pandavas accepted their exile to Varnavat. They had no supporters, resources, or negotiating ability.

After the fire at Varnavat, the Pandavas escaped and remained in hiding. They had little resources and pretended to be Brahmins. This allowed them to live off alms. After their marriage to Draupadi, they had the support of King Drupad. They discarded their disguise and returned to Hastinapur.

The Kauravas were tricked into believing the Pandavas had died in the fire in Varnavat. They later learnt that the Pandavas had survived and married Drupad's daughter. It was public knowledge that their marriage was set up by Krishna. The Kauravas changed tack as the circumstances had changed and the Pandavas were back in the race. They pretended good intent and sent Vidura to bring the Pandavas back. This is crucial when dealing with foes. The Kauravas would fight from inside their stronghold. The Kauravas maintained a humane and 'we are family' stance in Public. This was despite their behind the scene effort to remove the Pandavas.

Dhritarashtra knew of King Drupad's agenda. They needed to squash rumours that the fire in Varnavat was a failed assassination. Sending Vidura to bring back the Pandavas was a masterstroke. He was a supporter of the Pandavas. The Pandavas would not allow him to fail. They cornered the Pandavas, as a refusal to return would amount to breaking up with the family. They had no resources to support themselves or fund a war to win their right. The support of Drupad gave them protection. The Kauravas would now not attempt an assassination of the Pandavas. The story of Jarasandha's attacks on the Yadavas for widowing his daughters was testimony of the risks they faced.

Both sides knew of the strengths of their opponents. Dhritarashtra got the moral high ground by adopting the position of 'we are family.' This forced Drupad to adopt a family stance and it disarmed him too. Krishna could not fault the Kauravas. Dhritarashtra had converted the Pandava claim into a family matter. He ensured that, as the Head of the Kuru Family, he would have the final say. Also, the Pandavas were forced to bring their views to him and not through any outsider. He controlled the channels of communication.

CHAPTER 27

The Great Partition

Synopsis: In dealing with disputes, a foot in the door is better than nothing? Half in hand is better than nothing in a struggle to have the whole. Why is moral high ground the key to a successful negotiation?

The Pandavas had now returned to Hastinapur. They encouraged their supporters in the Court to lobby for their return to power. It now caught the Court in a difficult situation. They had assumed the Pandavas dead and had appointed Duryodhana as the Crown Prince. Their problem was how to return this position to Yudhisthir. The court could not agree on a solution. As a settlement, the King had to split the Kingdom. He agreed to give a share to the Pandavas on the condition that Bhishma would swear his lifelong loyalty to the Kauravas. When Bhishma agreed to this condition, he gave the Pandavas a territory called Khandavprastha. He also put two conditions on the Pandavas. They had to accept the supremacy of Hastinapur, and Kunti had to stay back.

Commentary

Partition a Masterstroke in Strategy: The partition served
several objectives. Bhishma, a vocal supporter of the Pandavas, had
to promise he would side with the Kauravas. This kept Vidura in
check. Dhritarashtra knew him to respect and follow Bhishma. As
Kunti had to remain in Hastinapur, the Pandavas would not have
her knowledge and unifying influence. All the key supporters of
Pandavas were under his watchful eyes. He also kept his status as
head of family. It weakened the Pandavas. They had no choice but to
accept the settlement offered. The partition gave them Khandavprastha.
A dense forest, occupied by hostile local tribes, surrounded
Khandavprastha. This ended the claims of succession. Each side now
had a share. The Pandavas got half instead of the whole. The
Kauravas ended up creating an entitlement for themselves. They also
ended up with at least half instead of nothing.

Dhritarashtra had settled the claim of the Pandavas. Krishna
could no longer support action against Hastinapur. King Drupad
was also disarmed as the claims of the Pandavas had been settled. The
Pandavas had accepted to be a vassal state of Hastinapur. Marriage
now related the Kurus and Panchal. The Kurus could now claim the
allegiance of King Drupad as their relative.

Pandavas as Winners and Lessons from their Perspective: The
Pandavas ended up getting a foot in the door. They had nothing.
They needed to start somewhere. The learning is to get your foot in
the door as one needs to start somewhere. The Pandavas taught us it
is better to take the best deal available. Declining the conditional
partition would have given the Kauravas the moral high ground. The
Pandavas had to accept the partition as it gave them something to
start with, such as the status of Royalty and the legitimacy of their
claim. The Pandavas had built a few alliances through marriage, but
without a kingdom they lacked resources to fund themselves. They
could not gather an army and finance a war to force a fair settlement.

For the success of any campaign, one needs relationships and sustainable resources. They were winners, yet received sympathy as the underdogs.

Kuru as Winners and Lessons from their Perspective: *Dhritarashtra acted fast. He got the Pandavas to return to the family fold and offered them a part of the kingdom. They could rule over this part under the overall guidance and control of the family. Apparently, the Pandavas were given a share of the kingdom and they had accepted it. They could no longer get any sympathetic support from their allies. The Kauravas in reality did not yield to any pressure or allow their competition to win the moral high ground. The Yadavas had to strike a very careful balance. Their aunt, Kunti had married into the Kuru Family and was living in Hastinapur. This frustrated King Drupad's agenda of leveraging the dispute to wage war. Dhritarashtra ensured that by giving the Pandavas one half, he legitimised the right of the Kauravas to at least one half, foreclosing Yudhisthir's right to be the crown prince and future king of Hastinapur.*

CHAPTER 28

Pandavas Take Charge of Khandavprastha

Synopsis: Mothers-in-law listen, Kunti's message can help your image. Parents, we need to learn to fend for ourselves, set our children free! When is leaving your parental home not irresponsible abandonment?

The Pandavas were heartbroken when they learnt Bhishma and their mother Kunti would remain in Hastinapur. Kunti advised her sons that in their new phase of life, Draupadi would be their guide and soul. As their wife and the queen of the new kingdom, it was her Dharma to provide guidance. The Pandavas along with Draupadi and their supporters now left Hastinapur to take charge of their allocated territory.

This territory was mostly taken up by a dense forest on the banks of the River Yamuna. Tribals occupied this forest. They depended on the forest for food. Being on the river bank, they caught fish and reptiles. They would call these tribes, Nagas or serpent tribe, as they may have used reptile skin as clothing.

They would have to vanquish local tribes to capture land for their settlement and subsistence. Pandavas engaged in such a war to take back land for their use.

The Nagas fought with snake venom tipped arrows. After their defeat, Arjun forced them to use an anti-dote to revive the infected Kuru warriors. In the battle, Arjun burnt down the entire forest. On this cleared area came up the beautiful capital of Indraprastha. In some versions, Arjun justified his action by claiming he had acted on the instructions of his elder brother. Some believe, Krishna accompanied Arjun and together they orchestrated this brutal deforestation. Another version has it that some celestial Gods desired that they raze the forest.

As Takshaka, the chief of the Naga tribe was away, he had escaped. However, his entire family and members of his tribe were ruthlessly butchered in the battle and perished in the fire. Also from amongst the vanquished tribes was Mayasura, the chief of Asuras, whose life the Pandavas spared.

Commentary

Arjun burnt down the dense forest, killing all the creatures living there. We cannot excuse this inhuman act. It cannot be his obligation towards Dharma. This event describes deforestation. It shows how urbanisation leads to the displacement of tribes and native communities from their original settlements. Other ethnic groups had skills and knowledge the Aryans lacked. They had medicinal capabilities evidenced by use of antidotes for snake venom poisoning. They used reptile skin as clothing, etc.

The Mahabharata changes course. Its initial focus was on Karma, Kula, Itihas, re-birth, parenting, marital relationships, education of children. The children had now grown up, taken up their careers and had married. We now deal with the parents after their children have entered the Grihastha Phase.

Role of a Mother Post the Marriage of their Son: *This event deals with the transition of the role of a mother upon the marriage of her sons. The Pandavas and Draupadi were upset and agitated when they discovered Kunti would not accompany them to Khandavprastha. Kunti told her sons she was confident that Draupadi as their wife was competent to guide them in their path of Dharma. It was their solemn duty to seek her counsel and concurrence in all matters, just as they had taken hers in the past.*

According to Kunti, a spouse has the right and is bound to stand by their partner in their Dharma. This approach places greater responsibility on a married couple and gives them the independence to find and create their own purpose in life. Parents must therefore move into the background and be available as advisors. Dharma requires a man and his wife to carve out their future path in consultation with each other.

This grant of space could benefit and enrich the much-maligned mother-in-law and daughter-in-law relationships. Generations since would have avoided the consequences of an estranged relationship. A mother-in-law in her relationship with her daughter-in-law could follow the Kunti principle.

Kunti's guidance to her children on their spousal duties are also part of the vows of a Hindu marriage taken walking around the ceremonial fire seven times. In some Hindu marriages, the couple take four rounds. They pledge to be together and for each other. They undertake to fulfil their goals of Kama, Artha, Dharma and Moksha. In some Hindu marriages, the couple take seven rounds where each round is a vow. These vows lay the foundation for a successful union. The couple vow to provide prosperity as a household to the family and will stand together against anyone who tries to hinder it. The couple vow to lead a healthy life by developing their physical and spiritual sides. They vow to earn a living by proper means so that their material wealth increases manifold. As a couple they will respect, love and understand each other, together they will strive for knowledge, happiness and harmony. They take a pledge to expand their family by having healthy, brave and honest children, for whom, they will be responsible. The couple takes a vow they will strive for a long marital relationship by exercising self restraint of the mind, body and ego. Finally, the couple will be true and loyal to each other, remain companions and best of friends for the lifetime.

The marital vows, the rules of Ashram Dharma and message of Kunti must all be read together to understand the role of a parent after their child is married. After the marriage of her sons, Kunti intervenes only once when her sons wanted to compromise their goal of winning back their legacy rights from the Kauravas. After the Pandavas won it, she devoted herself to the service of her 'parent like' in-laws Dhritarashtra and Gandhari. She also joined them when they proceeded to the forest. She explained to her sons, she had enjoyed all the privileges and pleasures of life as a royal and had no more to seek. After marriage, a parent's concerns can remain, but the responsibility and onus must vest with the couple. Detachment must be at both emotional and material levels. Mothers often desire to bring order, purpose and direction in the life and household of their married daughter. The mother-in-law is also doing things with the same intent. When two people are giving directions, it is likely there will be conflict. The rules in the home of a bride and her groom are likely to be different. If after marriage, both their mothers demand the newly wed couple to follow their rules, it will lead to conflict. There is a risk of the marriage failing.

What Happens to Parents when Children Fly the Nest? When Ashwatthama is crowned ruler of an annexed Panchal, his father Dronacharya sticks to his job even though he no longer needs it. He recognises that his son has come of age, gives him the responsibility, rather than becoming king himself with his son waiting as next in line. So often, we see parents not wanting to give up control and stay in charge into their old age whilst their sons remain in waiting. We are reminded of the Queen Elizabeth in the UK, strong into her 90s, with a waiting Crown Prince way into his 70s. The principles of

Ashram Dharma would have guided their family to allow for succession well before the present time. A son does not have to wait for a parent to die and remain till then a successor in waiting. If the first in line is less eligible than the one after him, it would be in order for the second in line to be enthroned. No progress is possible without change. The story of Dronacharya and Ashwatthama serves to guide a parent on transition and transfer of control, in much the same way that Kunti places the responsibility on Draupadi.

What happens when grown-up children want to or need to set up their own homes? This requirement may arise in the interest of domestic peace and harmony, or work needs or changed circumstances. We can base such separations on disagreement, on an agreement not to disagree or mutual agreement. Pandavas alongwith Draupadi leave Hastinapur to settle down in Khandavprastha, which is like a couple leaving their family home to work in another town or country. The location is unimportant because the act is often opposed. They accuse children of abandoning their parents in their old age. Rules of Dharma, the vows in marriage might be the basis for the decision of the young couple. Yet, we often accuse the bride of being a home-breaker. At other times, we might accuse the boy of being disloyal to his parents. They always consider the mother-in-law a troublemaker. Irrespective of whatever be the truth, children after marriage must have independence.

Kunti did not join the Pandavas when they moved to Khandavprastha and remained in Hastinapur even during the war. Dronacharya maintained his independence, he kept his office, his title and a life separate from that of his son. Every parent like Kunti and Dronacharya must allow their children to establish their independence. They must be free to choose their livelihood, their own home and the right to build their own family and destiny.

We Must Look after, not Merely Stay Together: *Mahabharata does not impose upon a child the responsibility to stay in the same home just to look after their parents in old age. Instead, it uses Ashram Dharma to provide guidance on how parents should conduct* *their life in old age. In our lives, we may live in separate homes, but we must maintain a connection with our parents. We must, if required, ensure they remain provided with their needs. We remain free to live our lives and perform our respective duties as per Ashram Dharma. As we grow up, it is usual for our interests and priorities and that of our parents to fall further apart. This does not amount to abandonment so long as we remain emotionally invested. Parents must not attempt to control their grown-up children using emotional or economic blackmail. They would then be as guilty as their children whose only interest in their parents arises from the property they may inherit.*

Parents know someday they will stop earning, their savings may be negligible and they may depend on their children. This can have ugly implications on elderly parents, and they must be prepared for such a situation. I devote a chapter in this book to relationship and trust; it identifies that the deepest of emotional relationships suffer with time. For all parents, who are fast moving into the latter stages of the Ashram dharma, Mahabharata recommends that we curb our desires and wants. We must focus on our basic needs and make our best effort to end any support from our children. Parents often expect to be financially supported in exchange for leaving a financial legacy in the form of money or assets. An ancient wisdom in this context may be very relevant. They believe if your children are worthy, they will not need your wealth; if they are unworthy, no wealth will be of any good to them. Parents in our present times must be financially smart and leverage their assets to provide for themselves. Many would agree that relationships between parents and their grown-up children are at their best when parents are financially independent.

The Pandavas had to be told when to give up the Vanprashta phase of their life. When Dhritarashtra, Gandhari, Vidura and Kunti entered their last phase they lived in a forest. Their children would visit and provide them with the essentials for their livelihood. One day, Dhritarashtra requests them to end all support, thus marking the end of their mortal connections. It subtly suggests that we shall alone cover the last distance of our mortal existence.

CHAPTER 29

Mayasura and the Building of the Capital – Indraprastha

Synopsis: Relevance of Vastu in a new home; basis of other ancient beliefs.

The Pandavas razed the forest to set up a new township. They appointed Mayasura, a renowned architect, to build a new capital. Asura, being natives of the region, had developed the knack of building structures with stones and coloured tiles, baked in kilns. The Aryans built their palaces with wood.

Mayasura is believed to have constructed a Palace of Doom, as a revenge for the horrific death of his family members in the forest fire lit up by Arjun. The uniqueness and the negativity of the palace built by him became clear in later events. The most amazing part of the Palace was the Royal Assembly, or the *Maya Sabha*. It had an amazing design. He used flooring tiles of different hues, which looked so natural that they resembled a water feature. Amid this flooring lay a pool which blended with the natural tiling. It could trick a person into falling into the water. Maya also has a negative connotation as in temptation, possessive attachment, negative influence or illusion.

They named the new palace and the settlement around it as Indraprastha, meaning the abode of Lord Indra. Supporters of the Pandavas initially settled down in the new capital, and those seeking better opportunities joined them later. The settlers enjoyed the judicious rule of Yudhishthir. The kingdom prospered and the Pandavas achieved Royalty.

The Pandavas lived there briefly before proceeding on a long exile. Even after the war, they preferred staying at Hastinapur, never once referring to Indraprastha post the war.

Commentary

Maya Sabha, Vastu and Hindu Beliefs: The Palace of Illusion was a spectacular piece of architecture. Hindus believe in vastu shastra dealing with the designs, layout, methods and rules of architecture. People also believe that faulty layout and the design of the building can block the natural flow of energy, wind and light. This can affect the health, spiritual wellbeing, prosperity and even the longevity of the occupants. Or adversely influence the behaviour of occupants and also bring about their downfall. People choose not to stay in their newly built homes as they believe it has bad vibes or has affected their progress or well being. They often call experts in Vastu or Feng Shui to help deal with the bad aura, etc.

Experts on Vastu base their guidance on an understanding of human hygiene and needs. They place bathrooms in such a way as to ensure that the winds can carry the odour away from the living quarters; the kitchen is so placed as to ensure that the wind does not draw the fire or the smoke towards the cook. They place bedrooms in a manner that people do not rest their head in the northward direction. There is evidence of raised blood pressure due to the influence of the earth's magnetic field when we sleep with our heads towards the north. They prefer the position of doors and windows in a direction that allows air to flow and circulate.

The Hindu idea of lighting a small ceremonial lamp daily after a bath in the morning and evening is to ensure a routine of hygiene. Most homes are dusted and cleaned before the lamp is lit. This ensures that the home remains free from insects, rodents, etc. as people would sleep on the floor at night.

Many people believe harsh behaviour will attract negative vibes. In a way, it arouses evil in the other person. The merciless killing at Khandavprastha would haunt the Pandavas. In fact, these killings would cause a revenge killing that a future generation would suffer. These superstitious beliefs come true when we read about the Pandavas in the chapters ahead. They often base superstitious beliefs on the experience of people. Sometimes, they base it on knowledge that has now been lost. They now perform rituals because it is customary. However, in their time, there was a value. This value may now not be relevant. In many homes, they sweep the house clean every evening. The lady of the house bathes and lights a ceremonial lamp, then prepares the family meal for consumption before retiring for the night. We may not attach any value to the practice. But there is logic in this routine. The houses centuries ago had open architecture. The woman would be engaged in farming whereas the men would be out hunting or trading. It was good hygiene to clean the house before sunset. They swept the floor clean where people would sleep. People used stories to explain their importance, if they dramatised them, they became superstitions.

CHAPTER 30

Life in Indraprastha – the Tragedy Begins

Synopsis: Learn the importance of developing a bond and understanding between couples.

Indraprastha continued to receive new settlers. It gained recognition as a centre of opportunity, peace and prosperity. The Pandavas were also happy, but their happiness would soon be short lived.

One night Takshaka, the surviving head of the Naga Tribals, raided the cattle sheds of the Brahmins in Indraprastha and took away their cattle. The desperate victims approached Arjun for help. He wanted to recover their cattle, but he could not access his weapons, as they were stored in Draupadi and Yudhishthir's bedroom. Nevertheless, he entered the room in their presence, out of a sense of duty, to grab his weapons and went after Takshaka, to recover the animals.

But then Arjun had violated the oath of privacy, which ensured the right of each of these siblings successively to spend a year with Draupadi as man and wife. Any violator would proceed on a year of exile, while surrendering his rights in favour of the one whose privacy he had violated. In this manner, Yudhisthir got an additional year of being with Draupadi.

Commentary

Duty, Promise, Apad Dharma and Punishment: As a kshatriya, Arjun was bound to protect the property of his subjects. But because of extraordinary circumstances, he could not avoid violating the oath of privacy. Yudhisthir and Draupadi could have condoned it as an act of Apad Dharma. But even a well-intentioned deed of Apad Dharma still violates some Dharma. Nor does it absolve the doer from punishment. It arises when we violate our obligation for executing a greater good.

Importance of Privacy: The privacy of a couple must be respected, not just when they are engaged in sex but also in togetherness. The privacy oath appears to bring order and discipline in the lives of Draupadi and her five husbands. It also implies that a married couple must spend time together to develop an understanding and a bond. Often this is possible during a honeymoon or courtship. Obstructing the development of this bond and understanding is an offence.

CHAPTER 31

Arjun's Year of Celibate Exile

Synopsis: Importance of Sanskar in marriage; compatibility in marriage; learn to eradicate problems, not contain them.

The Mahabharata narrates the experiences of Arjun in exile, when he undertook penance and received boons. He visited many places and married three women, including Ulupi, a Naga princess he met on the banks of the Ganges. This marriage helped appease a section of a local tribe of Nagas, not connected with the Nagas he had killed in Khandavprastha.

On his sojourn, Arjun reached Manipur where he wed princess Chitrangada, on the condition that a child born of their union would stay in Manipur. They named the child Babruvahana, successor to the throne of Nagaland. During exile, he returned to Manipur again to meet his wife and son.

Before his exile ended, Arjun reached Dwarka to meet Krishna, whose elder brother Balarama was already planning a Swayamwar for his sister Subhadra. He wanted her to marry Duryodhana and create an alliance with

Hastinapur to forestall Jarasandha's bid to attack the Yadava clan. But Krishna, who considered Arjuna a better choice, helped him abduct her. Balarama and Duryodhana wanted to punish Arjun for the abduction, but Krishna's intervention prevented Balarama from carrying out the act. He convinced Balarama to bless the marriage. Humiliated, Duryodhana returned to Hastinapur. He had again lost an opportunity to marry a princess.

Commentary

Marriage between First Cousins: Children born to two brothers could not marry as they shared the same Gotra. However, the child of a brother could marry the child born to his/her parent's sister.

Hindu Marriages: There are eight types of Hindu marriages. Brahma marriage is the marriage of one's daughter, after decking her with costly garments and presents of jewels. They marry her to a man of good conduct learned in the Vedas and invited by oneself. Daiva marriage is the marriage of one's daughter, decked with ornaments to a priest who duly officiates at a religious ceremony, during its performance. Arsha marriage is when the father gives away his daughter after receiving from the bridegroom a cow and a bull or two pairs of either as bride price. Prajapatya marriage is when a girl's father gives her in marriage to the groom, treating him with respect. He addresses them: May both of you perform together your duties. Gandharva marriage is a voluntary union of a maiden and her lover, which springs from mutual attraction. Asura marriage is when the bridegroom receives a maiden after having given of his own free will as much wealth as he can afford. This is given to the bride and her kinsmen. Rakshas marriage is when the bride maiden is abducted from her home after her kinsmen have been slain or wounded. Pisach marriage is one when a man by stealth seduces a girl who is sleeping, intoxicated, or mentally challenged. They considered the first four proper. Rakshas and Gandharva marriage was acceptable to Kshatriyas, as was Asura marriage for Vaishya and Shudra.

The Choice between Removal and Restraint: Balarama wanted his sister to marry Duryodhana. He was the guru of both Duryodhana and Bhima, and he knew them well. He knew the Pandavas would often resort to tricks. If his sister married into the Kuru family, the alliance would secure the Yadavas. Jarasandha would stop his attacks.

However, this would force Krishna to side with Duryodhana, which was bound to erode his influence with the Pandavas. Krishna knew Arjun well, and he did not trust the Kauravas. Duryodhana lacked Sanskar. His blind parents could not provide him the required guidance. Kunti as a mother had been hands on and ensured that the Pandavas understood and fulfilled their Dharma. He preferred the happiness of his sister over the security of the Yadavas. Krishna wanted to remove Jarasandha for good and ensure permanent peace, not a mere truce. An alliance with the Kurus meant he had to depend on Jarasandha.

Krishna showed that we cannot rely on another's goodwill for our well-being. He wanted to kill Jarasandha and ensure long term security for his clan, but could not wage war against him. The other option was assassination, perhaps at the hands of Bhima. He had to stop the marriage and the resulting alliance with the Kauravas and align the Yadavas more firmly with the Pandavas, who were already grateful to him for arranging their match with Draupadi. His sister's marriage would reaffirm their partnership. He asked Arjun to kidnap his sister, convincing Balarama to accept the alliance. His plan humiliated Duryodhana, who had lost to Arjun for the second time as a suitor, helping fan the hatred between the cousins.

Krishna's Intervention and Sanskar: We learnt the importance of Kula from the events at Draupadi's Swayamwar. Arjun and Duryodhana were members of the Kuru family and, therefore, shared *the same Kula. Krishna's intervention in a marriage on this occasion brings out the importance of Sanskar. Sanskar is the guidance we receive from our parents. It influences our values, social and moral conduct. Duryodhana's parents were blind, which takes on another dimension. It refers to their inability to provide guidance. Arjun grew up under the care of a single parent. But Kunti was hands on. Arjun had the benefit of Sanskar from his mother.*

Synastry and Marriage: *To complete the matchmaking process, it was necessary to establish the compatibility of the couples. They therefore added a process from astrology called Synastry. Every planet orbits the Sun from a different distance. The Earth orbits the Sun and the Moon orbits the Earth. The Planets, Sun and Moon are each uniquely located from our place and time at birth. Their locations are calculated and placed in an astrological chart. Astrologers prepare such charts for both the proposed bride and her groom. They then compare the charts. A planet based on its location may be good or bad. Planets may be good on the chart of both partners, or they may be placed badly. A planet based on its position can mean that the person is aggressive. If the planets denote the same characteristic in both the parties, then the marriage will be difficult. The astrologer can attribute a personality or behaviour trait to every planet. In this process, they can suggest if the bride and groom are compatible. We can attribute its later addition to advancement in knowledge of astronomy and the establishment of a uniform calendar. In a marriage search process, we need to look at the attributes a girl desires in her husband, his Varna, Jati, Kula and Sanskar. Today, we must also look at the attributes of a girl. It is possible that neither side may know the other. Therefore, it would be hard to assess the character and compatibility of the couple, Synastry helps resolve this.*

CHAPTER 32

Arjun Returns to Indraprastha with Wife Subhadra

Synopsis: Long-distance relationships. Lack of communication affects relationships between couples. How to respond to the other woman?

After their marriage, Arjun returned to Indraprastha with Subhadra and Krishna. Draupadi was determined that although the Pandavas could marry other women, they could not share the same roof with her. Arjun breached her rules by bringing Subhadra to Indraprastha, where Draupadi lived with the Pandavas.

Draupadi made an exception for Subhadra. She fell at Draupadi's feet, accepting her superior status and offering to be her handmaiden. Subhadra's humility melted the ice between the two women of immense beauty. Another version suggests that Draupadi wanted Arjun to realize that she surpassed Krishna's sister in every respect and hence more deserving of his love and attention.

Subhadra was Krishna's sister, a favourite of Kunti and a cousin of the Pandavas. Draupadi knew of the influence Krishna enjoyed with the Pandavas. She had a high regard and special relationship with Krishna. She also knew Arjun was third in line. Subhadra, as his fourth wife, was not a threat to her role as queen. Subhadra was also a favourite of her aunt Kunti. Draupadi therefore compromised and allowed Subhadra to share their roof.

Commentary

From Draupadi's Perspective: An ambitious Draupadi had married the five Pandavas. As Yudhisthir's wife, she was first in line to be Queen. She would be queen irrespective of who amongst the Pandavas became king. Subhadra's marriage had resulted in an alliance between them and the Yadavas. Treating Subhadra well would help her relationship with Krishna. If Arjun became King, she would still be the Queen. Subhadra was Arjun's fourth wife, her power and influence was relatively small. Draupadi valued her relationship with Krishna. He had managed her marriage to the Pandavas. They trusted him and accepted him as their advisor. He was close to Kunti. Krishna had the ability to manipulate events and circumstances. She needed him on her side. This would secure her position. She could use Krishna to influence the Pandavas.

Perspective of the Pandavas: Arjun had won Draupadi. Draupadi later in the Epic laments that Arjun was openly partial to Subhadra and her son Abhimanyu. He ignored their son. The other Pandava brothers knew Draupadi was partial towards Arjun. It upset Draupadi when Arjun brought Subhadra home. This affected her relationship with Arjun. They thought this would help them. They realised his marriage to Subhadra would affect the relationship between Draupadi and Arjun.

Impact on Marriage: *Draupadi did not feel rejected nor did she wallow in self-pity. She did not passively accept the situation, but responded to the challenge. She acknowledged Subhadra's existence. She wanted Arjun to realise who was more deserving. She was in charge and used her right to maintain her status. Draupadi knew Subhadra would never enjoy an equivalent status. Draupadi would always be first in line to be queen, whereas Subhadra was not really in the reckoning.*

Women have to deal with the challenge of extra-marital relationship in their marriage. The Epic advises her not to resort to self-pity. She must protect her economic interest. She must not resort to self-denial or confrontation. If the affected party feels they still desire the other, they should give their relationship a second chance. This event offers guidance to couples of the risk they face in extra-marital relationships. It warns them of the risk of a permanent divide.

CHAPTER 33

Krishna Returns to Exert His Influence over the Pandavas

Synopsis: Feel manipulated? Advisors have an agenda. Pandavas lacked a strategy and were exposed to manipulation. In group working, everybody must contribute, pay a price or make a sacrifice, so did Krishna.

Arjun and Subhadra's arrival in Indraprastha marked the return of Krishna into the lives of the Pandavas, now established as rulers. Their coffers were flowing with revenues from their Kingdom. As just rulers, they commanded the loyalty of their subjects. However, they wanted to be independent and be recognized for good work. Krishna knew the partition was unfair. It forced the Pandavas to leave their mother behind and accept the supremacy of Hastinapur.

Drupad wanted to teach Hastinapur a lesson. He held them responsible for losing half his kingdom. Krishna wanted to secure the future of Yadavas by eliminating Jarasandha and removing the threat to his subjects, while avenging his humiliation.

Pandavas trusted Krishna. He had been instrumental in securing the hand of Draupadi and Subhadra for them. They needed Krishna's experience of politics and strategy and regarded him as their advisor. The Epic now introduced demi-god Narada into the story. He asked the Pandavas to perform Rajsuya Yagna to establish Yudhisthir as an emperor. The Pandavas approached Krishna for a solution. He pointed out how more than 95 kings had accepted the supremacy of Jarasandha. They therefore needed to remove him and gain the support of those rulers.

Commentary

Manipulation and Personal Agenda of Advisors: *Krishna was very focused on removing a powerful enemy like Jarasandha. It had to be done covertly. The Pandavas were playing to his plan to avenge his defeat and negate his reputation as Ranchod and establish him as Vasudeva, a title given to a person in a generation. They would consider him as an incarnation of Vishnu.*

Duryodhana understood the importance of making friends and allies. He used this ability to build a team loyal to him. The Pandavas lacked a strategy. They achieved results but had no strategic plan. Krishna recognised their weakness and stepped in to fill this void.

CHAPTER 34

The Assassination of Jarasandha

Synopsis: Been in a mess that was not your doing? Why were you there when it was not your problem? Like all other faiths, did we have our own divisions between followers of Shiva and Vishnu?

Krishna came up with a plan to assassinate Jarasandha. Bhima with his brute strength was the only person Krishna could trust to duel with Jarasandha. Jarasandha had defeated about 95 neighbouring kingdoms and held their rulers in captivity. This was a dramatic license. Jarasandha was a devout follower of God Shiva, well versed in Dharma. Jarasandha's death would release these kings, and they could then accept the supremacy of the Pandavas. This apart, Krishna could avenge his personal humiliation.

Krishna accompanied by Bhima and Arjun set out for Magadha, disguised as Brahmins. Jarasandha a man of faith never turned back or denied a request received from a

Brahmin. He also would not refuse a challenge to a duel as a Kshatriya. Krishna exploited this charitable characteristic of Jarasandha. They gained admittance to the Emperor's palace as Brahmins. They then trapped him into choosing either to challenge Arjun in a bout of archery or Bhima in a bout of wrestling. The fair-minded Jarasandha was a wrestler and chose Bhima as he was a closer match to him in physique. The wrestling bout lasted several days. Bhima killed Jarasandha. They dramatised the story of his death. This built up Bhima's profile on the one hand and demonised Jarasandha.

In the story, Bhima in a manoeuvre would tear the body of Jarasandha into two halves and take him to be dead. However, in a few moments the body would join and Jarasandha would rise again, ready to continue battle. They glorified Krishna because he told Bhima to tear his body apart and throw each half in the opposite direction. When the body sought to join again, the parts would not align as these faced the opposite direction. They killed Jarasandha, releasing the kings owing allegiance to him. They were now open to accepting the supremacy of the Pandavas.

Commentary

This story was brilliant from a folk tale perspective, but unacceptable to the modern mind. A body once ripped into two equal parts will not join or return to life. This over-dramatisation of the assassination and fighting for several days was just to drive home the point it was a big fight.

People Hate Paying Taxes and Resist Domination: *The story that he had captured 95 kings and needed to be checkmated because* he was looking to sacrifice a hundred kings made him appear like a villain. It is unlikely that he would have imprisoned kings or sacrificed them. As an emperor, he would have received their allegiance and tributes. However, it was more likely that the kings who were forced into submission (held in captivity being a dramatisation) were unhappy with the tax burden.

Killing Without Cause: After the Yadavas moved to distant Dwarka, there was no record of Jarasandha trying to invade them. In fact, the Yadavas had become irrelevant. Disguised as a Brahmin, Krishna breached the Dharma of Jarasandha, to gain access to his person and eliminate him. A legendary wrestler, Jarasandha was much older than his rival Bhima. The commentary of a battle is unreal and was done to glorify Bhima, masking his dubious intentions.

Lessons from the Assassination of Jarasandha: They killed Jarasandha without a cause. They tricked him into a wrestling bout by exploiting his Kshatriya code. Had Jarasandha acted with discretion, he could have avoided death. When we make a habit of our charitable behaviour, it turns into vanity leading to our undoing. We must not forget that charity begins at home and that we must act our age.

All Things Must End: The end of Jarasandha's supremacy points to the evolution of mankind, where all things must end so that the new can begin. The Mahabharata introduces us to the idea of Yuga. Jarasandha, Dhritarashtra and Bhishma are examples of people who never transitioned their lives from the second to the next stage.

CHAPTER 35

Rajsuya Yagna and the Seeds of Discord

Synopsis: It is important to say No. Learning to say no is important, beware of people who can use your ambition to exploit and manipulate you.

The rulers looked to becoming a samrat or emperor for a much higher stature. Several kings would acknowledge their supremacy and pay their obeisance. In the Aryan world, if a ruler lost a battle, his life would be spared if he submitted to the victor's authority. When he died in battle, the victor would designate the next of his kin as a successor. If he happened to be a minor, a regent would be appointed to manage affairs of his kingdom until he came of age. Defeat in battle did not always lead to annexation and execution of the defeated royals.

A king is the upholder of Dharma, who must defend and protect his subjects. When faced with the prospect of invasion, it is his responsibility to avoid war through diplomacy, loss of lives and wealth. He would invite other kings to a 'Rajsuya Yagna.' Accepting the invitation implied their acknowledgement of his supremacy. After killing Jarasandha, the Pandavas freed the 95 kings and invited them to Indraprastha for the Yagna. Many of them accepted. Bhishma, senior Kurus, Duryodhana and his brothers attended on behalf of Hastinapur.

Commentary

Inability to Say No, the Ambition Trap: The Pandavas had unwittingly walked into a trap, after being manipulated by their allies. Yudhisthir performed a Yagna to elevate himself as an Emperor and invest himself with a status higher than Dhritarashtra. Kuru elders and their Kaurava cousins attended the event, displaying astute political sense, confident in their power and supremacy. Why did the Pandavas not take cognizance of Narada's mischief making and reject his suggestion on the Yagna?

CHAPTER 36

Honouring of Krishna and Assassination of Sisupala

Synopsis: *Experienced but passed over for promotion; beaten by a junior to the post; accord respect to your elders. Grant position based on competence and wisdom.*

At the Yagna, the opulence of the Maya Sabha enchanted the guests. Aryan architecture was wood-based, whereas they used stones and coloured tiles in the Palace. Visitors were jealous of the success achieved by the Pandavas. They required Yudhisthir to honour all the attendees, including King Drupad, Ved Vyas, Vasudeva (Krishna's father), Bhishma, many learned priests and Kshatriyas. The issue before Yudhisthir was whom should he honour first. Yudhisthir could have honoured Bhishma first. He could have honoured his biological grandfather the very learned Ved Vyas. Or he could have honoured his father-in-law Drupad. They would have regarded each of them as a father or grandfather. These were men of great honour, achievement, knowledge and wisdom.

Yudhisthir sought Bhishma's advice about whom he should honour first. The patriarch pointed to Krishna because he made the ceremony possible. However, Krishna's cousin Sisupala was upset with the choice.

The roots of their enmity went back to the time when Krishna abducted and married Rukmini, after it had been settled that she would wed Sisupala. Rukmini sent word to Krishna to rescue her, with whom she was in love. Sisupala supported King Jarasandha and blamed Krishna for killing him. Many of the rulers present at the Yagya resented the sudden rise of Pandavas. Sisupala's objection to the choice of Krishna found many takers. Sisupala's behaviour shocked the Pandavas. He insulted Krishna and accused Bhishma of being impotent and dismissed the Kuru Dynasty as incompetent. He insisted that the Kurus should have punished the Pandavas for killing their allies and Krishna for creating a rift in the family.

Krishna realised that support for Sisupala by the royal assemblage was virtually jeopardizing the Yagna. He permitted the latter to mock and abuse him 99 times, just as he had promised his aunt, but killed him when he crossed the 100th mark. The authors of the Epic presented Sisupala with a demonic profile, possessing extra limbs, one who had been Ravana in his past life. His death, at the hands of Krishna, liberated his soul. But the sudden violence shocked the entire assembly. Krishna and the Pandavas calmed their guests and the Yagna ended peacefully.

Commentary

Yudhisthir the Dharma Raj? Bhishma knew Yudhisthir wanted to honour his mentor/advisor Krishna and violate conventions. He

*could have chosen Guru Dronacharya or his father-in-law Drupad.
Each of them was like a father figure and deserved the honour.*

Honour the Deserving: *Yudhisthir's actions convey an important
and subtle learning. We must honour and respect the deserving, and
it need not be based on seniority.*

Krishna's Emerging Role as King Maker. *The notion that many
of the royal guests recognised Krishna as an incarnation was inserted
much later. The Pandavas depended on Krishna for strategic help
and support. He led the way in the court of Indraprastha.*

Obligations of a Guest: *Krishna's slaying of Shishupal is a
contentious issue. We must revere a guest as god as the saying
'Attihi devo bhava,' goes. It was the solemn duty of the Pandavas to
protect every invitee and prevent any altercation between guests. On
his part, a guest must not abuse his welcome and take advantage of
the host. If a guest disagrees with the host, he may leave, but never
disrupt the occasion. Sisupala's story is a message on the rules of
conduct and the obligations of a Guest.*

A Lesson on Strategy: *Sisupala's killing served the interests of
both Krishna and the Pandavas. Krishna killed anyone opposed to his
agenda, which included the likes of Kansa, Jarasandha and Sisupala.
He ended up being the power behind Yudhisthir and wanted to
become the Vasudeva of his time.*

Krishna Slaying of Sisupala: *Krishna could have exercised self-
restraint rather than being intimidated by Sisupala's outburst or
succumbing to the ego. He had made off with a woman whose
betrothal was planned with Sisupala. Stories of Sisupala being born*

with extra limbs or being Ravana in an earlier life were meant to demonise him. The authors of the Mahabharat are sending forth the message that God is forgiving, but a devotee must not take him for granted. Even in law, repeat offences may invite the death penalty.

An End for a New Beginning: *The killing of Jarasandha released several kings from subjugation and was necessary for conducting the Yagna. But it did not justify the act at the insistence of Krishna. The message here is that everything must end to herald a new beginning. Also, power can blind and corrupt and serves a warning to act with restraint.*

CHAPTER 37

Emperor Yudhisthir and Duryodhana's Humiliation

Synopsis: An age old wisdom. Show respect, keep a smile, avoid harsh words and controversy.

The events at Indraprastha had sown the seeds of a rift between the Kauravas and the Pandavas. Yudhisthir could have chosen a Kaurava elder for the high honour. Maybe he could have averted all the ensuing negativity and bitterness.

After the Yagna, the guests returned home, but Duryodhana stayed back for a few more days. He wanted to identify weaknesses to use against the Pandavas and neutralise them. He was quite taken in by the architecture of the Pandava Palace and Maya Sabha's design, with its multi-coloured tiles and integration of water features.

Being unfamiliar with the layout, Duryodhana trod carefully so as not to wet his attire, all the while being watched by Draupadi. When he fell into a pool of water, she burst out laughing, remarking insensitively 'blind like the father, the son.' Duryodhana swore to avenge the humiliation. Draupadi should not have made light of Duryodhana's embarrassment, who after all happened to be her guest.

There are several versions in existence. One of them is that Draupadi made no comments. Bhima helped Duryodhana get up from the pool of water, but he acted rudely, which offended Duryodhana. In another version, she and Bhima exchanged meaningful glances, enjoying Duryodhana's discomfiture, which was bound to upset him.

Returning to Hastinapur, Duryodhana shared his experiences with the loyalists, who wanted to checkmate the Pandavas' growing clout and assertion of their independence. Dhritarashtra sought to dissuade Duryodhana from taking any action, insisting that Kauravas and Pandavas were brothers and shared the same family tree. He wanted Duryodhana to focus on what he had, instead of being envious of Yudhishthir's success, just as the Pandavas did not resent him or his kingdom.

Duryodhana performed a Digvijaya Yagna and established alliances with several kings. He wanted his forces, combined with that of his partners, to be larger than the Pandava army and their allies, believing that it would assure him of victory. The Kauravas began to identify ways to isolate the Pandavas and re-establish their supremacy over the entire Aryan race.

Commentary

This event may have been dramatized and the extra bits added to help move the epic to the next level. Some versions might not seem real.

The narrative lacks the finesse of an educated royalty. However, it has helped to paint negative forces and make light of societal obligations.

Sometimes it is Wise to Shut Up: *Having accepted the supremacy of Hastinapur, it was reasonable to treat its Crown Prince with respect. Tradition prescribes that a wife must treat her husband's elder siblings with consideration. The poolside event also reflects a lack of sensitivity to someone's embarrassment, which was bound to cause bad blood among princes.*

Pandavas Could not be Trusted: *Pandavas had agreed to the terms of the division of the empire and then violated them. Rajsuya Yagna, which enthroned Yudhisthir as an emperor directly challenged his cousins. They killed Jarasandha, an ally of Hastinapur, by trickery to benefit Krishna. Bhima married a tribal woman so that he and his family could live safely in the jungle. But he callously abandoned her after the birth of their child and moved on. Only to approach them when he needed their son to fight for him. Clearing the forest for establishing Indraprastha may have been essential. But killing its denizens senselessly, with Krishna and Arjuna's involvement, could have never been justified. They only created enemies. In a formal setting they honoured Krishna, insulted Duryodhana and made fun of an elder's disability. Given their status and education, this was shocking. Five men marrying a woman violated the principles of a society. Parashuram punished Karna for lying, who pretended to be a Brahmin.*

CHAPTER 38

Shakuni and His Plan

Synopsis: The Power of Thought. Uber may have found its business model in Shakuni's Plan? Beware Apple some day a giant killer will rise, inspired by Shakuni's game of dice plan.

The Epic creates the hero and the anti-hero. Krishna and Shakuni serve as the advisor and guide to the Pandavas and Kauravas, respectively. Shakuni imposes his own brand of logic and guidance to ensure that the Kauravas can defend their rights.

After his return to Hastinapur, Duryodhana looked at his options to clip the wings of the Pandavas, but also knew of the divided loyalties within his own court. He needed a solution to remove the Pandavas without engaging in a contest of arms, which entailed huge loss of life, in keeping with the Kshatriya Dharma to avoid conflict and destruction.

The Kauravas thought of ways to divide the Pandavas. They thought of using Draupadi's affection for Arjun to create jealousy, but rejected it because of the bond among the Pandavas. Shakuni, an acknowledged master in gambling, who knew of Yudhisthir's weakness for the game, suggested inviting Yudhisthir to a game of dice.

Following the Yagna, Shakuni wanted to capitalize on the loyalty and commitment of the Pandavas towards Yudhisthir. He knew they would not challenge his decision. Shakuni planned to trap the Pandavas by inviting them to a game of dice. Initially, the Kuru elders rejected the idea when it was first presented at the court. But Duryodhana overcame their objections. A reluctant Vidura conveyed the invitation to the Pandavas. After the Rajsuya Yagna, Yudhisthir, vexed by premonitions, sought the advice and blessings of his elders for their well being. He was warned about their future being fraught with grave risks and advised to be extra cautious and avoid any conflict or confrontation.

The Yagna and its events had sowed the seeds of a conflict between the two clans. It left Yudhisthir with no options, but to participate in the game, even if reluctantly and with serious misgivings. Refusing the invite would weaken Vidura's position, his biggest supporter. It would also offend a father figure and family elder like Dhritarashtra, who had sent it in the first place. Personally, it tempted Yudhistir as a gambler. Unfortunately, in Krishna's absence, Yudhisthir had to rely on his own counsel.

Commentary

Exploiting a Weakness, Timing is the Key: Duryodhana and his advisors showed their mastery in the management of the Pandavas. Yudhishthir's acceptance acknowledged the supremacy of Hastinapur at both personal and political level. A refusal would mean that the Pandavas wanted to break their relationship with the rest of the family. The Pandavas were not well-versed in the art of statecraft. The Kauravas exploited Krishna's absence. The design and execution of the plan is a great management lesson. Ostensibly the invite would promote friendship between the two clans. No one could find a fault with the invitation or its intent. They would construe a refusal as a hostile act.

Understanding Weakness of the Opponent: *Shakuni exploited Yudhisthir's weakness for gambling. A gambler who has lost is often carried away by a belief that luck will turn in his favour. He will keep increasing his stakes hoping to recoup his losses and to win ultimately. Shakuni knew the Pandavas would blindly support Yudhisthir. Their greatest strength which lay in unity would become their biggest liability when Yudhisthir blundered. Not being an astute politician, Yudhisthir never sought counsel before accepting the invite. Nor did he identify the risks. Despite his strong and uncompromising views on Dharma, he suffered from a flaw: gambling. He felt confident that he could gamble and win the other half of the empire from the Kauravas. The Kauravas leveraged this weakness of Yudhisthir. The Pandavas' strength became their weakness.*

Uber as a Model Exploits a Human Weakness: *A modern day example of The Plan is the business model of Uber.*

They regulate taxis as a trade. One needs a licence to operate a taxi. The metre determines the fare. This assures the customer of safety, security and transparency. However, all this comes at a cost. Riding a taxi is expensive.

Uber challenged this model. They provided a driver and a decent car. The fare could vary based on demand, traffic conditions, time of day, etc. There were no major entry barriers to the trade. Any driver with a decent car was eligible to operate under the Uber network. The lower entry costs and use of a less expensive vehicle helped them to keep the fares low. The fare could be lower, during non-peak hours or when traffic was not busy. The ride could be booked and tracked. The user was now tempted. The user was like Yudhisthir willing to gamble for a saving. A trip using Uber might cost less than a taxi. He may or may not save, but he was hoping to save. Uber converted the strength of the Taxi trade into a weakness. They offered the temptation of a possible saving thus leveraging a customer's gambling instinct. The strength of the taxi business which offered price regulation now became a weakness. Transparency was equalled by using satellite navigation technology to guide the drivers to take the most optimal routes based on real time traffic information. A tracking software allowed a well-wisher to keep track of the rider's enhanced security.

CHAPTER 39

The Game of Dice

Synopsis: Downfalls are always sudden and deep; success can be shortlived and deceiving. The higher you go, the more cautious you need to be. Mahabharata and legal ideas like Trustee, Ownership, rules that void a contract. Can a partner commit their spouse?

On the fateful day in presence of an assembly of kings, royal invitees and courtiers, the Game of Dice got underway as scheduled. Duryodhana announced that Shakuni would play on his behalf. Shakuni was well-versed in the game and understood how the rules of probability operated. Yudhisthir, being a novice and a gambler, believed in luck and joined the contest.

It is believed that Shakuni possessed an enchanted dice, fashioned out of the bones of his own father, which responded to Shakuni's wishes. Yudhisthir staked all his wealth and then his kingdom. He then staked his brothers and he lost them all. Finally, he staked himself and then Draupadi.

Duryodhana summoned Draupadi to the royal court as she was no longer a queen and he had won her in a wager.

When Draupadi refused to honour his summons, he sent his brother Dushashan to bring her to the court.

A lot of versions exist of what happened that day. As per one, Dushashan dragged her by her hair and pushed her into the court. They thus brought her in the presence of King Dhritarashtra, Bhishma and many elders, including Vidura.

Once dragged to the court, she demanded to know how an enslaved Yudhisthir staked her when he himself was not independent. She also asked the present Kuru elders how could a royal princess and daughter-in-law of the Kuru family be dragged so shamefully to the court.

No elder present offered a definite answer, and the Pandavas remained silent with bowed heads. At some point, they asked the enslaved Pandavas to discard their royal attire and wear one befitting a slave. Draupadi, dressed as a queen, ignored this and as some versions claim, Dushashan tried to disrobe Draupadi. In other versions, Karna avenged his humiliation by pointing out that a woman in a relationship with five men deserved no respect. This comment spurred Dushashan to disrobe Draupadi, who sought divine intervention to protect her honour, which was granted. Dushashan could not pull off the infinite length of sari.

Another version says Duryodhana asked Draupadi to sit on his lap. Had she accepted the offer, it would have implied that she had left her five husbands and had taken refuge of Duryodhana as his queen.

This is the only time when Yudhishthir's brothers challenged his authority and actions. Bhima vowed to break Duryodhana's thighs for insulting and humiliating Draupadi. He also vowed that he would rip out the hands of Dushashan and kill every Kaurava Prince. He was so angry he wanted to burn Yudhishthir's hand.

Dhritarashtra realised that the behaviour of his sons was unpardonable. They had ruined the reputation of the Court. They had not only endangered their lives but also risked losing support of their present allies. He even feared risk of internal challenges to the throne. He called for an immediate stop to the events and restored sanity in the court. He apologised to Draupadi for her humiliation and granted her three wishes. Draupadi asked him to release her husbands and to return their weapons to them. Dhritarashtra restored all that the Pandavas had lost. He asked them to return to their Palace and forgive their cousins for all that had happened.

Duryodhana upset with Dhritarashtra's decision compelled the Court of Hastinapur to allow another game. This time the stake was that the loser would relinquish the throne and proceed to twelve years of exile followed by one year of exile in disguise. If in that last year, someone discovered them, then the loser would have to return to a further cycle of exile and a further year of exile in disguise. The Pandavas returned to the game and Yudhisthir once again lost. As a result, the Pandavas and Draupadi had to relinquish their kingdom and proceed on exile.

The Kauravas had achieved their aim of recovering their Kingdom. The Pandavas returned to a life of penury. This apart, they lost their right to stake a claim to any part of the Kingdom of Hastinapur.

Commentary

A lot of different versions exist of the events that happened that day. They have dramatised many, of which some were later additions.

__A More Reasonable Set of Events:__ The assassination of Jarasandha an ally of the Hastinapur was an act against the state of Hastinapur. Pandavas at Rajsuya Yagna challenged the supremacy of the Court of Hastinapur. They honoured Krishna over the Crown Prince of Hastinapur and the Regent of Hastinapur. Kauravas viewed these acts as rejecting the Supremacy of Hastinapur. These acts against the state of Hastinapur justified the removal of the Pandavas as rulers of Khandavprastha and their exile.

__Additional Melodrama Serves to Provide Guidance:__ They introduced the additional melodrama to add a touch of divine to Krishna and to paint the dark act darker. It may be an attempt to justify Bhīma's future actions. He targeted Duryodhana's thighs in their final fight with the mace. He inhumanly killed Dushashan, drew and drank Dushashan's blood. He allowed Draupadi to wet her hair in that blood. This apart, he used the excuse of an oath to kill every Kaurava cousin.

__Pandavas and Their Unexplained Behavior:__ On the day of Violation of Draupadi's modesty Bhima sought to avenge her humiliation with an oath to kill all his Kaurava Cousins. Dhritarashtra urged Draupadi to pardon all the wrongs done to her and in return granted to her three wishes, which she exercised. Dhritarashtra not only acted on her wishes but also restored the kingdom, assets and title of the Pandavas. Though the Pandavas were recalled to play the game again and lost is another matter. Should the oath of Bhima survive? Why did Yudhisthir agree to yet another game? As both Bhima and Arjun were agitated by Yudhisthir's irresponsible behaviour, why did they allow him to play again? Was the Game of Dice a later addition? Was it incorporated as a study of responsible behaviour?

Guidance on Responsible Behaviour: Mindless acts can destroy peace and tranquility. The cycle of change is beyond the control of the persons involved. Success is blinding and we often indulge in acts that can bring grief. It cautions us to be mindful of one's commitment, listening to counsel, acting wisely and ensuring we guard against our weakness.

In later events, they quote Krishna as stating that he would not have allowed the Pandavas to accept the invite to the Game of Dice. Krishna's brother Balarama maintained that staking one's wife was unforgivable and refused any support to the Pandavas. Drupad's desire to avenge his personal humiliation was his personal agenda, it created no obligation of Kshatriya Dharma on the Pandavas. Drupad's mindless act of promising half his Kingdom was wrong. When a desperate Dronacharya asked for his promised share he should have acknowledged and explained his inability to his childhood friend. The Kingdom was not his personal property, and he had no right to give it away.

With success and wealth, we often become arrogant, our conduct can turn offensive. We are often in denial of events, circumstances, friendships from our times when we were struggling. This denial is an example of how success blinds. Yudhisthir sought no counsel before accepting the invite. His advisor Krishna would have asked him to reject the invite. Yudhisthir lost the first time, but Dhritarashtra returned to him all that was lost. His obedient brothers opposed his behaviour, yet, Yudhisthir returned for another round of gambling. He lost again. His actions lacked wisdom and showed his weakness.

The desire to get rich quick or depend on wager rather than wage. Yudhisthir did not decline to wager once he had lost all his material possessions. This reflects the typical behaviour of a gambler and his belief that luck will turn in his favour soon. Even after all was restored to him, he agreed to wager again. It is important to realise one's folly.

Yudhisthir got the throne by the efforts of Krishna, Bhima and Arjun, with little or no effort on his part. Often, we squander away inherited wealth because we are not aware of the efforts and sacrifices made to earn it.

When Duryodhana invited Shakuni to play on his behalf, the Game of Dice was no longer a social event between the hosts and guest king, which Yudhisthir did not recognise. Even when bets were being placed, i.e. when Yudhisthir bet Draupadi, the Kauravas did not place an equal stake again demonstrating his catastrophic lack of judgement.

Pandavas Lives before the Game of Dice: *Married to Draupadi, the Pandavas were living a contented life in Khandavprastha renamed as Indraprastha for bringing prosperity to their subjects. Having accepted the supremacy of the court of Hastinapur, there was no provocation to alter that arrangement. Listening to others who were the greatest beneficiaries of the Rajsuya Yagna was not sound political judgement. It showed their lack of political skills and understanding of affairs of the State. The killing of Jarasandha served Krishna's personal agenda as the Pandavas had no justifiable cause against him. Engaging in a game of dice where they staked and lost public property was Adharma and even worse they staked Draupadi.*

Game of Dice - the Legal Response to Molestation of Women?
The game of dice highlights the plight of women when they are objectified. Yudhisthir also called Dharma Raj staked his wife. They treated Draupadi of royal birth and a queen as an object, so imagine the plight of women less fortunate?

Bhishma, Vidura, Kripacharya and Dronacharya, all well-versed in matters of Dharma remained silent. This points to the ordeal of oppressed women when Dharma or its enforcers do not act proactively. The Mahabharata cautioned that even the thought of molestation must be punished. It then brings into the frame our laws and enforcement. The inability of the members of the Court, who were experts on Dharma, to respond to Draupadi's question is how our laws operate. They wait for a complaint. Then they spend time to 'investigate' and respond only after they have 'conclusive evidence.' This happened, the Judge (blind Dhritarashtra) well after the act and the investigation are over, declares the event as void. He awards the victim with compensation, namely the three wishes granted to Draupadi. The victim accepts the compensation, but her emotional trauma remains. She cannot forget her ordeal. She berates her perpetrators, Yudhisthir, and Dushashan and his accomplices. She was upset with the other Pandavas and Kauravas who watched but did not come to her rescue. She does not tie her hair till she can wash away her trauma with Dushashan's blood. The Mahabharata tells us a victim must receive compensation. We must punish her perpetrators, and we must also deal with her mental trauma.

It details the saga of oppression of women in the Epic from even times long past. Madri was bought and then married into the family. Queen Satyawati forced her widowed daughter-in-laws to bear children to provide for succession. They forced Gandhari to marry against her wishes after they starved her family. Bhishma abducted three princesses for marriage to his half-brother.

The temptation to covet another man's wife because of her beauty is well-known. So is the lop-sided view of the society that accepts a man's polygamy but rejects a woman's polyandry. When Draupadi was brought before the court, she raised objections. When the Pandavas and Draupadi were asked to dress as slaves, Draupadi objected. They asked Dushashan to ensure that she took off her royal clothes. He was unwilling to use force until Karna stated that a woman in a relationship with five men was a whore and should be treated as one. Men of that time had several wives, but that was not objectionable.

Draupadi's Questions on Dharma was a Legal Challenge: Was Yudhisthir justified to stake his brothers or their wife as an object in a game of dice? Was Yudhisthir capable of staking his wife after he had staked himself and lost? Draupadi posed questions to the attendant elders. They deployed deep thought and remarkable intelligence in constructing the events around the Game of Dice. The first event was treated as cancelled because the game had degenerated into staking of relationships. Yudhisthir could not stake his brothers or his wife. As per an established legal principle, bankruptcy courts cannot attach the revenue or assets of a spouse even where his/her partner is a bankrupt. The drag along provisions for a bankrupt cannot extend beyond the assets owned.

As he was no longer independent, they could say he disqualified himself from executing a contract. Another dimension to the argument is that a slave may also have personal possessions. In those times, a wife was considered the property of a husband and a slave was entitled to own property. However, the obligations between a couple are based on their marriage vows and this make them partners and a wife is not a property of her husband.

Experts like Bhishma and Vidura knew the answer would have not resolved the crisis that faced the Court because it entitled the winner to take possession of his winnings. A response to Draupadi's question would have added to her distress and encouraged the Kauravas to add to her woes. The silence of the present elders to the valid questions of Draupadi points to the objectification of women. Oppression against women was not objected to, even her rightful questions and objections were ignored. There has been no real improvement in the plight of women to this day.

Partnerships and Unlimited Liability: *In partnerships, a partner's personal assets are at risk for any commitments made by the firm or by any of its partners. Yudhisthir and his brothers were all married to Draupadi, they owned Draupadi. Yudhisthir staked his wife and created a drag along risk similar to how a partner can risk the firm and the asset of all its partners.*

Can a Spouse Make a Promise on Behalf of the Partner? *The answer is no. Dhritarashtra awarded Draupadi three wishes on the condition that all that happened on the first round of the Game be forgiven. Draupadi exercised the wishes but the Pandavas viz. Bhima still fulfilled his vow of killing all his Kaurava cousins, and none of the brothers or Draupadi objected.*

Courts will not convict a spouse as a partner in a crime where consent or complicity is not established. Not even when the spouse has enjoyed the proceeds of the crime. This is best exemplified by the legal action taken against Mr. Bernie Madoff, who defrauded investors of billions of dollars through his Ponzi scheme. As much as

a spouse cannot automatically drag a partner into a crime, the
partner can also not commit the other.

Nobody Answered Draupadi's Questions on Dharma: *It was
an example of how the principles of Apad-Dharma can only be
applied by the affected individual. It is difficult for any person
though present but not involved to opine on whether someone
breached Dharma.*

*The writers of the epic may have wanted the readers to
understand that one can easily understand Dharma and Adharma in
the normal circumstances. Apad-dharma requires the individuals
involved to act based on their own cause. Well-versed stalwarts on
Dharma like Bhishma, Vidura, Kripacharya and others were quiet
and stood in silence showing the individualisation involved in
matters of Apad-Dharma.*

*In the Mahabharata, they often refer to Yudhisthir as Dharma
Raj; however, it is Krishna who compels them to look at the
circumstances from a perspective of Apad-Dharma. This shows the
difficulty that even individuals with the highest level of knowledge
and understanding of Dharma face with choosing the "right path" in
extraordinary circumstances or situations. Krishna later commented
that had he been present, he would not have allowed the 'game of
dice' to take place.*

*The Game brought home the point that in challenging times we
will all need a Krishna to help us fulfil our obligations of Dharma. It
also follows that we need to seek wise counsel when in doubt. There
is also an age old wisdom that suggests 'when in doubt, stay out.'*

*Yudhisthir applied Dharma in isolation when invited to a game
of dice. He viewed the invite as coming from his uncle Dhritarashtra
and to refuse an invitation from the eldest in the family would be
disrespectful. Second, the invite was in Kshatriya tradition and
intended to promote friendship and refusal would create discord.
They also aroused the gambler in him, and he hoped that he could
win the other half of the Empire that the Kauravas had kept.*

Role of Trustee: *Yudhisthir did not realise he was now a Samrat and that the Kauravas practised in the art of state-craft could hurt his kingdom and this would violate Raj Dharma. When the stakes involved the treasures of the state, the game had degenerated and Yudhisthir violated all principles of Dharma. He did not discriminate between his personal assets and assets of the State. Dharma entitled him to stake his personal property, because he had absolute ownership over it. He could not have staked his wife Draupadi because he did not own her and more so because she was also the wife of his brothers. He had no right to stake the assets of his kingdom because he controlled it only as a trustee.*

They convey the principles of sole and joint ownership, trusteeship and the rules relating to private property through this event. In Indian households, the eldest male member is the head of the family. They do not question his authority, absolute discretion and control, the silence of Yudhisthir's brothers reflects this respect that is accorded to the head. They broke this silence when Yudhisthir dealt with Draupadi because she was not property but their spouse.

Management Lesson: *Kauravas leveraged the weakness of each of the Pandavas. Yudhisthir had a weakness for gambling. Bhima's flaw was his brutish behaviour and his inability to control his anger. Arjun's only focus was to show his ability as the best archer of all time. Twins Nakul and Sahadev, overwhelmed by their elder siblings, blindly followed them. The Kauravas manipulated the Pandavas without the guidance on state-craft and politics from Krishna.*

A King must have loyal and able advisors free to offer correct advice without fear or favour. Until the division of the kingdom, Bhishma supported Dhritarashtra ably, loyally and fearlessly. It is this right of dissent that Dhritarashtra took away from Bhishma as a condition for granting Pandavas the right to rule over Khandavprastha. Vidura also stood up and voiced his dissenting opinions on matters of governance and Dharma. At one point, they banished him from the court for voicing his dissent.

When Yudhisthir lost everything including their common wife, his loyal brothers stood as mute spectators, nor did they stop him from mindless betting. The writers have conveyed how a single human weakness could destroy everything; even negate the combined strength of their collective virtues and strengths. The biggest takeaway is that at the height of success, one feels one can conquer the world, but this is fraught with untold dangers.

The brothers' ignorance of Raj Dharma and zero experience of state-craft stood thoroughly exposed. Yudhisthir was divested of his role as crown prince and banished to Varnavat. Later, as the Emperor, Yudhisthir lost everything in a game of dice. Quite possibly these events leading to their exile was dramatized to provide us with guidance, not as a justification of the causes leading to the great battle.

Krishna's Presence Supports the Turn of Events: Krishna joins the story at the Draupadi Swayamwar, and his manipulation of the events begins from that day. His role in the assassination of Jarasandha, the suppression of of the rebellion led by Sisupala and his killing at the Rajsuya Yagna. Krishna's being endowed with the highest honour at the Yagna is an impressive buildup of his profile.

The Concept of Hero and Anti-Hero: Based on the events so far, it might be a possible for us to look at the several characters in a more realistic manner in the light of the epic as a Dharma Granth.

Kunti and Gandhari: Kunti married Pandu in a swayamwar. They vanquished Gandhari's family, and she had to marry a blind Dhritarashtra. Both the queens of the time shared a contrasting relationship with their husbands.

Gandhari never saw her husband as she remained blindfolded for most of her life. This blindfold may have symbolically conveyed that she never accepted her husband as a partner in marriage. Kunti suffered rejection because a beautiful Madri, his second wife, besotted her husband Pandu. Despite her suffering, once widowed, she looked after the children of Madri as her own and returned to Hastinapur to stake a claim for her children to succeed Dhritarashtra. This is a sharp contrast of two royal ladies and how they performed their Dharma.

Krishna and Shakuni: *They were great thinkers, artful manipulators, strategists with unique capability and leaders who got their respective followers to do their bidding. Krishna used his skills to bring in a new era and draw people back to the path of Dharma. Shakuni's actions were consistent with the ways of the time. Throughout the Epic, Krishna guides and directs the Pandavas. Often these actions seem prima facie wrong but maybe right from a perspective of Apad-Dharma under the circumstances.*

These events / actions may at times appear as later additions intended to present the Hindu Way of Life. Their actions are not always about being right or wrong but serve as examples of the Indic way of Life.

Shantanu and Dhritarashtra: *Their characters best illustrate the diversity of relationship between a father and son. Shantanu took away from his son his right to the crown out of his love for Satyawati. He is the same Shantanu who broke his oath and marriage with Ganga to save his son.*

Dhritarashtra, a doting father, was blinded by his love for son. He allowed Duryodhana a free rein, often going against the counsel of his advisors. It is maybe because of his failure to discriminate between Dharma and Adharma that they called him blind.

Parents often live the life they wanted to through their offsprings. Many force their children to become singers, actors, doctors etc. not based on their children's aptitude but because it was something they wanted to do. The attempt and consequences to live our dreams through our children are best reflected in the relationship between Dhritarashtra and his children.

Kauravas and their Pandava Cousins: *In this most melodramatic of all portrayals, the writers of the Epic may have portrayed one or some of them as several characters to highlight the human desires and attributes.*

The Pandavas were not five but fewer or even maybe one. Kunti may have got one child as permitted under the principles of Niyoga. Madri had no children, and that could explain why King Shalya sided with the Kauravas as he shared another relationship by marriage with the Kauravas.

The 101 children born of a single ovum, nurtured in a tube outside the womb, remains as unacceptable as the possibility that Gandhari could have by herself given birth to them concurrently or in any order.

Nowhere in the epic did they accuse Kauravas of misrule or oppression. We cannot accuse them of conspiracy as they were protecting their right to succession. Pandavas' actions in Varnavat, unprovoked killing/murder of Jarasandha, the massacre of tribals in Khandavprastha and the heartless abuse of love of Hidimbi by Bhima, all point to their questionable ways.

Karna and Pandavas: *This is a classic example of two representations of perfection. Karna is everything the Pandavas (when put together and seen as one) were. Both Arjun and Karna were outstanding archers; Arjun killed Karna when the latter was unarmed.*

Karna was a man of great honour who always kept his word. He was neither tempted by women or wealth, nor was he known to have any weakness, or lying even for the greater good. He honoured his commitments despite all odds. Karna's only shortcoming was the mystery behind his birth and his constant battle to gain acceptance for his worth rather than his birth.

Chapter 40

The Exile

Synopsis: Why we must always act with faith and good intent? While facing unsurmountable problems in life, focus on your inputs and efforts to give it your honest best.

The Pandavas proceeded on exile with Draupadi, leaving her children under Dhrishtadyumna's care. Subhadra returned to Dwarka with her son Abhimanyu, who grew up under the care and guidance of Krishna. The other wives of the Pandavas also moved back to their parental homes while Kunti remained in Hastinapur.

The Pandavas set up camp in the forest, living a life of hardships, minus the pomp and royal comfort. They spent their days hunting for food for themselves and their followers. Yudhisthir spent much of his time in meditation, contemplation, and performing sacrifices. Draupadi would prepare and serve meals to the residents of the Hermitage.

Many sages and religious travellers visited the Pandavas, with whom Yudhisthir discussed Dharma. Other siblings hunted for food, while Draupadi served guests diligently.

Once Sage Durvasa, much feared for his wrath, decided to approach the Pandava hermitage with his followers for a meal, but Draupadi did not have a single morsel to offer them. She possessed a magical vessel called Akshay Patra, which never ran empty, until all had eaten. A panicky Draupadi invoked Krishna, who materialized. She revealed her predicament about Durvasa by pointing him to the empty Akshay Patra.

Krishna, who noticed a single grain of rice still sticking to the bottom of the pan, partook of it and told Draupadi that he felt satiated. At that instant, he also quelled the hunger pangs of Durvasa and his followers, who were bathing and freshening up before the meal and caused them to go another way.

Commentary

Atithi Devo Bhava: They feared Sage Durvasa for his wrath. His curses could devastate and ruin lives. He was always received with great reverence out of fear. However, when served well, he would often bless his hosts. As a character, he has appeared in many epics and Puranas. Once again the Mahabharata allows readers to draw a world of meaning from a single incident.

It has been the convention in most homes that the person who cooks the food eats last. Draupadi would cook food for the Pandavas and eat only after she had served all.

Sage Durvasa's visit to the hermitage also gives rise to an obligation under Dharma. It is called "Atithi Devo Bhava," meaning that we should treat a visitor like God. We must be hospitable, treat him well and offer him all that we have, even if it is the last bite of food.

204 Mahabharata: Relevance and Application in Contemporary Thought

Faith can Move Mountains: *The Akshay Patra event would appear unreal, but when enacted as a play it helps convey many significant messages. A devotee can seek divine intervention and expect fulfilment when sought with pure intent, as exemplified by a distraught Draupadi's invocation of Krishna. He resolves her dire problem in an instant. When Krishna feels satiated, then the whole world is also satiated.*

The message is that the Lord accepts even a blade of grass if offered with pure intent, as Krishna himself declares in the Gita. Similarly, a royal guest must accept the offerings of his humblest subject. For instance, a king on a hunt saw a poor villager performing a religious ritual. He stopped to bow before the ceremonial fire, but declined to accept the prasad, which angered the gods. They punished him with blindness or loss of memory. We may never experience such events in our own lives, but the Epic intends to convey the same message.

CHAPTER 41

Abduction of Draupadi

Synopsis: It is not wrong to desire someone in life, but he or she must reciprocate. Respect the right of the other to say no.

One day, Jayadratha came to the hutment of the Pandavas when they were out hunting. Draupadi welcomed him as a guest, but her beauty so enamoured Jayadratha that he abducted her, wanting to marry her, even though she had declined. He thought he was rescuing Draupadi from hardship of exile. He happened to be the husband of Dushala, the only girl in the Kuru Clan.

When Arjun and Bhima learnt of her abduction, they chased and caught Jayadratha and brought him before Yudhisthir, wanting to kill him. But this would have widowed the only daughter in the Kuru clan. So they spared his life, but shaved his head as punishment. Jayadratha returned to his kingdom and performed severe penance for a boon to defeat the Pandavas, which the Gods granted for a single use.

Commentary

The Principle of Consent: In this Epic, even though women were abducted, they were not molested or sexually abused.

Indic thought which precedes Christianity recognised desire as the driving force behind human actions. It permitted a married man to take another wife, nor restricted a woman from making her choice. Women were granted the right to choose or change their partners.

CHAPTER 42

Arjun Rescues Duryodhana

Synopsis: When down, stay down? When to reveal your hand.

Even as the Pandavas went through a phase of hardships during the exile, Duryodhana busied himself in consolidating his control over a reunited Hastinapur, with the help of Bhishma, Vidura and other senior advisors. However, he spared no efforts to vex his rivals. During a royal hunt, he would peg his tents close to the Pandava quarters. One day, having settled in a Gandharva area, Karna and Duryodhana attacked the Gandharvas. These locals responded valiantly and overwhelmed the Kauravas. Karna ran away, but they took Duryodhana a prisoner.

Yudhisthir, who learnt about the capture, asked Arjun to rescue Duryodhana. But he felt loathe to antagonize the Gandharvas, with whom he shared good relations. Upon Yudhisthir's insistence, Arjun used his goodwill to persuade the Gandharvas to release Duryodhana, who thanked Arjun and promised him a boon.

Commentary

Impact of Yudhisthir's Decisions: The Pandavas secured the release of Duryodhana. This showed their commitment to Hastinapur and the Family. This also ensured for them a troublefree exile. It worked for them in much the same way as Bhima's marriage to Hidimbi.

The release of Duryodhana showed they treated the Kauravas as a family. They had also spared the life of Jayadratha. These actions were to be a message to their cousins and Dhritarashtra. It gave the impression they harboured no ill-will for the exile and the treatment of Draupadi.

Lessons from Yudhisthir's Decisions: Focus on your long-term goals. Stay close to your enemy, do not reveal your real intent. Using shock and awe against an under-prepared enemy would vastly improve the chances of success. The more comfortable the enemy becomes, the less prepared he is when he is confronted. Bide your time, prepare yourself before you take on your powerful enemy. Save your bullets for the right time.

The Pandavas could not allow the Gandharvas to rule Hastinapur. This would have ended the legacy and future of the Kuru Dynasty. The Pandavas not be able to reclaim their kingdom after the exile. King Drupad would have lost interest in Hastinapur. Without the Kurus, he would have no justifiable cause. He would not engage his resources. The Pandavas would have no future. Yudhisthir had now matured as a leader, as we all will with age and experience.

CHAPTER 43

Pandavas brought Back to Life

Synopsis: Is humility, substance over form? Is it knowing the limits of your capacity? Why did all the Pandavas except Yudhisthir fail?

As Pandavas neared the last year of exile, they needed to remain undiscovered and so asked their followers to leave. In their journey into the unknown, they arrived in a forest and needed to quench their thirst. A sibling sent out to locate a water source, stumbled upon a lake. As he bent down to drink, a mysterious Voice asked him to seek permission first. But he ignored the directive and gulped some water and fell unconscious. The same thing happened with the next sibling. Four Pandavas passed out under similar circumstances. Finally Yudhisthir, who went looking for them, found them. He agreed to answer the Voice, before drinking the water.

The Voice questioned Yudhisthir on Dharma. Pleased with his wise and correct replies, it offered to resurrect one of the siblings. When Yudhisthir chose his half-brother

Sahadev, it wanted to know why. He explained that he as Kunti's child was alive, so he also wanted his step-mother Madri's child to be revived. Pleased by his sense of fairness, the Voice not only revived all the Pandavas but wished them success in exile. He urged them to spend that year in Virata.

Commentary

Substance is more Important than Form: The introduction once again of a Divine Character, the test of Yudhishthir's knowledge of Dharma and his selfless behaviour all point to the Mahabharata's promotion of the principles of righteousness.

The mysterious voice later introduced himself as the Yudhishthir's divine father. He brought back to life all the Pandavas. He then advised them where they should spend their last year in hiding. This is a little hard to believe. However, as a play, this was a good device to take the story forward.

Importance of Humility and Judgement: The Pandavas, who passed out at the pool, were valiant and learned, but they were undone by their arrogance and impatience. Yudhisthir used his knowledge and intelligence to avoid the fate of his brothers and also became instrumental in their revival. The event teaches us the need to be patient and act intelligently and rationally.

Some of the Questions, Answers Reproduced below:

Q: *Where does the Sun establish himself?*

A: *Sun establishes himself in truth, because truth brings to light.*

Q: *How does a man become secure?*

A: *Man becomes secure by courage.*

Q: *How does a man becomes wise?*

A: *He becomes wise by living with learned wise men.*

Q: *Which strong, rich and clever man is considered as not breathing, even if he breathes?*

A: *The one who does not look after Gods, guests, servants, ancestors and his own self is considered as not breathing, even if he breathes.*

Q: *Which is heavier than earth?*

A: *Mother is heavier than earth.*

Q: *Which is taller than the sky?*

A: *Father is taller than the sky.*

Q: *Which is faster than wind?*

A: *Mind is faster than wind.*

Q: *Which is more in number than grass?*

A: *Worries outnumber grass.*

Q: *Which does not close its eyes even while sleeping?*

A: *Fish does not close its eyes while sleeping.*

Q: *What does not move even after birth?*

A: *Eggs do not move even after birth.*

Q: *What does not have a heart?*

A: *A stone does not have a heart.*

Q: What grows further with speed?

A: The river grows further with speed.

Q: Who is the friend, for one who goes abroad?

A: Education is the only friend of people who goes abroad.

Q: Who keeps company to the one who stays with in his house?

A: Only his wife keeps company to such a person.

Q: Who is the friend for the sick person?

A: Doctor is the friend of the sick person.

Q: Who is the friend of the one who is going to die?

A: Charity is the only friend to such a person.

Q: Who travels alone?

A: Sun travels alone. Sun represents truth and therefore travels alone, because there is only one truth.

Q: Where does "fame" normally reside?

A: "Fame" resides mainly in charity.

Q: Where does "heaven" normally reside?

A: "Heaven" normally resides in truth.

Q: Where does "pleasure" normally reside?

A: "Pleasure" normally resides in good conduct.

Q: What is the soul for man?

A: Child (athmaja-born out of soul) is the soul for man.

Q: Who is the companion made by God?

A: Wife is the companion made by God.

Q: What is the place where man ultimately reaches?

A: "Charity" is the place where man ultimately reaches.

Q: Which is the best giver of wealth?

A: "Tireless effort" is the best giver of wealth.

Q: What is the best among things?

A: The knowledge that we get from learned is the best thing.

Q: What is the best among "blessings"?

A: "Life without sickness" is the best among blessings.

Q: What is the best among "pleasures"?

A: "Contentment" is the best among pleasures

Q: Which is the best among "Dharma (just actions)"?

A: Non-violence is the best among "just actions".

Q: By controlling which man will never be sad?

A: By controlling the mind, man will never become sad.

Q: Friendship with whom lasts for ever?
A: Friendship with godly persons will last forever.

Q: By leaving which, will man never become sad?
A: By leaving anger, man will never become sad.

Q: By leaving which, will man become rich?
A: By leaving out desires, man becomes rich.

Q: By leaving which, man will be able to lead a happy life?
A: By leaving out miserliness, man would be able to lead a happy life.

Q: Why should we give it to servants?
A: It is for making them obey you.

Q: By which is the world covered?
A: World is covered by ignorance.

Q: Why do friends go away?
A: When they get nothing from you, they go away.

Q: Why does not man reach heaven?
A: Man does not reach heaven due to attachment.

Q: When does a country not have life?
A: When it does not have good rulers, it does not have life.

Q: *What is poison?*

A: *Begging from others is poison.*

Q: *What is the "best mercy"?*

A: *Wishing for pleasures for all is the "best mercy".*

Q: *What is righteousness?*

A: *Having the same attitude towards everybody is righteousness.*

Q: *Who is the enemy who cannot be defeated by man?*

A: *Anger is the enemy that cannot be defeated by man.*

Q: *Who is considered as a holy man?*

A: *He who loves all and does good for all, is considered a holy man.*

Q: *What is honor?*

A: *The pride in oneself is called honor.*

Q: *What is laziness?*

A: *Not doing Dharma (just action?) is laziness.*

Q: *What is sorrow?*

A: *Ignorance is sorrow.*

Q: *What is a good bath?*

A: *Cleaning the mind of the accumulated dirt is the good bath.*

Q: What is the best charity one can do?
A: Saving life of others is the greatest charity one can do.

Q: Which is considered as "unhealthy competition."?
A: Unnecessary turmoil of the mind is "unhealthy competition."

Q: What is pride?
A: Ignorance is pride.

Q: What is snobbishness?
A: Telling others that "I am the only follower of Dharma" is snobbishness.

Q: What does one who tells sweet words get?
A: He becomes friends for everybody.

Q: What does one who does planned actions get?
A: He attains success.

Q: What does one who has many friends get?
A: He lives happily.

Q: What does one who is attached to Dharma get?
A: He attains salvation

Q: What is a surprise?
A: The fact that people thinking of themselves as stable and permanent, in spite of seeing several deaths daily is surprising.

CHAPTER 44

Pandavas and their Final Year of Exile in Disguise

Synopsis: Learn the art of managing your boss or being one, working in teams. Working in a team, recognise the politics and traps that can cause trouble.

The Pandavas sent off their helpers and companions, just before the final phase of their exile. Family priest Dhaumya gave them parting advice on how they should conduct themselves at the Royal Household and with the king. Pandavas travelled to the Kingdom of Virata, as advised by the Voice. King Virata happened to be just and fair, with an army capable of resisting Hastinapur. His brother-in-law Kichaka led his army.

The Pandavas disguised themselves as minions at the royal household. Yudhisthir served as a courtier to the King of Virata, claiming to have worked for his namesake in a similar capacity at Indraprastha, besides being proficient in playing dice and in astrology. Bhima took up employment as a cook, ostensibly after a stint with the royal Pandava kitchens, specialized in preparing culinary dishes. Arjun disguised as a eunuch, taught princess Uttara dance and music. Nakul minded the horses. Sahadev tended the cows. Draupadi served the queen as a beautician and chambermaid, after being in the employ of her namesake.

C Rajagopalachari has summarised this advice given by Dhaumya in his book *Mahabharata*:

"Those who are engaged in service under a king should always be vigilant. They must serve without talking too much. They may give their counsel only when asked and never obtrude it. They should praise the king on befitting occasions. They may do all things only after informing the king who is a veritable fire in human form. Do not go too near him, nor appear to avoid him. Even though a person may be trusted by the king and have great authority, still he should always behave as if he would be dismissed immediately. It would be foolishness to place too much confidence in a king. One may not sit in the conveyance, seat or chariot of the king, presuming on his affection. A servant of the king should be ever active and self-restrained. He should not be excessively elated; nor unduly depressed, by being honoured or dishonoured by the king.

He may not reveal the secrets confided to him, nor may he receive anything in the form of a gift from the citizens. He should not be jealous of other servants. The king may place fools in positions of authority, leaving aside the wise. Such waywardness should be ignored. One cannot be too careful with the ladies of the court. There should not be the faintest suggestion of indelicacy in one's conduct towards them."

Matters were proceeding smoothly until Kichaka noticed Draupadi. Inflamed by her beauty, he plotted ways to corner her and satiate his craving, even offering to make her his wife. A desperate Draupadi complained to the queen and to her husband, Yudhisthir. The queen brought it to the king's notice, but in vain. He could not restrain his powerful commander-in-chief. Yudhisthir and Arjun were unwilling to act as this could compromise their identity. A helpless Draupadi realised that Bhima was the only one who could protect her.

Commentary

Leadership, Team Management and Processes: Dhaumya prepares Yudhisthir for his role as a courtier. He identifies the potential risks from his role based on possible weaknesses in a leader and those within his team. This message will help both the Leader and the Team Members. It is a guide on how to manage and work with Teams and guide their conduct.

This is a management lesson that sets out the code of conduct, responsibility and challenges for team leaders and members. Dhaumya advised Yudhisthir to accept the actions of the king. He warned him of the perils of groupism. Sometimes, the favoured would benefit more than the deserving. He should not criticise the King or the members of his court. Instead, he could present options with clear advantages from the decision maker's perspective. An advisor must give the king his personal space and he must never usurp his role or right as the leader. As a courtier he must maintain a respectable distance, avoid groupism and not create conflict within the team.

In a leadership role, we must focus on the fairness of action and the result. We must not abuse our power or our privileges as a leader. We should ensure that differences do not divide the team. It is important that they all commit to their task and the common goal.

Teams should be aligned in action and must always be unified in agenda and outcome. We must allow the team to operate in a healthy environment. We must allow the team to be honest, free from fear, and we must promote fairness.

Raj and Parivarik Dharma: *We can fail in our duties, when we are distracted by our ambition. We might neglect our family. The Pandavas ignored their responsibility towards Draupadi, whom they did not protect. Bhima was an exception. The other Pandavas did not want to risk being discovered, so that they could complete their exile uneventfully. They were only focused on getting back their kingdom. Their ambition had affected their sense of judgement and responsibility.*

Attitude Towards Women: *Draupadi attracted Kichaka. He desired her, even offering marriage. His behaviour upset her. Working women are often harassed. Powerful men would molest them. They lacked protection from unwanted attention. In this Epic and other stories, women were kidnapped or held against their wishes. They were not raped but offered marriage by their besotted abductors. There are still several instances of oppression against women. Satyawati forced her widowed daughter-in-laws to provide children. They forced women to marry as part of a strategic alliance and at times also forced them to have sex with the men they served.*

Women are the greatest oppressors of their weaker sisters, in much the same way, the harshest and most efficient slave drivers are often former slaves themselves. It is not necessary that only the rich and powerful will exploit the poor, but also the strong can abuse the weak. Not much has changed. The treatment of women by men and society has changed for the worse.

Leaders and their Leadership Styles: *Mahabharata provides examples of different kings and their style of leadership. Leaders of* *our time can use these examples to recognise and avoid weaknesses. Jarasandha was wise and powerful, but a domineering tyrant. Krishna played upon his emotions to get him to fight a much younger and stronger Bhima and paid with his life. Kansa, an insecure tyrant, feared death at the hands of his nephew. He imprisoned his sister and her husband and killed all their new-born children. King Virata was a nominal leader as he allowed his commander-in-chief to usurp his power. King of Ekachakra was weak. He allowed a cannibal Bakasura to oppress his subjects. This weakness was suggested by staging a fight in which Bhima killed Bakasura. Dhritarashtra suffered a personal disability, he was blind and like an absentee king he allowed his son to usurp the throne. His personal agenda blinded King Drupad. To avenge his humiliation, he used all his three children as chess pieces. He lost everything in his plan to avenge himself. King Shantanu's biggest failing was his weakness for women. He denied his son his right of succession.*

CHAPTER 45

Kichaka and Bhima and the Fight to Finish

Synopsis: Making yourself indispensable is an art. Learn the power of strategic thinking. When it is heads, you win and when it is tails, they lose!

When Kichaka continued to force his unwelcome attention on her, Draupadi appealed to Bhima for help. They decided that she should offer to meet him at night in the privacy of the music hall, where Bhima would lie in wait. As soon as Kichaka stepped into the spot he found Bhima, who killed him in a duel.

The next day, they found Kichaka's mangled remains. The entire town wondered how a strong and well-built man could have met such a horrific end. Draupadi boasted that her Gandharva husband had come to her rescue, angry with Kichaka for constantly harassing her, whom he killed in a duel.

The news of his death spread quickly. Duryodhana had spies searching for the Pandavas. They took this news to the court of Hastinapur. Duryodhana and his advisors realised that Bhima could have killed Kichaka and suspected the Pandavas were hiding in Virata, under the protection of its ruler.

Duryodhana and his allies attacked Virata. They wanted to force the Pandavas to fight on behalf of Virata, which they could not refuse as its residents.

Commentary

Some Important Lessons on Strategy: The Pandavas were stateless with no source of income or wealth. They could count on the backing of the state of Panchal and the Yadavas. But that was not enough to take on the might of Hastinapur. King Virata was a nominal head of the state and depended on his General Kichaka. On his death, King Virata needed another general to secure his rule. The Pandavas may have decided to remove him and create an opportunity for themselves.

Any attack as the one planned by Duryodhana would have brought down King Virata. It was the perfect situation to exploit. Duryodhana realised that in the event of an attack, the Pandavas would come out to protect King Virata. Being thus exposed, the Pandavas would have to go back to exile for another thirteen years, setting back hopes of regaining Indraprastha. One possible end to the story was here. They discovered the Pandavas before the end of their exile, who could be subjected to another thirteen year exile. But this is not how it ended.

Pandavas Create Economic Space: The Pandavas exploited the dependence of King Virata. They removed his source of strength. They positioned themselves as a possible replacement. If we can identify a weakness and offer to overcome it, then we can achieve success.

The Pandavas had no military and financial support. They lacked the resources to claim Indraprastha. They needed powerful supporters. They were the power behind the King of Virata. It gave them the influence to make King Virata join their fight.

Heads Duryodhana Won, Tails Pandavas Lost: The knowledge and strategy of Duryodhana and his advisors stand out. Any attack of Virata would force the Pandavas to expose themselves. They needed the cover of Virata till their exile ended. They had to help the king in his hour of need. Otherwise, it would have damaged their chance of getting King Virata on their side.

The Kauravas had placed the Pandavas in a tight spot. If they continued to hide, the Kauravas would defeat King Virata. If the Pandavas took up his defence, they were bound to be discovered. They were literally caught between the Devil and the deep blue sea.

Draupadi's Lie and the Power of Disinformation: Kichaka's killing would spur a manhunt for the killer. Draupadi cleverly claimed her Gandharva husband had killed Kichaka for harassing her. Gandharvas had defeated and imprisoned Duryodhana. A weakened Virata knew he could not take on the Gandharvas, who had even Karna on the run. Still, the Pandavas did not want to be discovered. She wanted to mislead investigators.

There is another insight into human behaviour. Humans tend to overstate their success or boast, which is often a lie, a kind of disinformation which can throw us off guard. We need to be cautious, as people may have a private agenda. These are the skeletons in the cupboard. Disinformation has another offspring; it is flattery, undeserved praise or recognition.

Why did the Pandavas not Just Lie Low? The Kauravas suspected the Pandavas were in Virata, but did not know whether they were hiding there with state support or they were there on their own.

The Pandavas would reveal their identity to King Virata and to avoid war, he would banish them. Then their presence would have been discovered.

Conversely, the Pandavas could have remained in disguise and let King Virata deal with the invasion. This was not an option, and we must credit the Kauravas for their brilliance. The Pandavas had killed Kichaka. Without a general, King Virata's army lacked leadership. The Kauravas would defeat King Virata minus Pandava support. He would become a vassal of Hastinapur and the Pandavas would lose their cover. Alternatively, the Pandavas could join the battle to defend Virata against the attack, the Pandavas would still be cornered and forced out from their hiding.

A counter-terror expert can learn a vital lesson from this event. The Kaurava strategy was brilliant. They used the agenda and Dharma of the Pandavas to force them out of their hiding place. Their strategy ensured the Pandavas had to respond. The Pandavas were cornered and would be flushed out.

A Woman's Indifference to Another's Plight: Draupadi complained to her two husbands Yudhisthir and Arjun, who were close to those in power, but they did nothing out of selfishness. The former was an advisor to the King and part of his court; the latter was a tutor to the princess. She sought the intervention of the queen, whose duty was to protect her employee. She could have asked her brother to stop, she could have asked the King to order her brother to stop, but she did nothing. The Mahabharata documents yet another instance where a woman shows no empathy with another woman's pain.

CHAPTER 46

Kauravas Wage War on Virata

Synopsis: When enough is enough, a mission ends when an aim is achieved; understand the power of self-restraint and responsibility.

The spies reported the assassination of Kichaka. The court of Hastinapur suspected this could be the handiwork of Bhima.

Duryodhana launched a two-pronged attack, initiated by a Kaurava ally, which engaged the entire Virata army. Taking advantage of the situation, Kauravas launched the main assault, compelling an inexperienced prince Uttar to lead the defence. Draupadi persuaded him to take Arjun as his charioteer. They set out for the battle.

The size and ferocity of the attack overwhelmed Uttar, who wanted to withdraw. Arjun revealed himself and started shooting arrows at the feet of Kaurava elders as a mark of respect. They realized the archer was none other than Arjun, but they could not sight him. Having achieved their aim, the Kauravas withdrew after a short battle. To maintain their disguise, Arjun asked Uttar to take credit as the architect of this brave defence.

When the Pandavas presumed their period of exile was over, they revealed themselves to King Virata. Overwhelmed, he expressed his gratitude for their support and protection against the Kauravas. He offered his daughter Uttara to Arjun. This was politely declined.

Commentary

Kauravas Strategy and Knowledge of Raj Dharma: King Virata should have made Hastinapur a vassal state. The Pandavas could have taken control of the entire Kuru kingdom, they were the power behind King Virata.

Once again, the Kauravas showed their knowledge of Kshatriya and Raj Dharma. They engaged in a surgical strike but withdrew after achieving their aim, minimizing loss of life and wealth as these were in the interest of the state and welfare of its people.

Relationship between Teacher and Student: The relationship between a student and teacher is like that of a parent and a child. It is in this context Arjun declined the offer of marriage of Uttara. Instead, Abhimanyu married Uttara.

Why Abhimanyu and not the Children of Draupadi? Uttara was the daughter of a Suta wife of King Virata. Once again, the Pandavas showed their obsession with lineage. They wanted to avoid any controversy. They wanted to ensure the parents on both sides were Kshatriyas. Their sons from Draupadi were born before Abhimanyu. Abhimanyu was therefore not first in line to be a successor. They offered to marry Uttara to Abhimanyu. This resulted in their alliance with Virata and yet it would avoid the chances of a Pandava Dynasty having a chief queen with a Suta lineage. The planned marriage of Abhimanyu with Uttara would also give them a good reason to invite and involve Krishna.

Military Doctrine of Surgical Strike Introduced: *In military doctrine, they use surgical strikes on specific targets and such strikes have a limited aim.*

CHAPTER 47

Kauravas: A Divided Camp

Synopsis: Trace the evolution in the legacy right of children born within or out of wedlock.

The Kauravas had discerned the presence of Pandavas during the war with Virata, who had completed their thirteen years of exile during the war. But Duryodhana claimed to have discovered them before the completion of their exile and wanted to extend their exile by the same period. In his consideration, completion of exile only permitted the Pandavas to return to Hastinapur, not entitled them to a return of the kingdom. There were two distinct parts in the bet, loss of kingdom and exile. It was not a loss of right to rule for 13 years.

The Kauravas had used the exile of the Pandavas well. They had consolidated their control over their kingdom, forming several alliances. Duryodhana refused to engage in any discussions with the Pandavas, insisting that Kunti birthed them through a boon, not Niyoga. How could they then claim to be descendants of Pandu? Conversely, Kauravas possessed royal blood and the right to succession.

Hence, the crown should legitimately pass to Dhritarashtra's eldest son, Duryodhana. Yudhisthir was not entitled to a share of the kingdom, named as Khandavprastha. In the Game of Dice, he had lost his kingdom and wealth to Duryodhana. The Pandavas had failed to fulfill their conditions of exile beyond doubt. Kauravas discovered them before their term ended. Most kings did not support Pandava claims, who were not sired by any Aryan males. The Pandavas had also violated Dharma by marrying into a Rakshas family, not to mention Draupadi's polyandry.

Commentary

Issues Bearing on Progeny, Pandavas were Non-Conformers: *Bhima married Hidimbi, a Rakshas. They had a child named Ghatotkacha, raised by his mother, who became the leader of the Rakshas tribe. He succeeded his uncle, who had been killed by Bhima. The Pandavas did not consider Ghatotkacha as a Pandava and denied a child his patriarchal lineage.*

In exile, Arjun married Chitrangada, the princess of Manipur. Her father consented to the marriage on the condition that their future child would remain with the mother. He would rise to be the king of Manipur, where matriarchal lineage formed the basis for succession. They named him Babruvahana.

Sage Parashara fathered a child with an unmarried Satyawati. He insisted that the son so born would enjoy his patriarchal lineage. He trained him to be an expert in the knowledge of the Vedas. This son, Ved Vyas authored the great epic, was the biological grandfather of Vidura, Pandu and Dhritarashtra.

Rights of Biological Children vs. Children Born under Niyoga: *The Aryans followed a patriarchal system. The woman once married* moved to her husband's home, their children drew their identity from their father and succeeded him. It entitled the father to enjoy the fruits of the union.

The son inherited the property and rights of his father. The internal conflict was the Kaurava children had a Kuru seed. The children of Kunti were not from Pandu's seed or from Niyoga, but they were from a boon. They could not treat the two at par. The Kauravas refused to accept the sons of Kunti and Madri as Pandavas.

A big moral divide faced the Aryan race when Kunti presented herself with the five Pandavas. She herself was apprehensive, but Bhishma ensured she and her offsprings were accepted into the family. Today DNA tests are conducted to prove paternity while establishing a claim to property.

Rights of Children Born out of Wedlock vs. Legitimate Children: The patriarchal rights of a child were not always absolute. Children born to palace maids by kings were called Dasi Putra. Although they were sired by the king, they were not entitled to the right of succession. Yuyutsu, fathered by Dhritarashtra but born of a palace maid, was a good example. The legal system over the years has evolved and gives equal rights to children born out of wedlock.

Children in Indian Families: When Vidura returned to Hastinapur, he informed the king that Kurus had won. A pleased Dhritarashtra ordered a royal celebration. He thought Duryodhana had won Draupadi, but when Vidura clarified the winner was Arjun and not Duryodhana, Dhritarashtra felt disappointed, but allowed the celebrations to continue. Vidura also pointed out that he should consider Pandu's children as his own. In many families, the head treats the children of his younger sibling as his own. Yet, in another conversation, he distinguishes between his sons and those of Pandu by clarifying that his sons unlike those of Pandu are his flesh and blood.

The Fight of Right over Entitlement: *The Mahabharata is a story of a fight between two groups of cousins. It based the Kauravas claim as a right, as they were born Kurus. Rights differ from entitlement, because society or rules grant entitlement. The Pandavas were born through a boon or Niyoga. A sage granted Kunti a boon. She used this boon to bear children. She fulfilled a wish of her husband. Pandu gave these children his paternal lineage. This entitled the Pandavas to a claim. This was a claim to succeed Pandu. The Kauravas had a right. This right is God given i.e. by birth. They had to fight to protect it.*

In the normal case, the holder of a right tends to be in possession of the property. The holder of an entitlement is one who wants to take possession of the property. This is because some rule of law or convention entitles him to it. In a dispute, the holder of a right has to defend it, whereas the holder of an entitlement has to pursue his claim and win the right. In the Mahabharata this is presented with great intelligence. The Pandavas had to declare war on the Kauravas, they had to win their entitlement.

CHAPTER 48

The Claim for Return of Kingdom

Synopsis: Back channel diplomacy. Strategy wins over might. What happens when a husband gives greater importance to his ambition over his commitment to his wife?

Krishna arrived in Virata and attended Abhimanyu's marriage with Uttara. The Pandavas had now settled down in the city of Uplavya, part of the kingdom of Virata. Post marriage, the Pandavas met with their supporters and discussed the strategy for a dialogue with Hastinapur. They also wanted to assess the Kaurava reaction to the completion of the exile and claim their kingdom. The Pandavas, Drupad, Virata and the Yadavas made up a strong group. They could not be ignored by the Kauravas.

An emissary from King Drupad's court arrived at Hastinapur to notify them of the completion of their exile. They were looking forward to peaceful co-existence with their cousins, subtly hinting at the restoration of the Pandava kingdom. Hastinapur sent Sanjay to convey their good wishes, besides seeking peaceful co-existence, but remained silent on return of the Kingdom.

The Pandavas and Kauravas had begun reaching out to rulers, tribal leaders and other groups for support. But the Yadavas were a divided house. Balarama refused to support either of the clans and accused Yudhisthir of Adharma, who he insisted had no right to gamble away his Kingdom and to stake his wife. In his view, completion of the exile enabled the Pandavas to only win back their freedom, and did not entitle them to the return of the kingdom. Krishna agreed that Yudhisthir was at fault in gambling away his kingdom, which the Kauravas had rigged and won, but they could reclaim their kingdom post exile.

According to the Epic, both Arjun and Duryodhana arrived in Dwarka to enlist the support of Yadavas. They wanted to meet Krishna, but as he was asleep, Duryodhana sat near Krishna's head and Arjun sat near his feet. Upon awakening, Krishna's eyes fell on Arjun. He noticed Duryodhana too. Both wanted his support, but Krishna wanted Arjun to choose first, to which Duryodhana objected, because he had arrived first. Krishna gave the opportunity first to Arjun as he was the younger one. He could either choose the Yadava Army or Krishna, but also clarified that he would not take up arms. Arjun chose Krishna and an elated Duryodhana accepted the Yadava Army.

Krishna's presence strengthened the Pandava camp. He would now represent their claims. The Pandavas wanted to avoid war, with no kingdom or source of revenue. Kauravas had unlimited resources, many allies and a huge army that would outnumber the forces of the Pandavas. They allowed Krishna to settle their claims as best he could; even accept five villages as a compromise.

It upset Draupadi to see Krishna siding with her husbands. She reminded him how they had forgotten all about her humiliation, even though they had promised to avenge her, which they owed her. How could they ignore her sacrifice and role during the exile? Krishna assured her he would punish the guilty.

Commentary

Negotiating from a Position of Weakness: Living in an alien land, the Pandavas lacked resources and means. They depended on Krishna, Drupad and King Virata for sustenance. They were willing to accept five villages, reflecting their dire circumstances. So they bided their time.

Strategy over Convention: Being aware of their poverty, the Pandavas built alliances through marriages at every opportunity. Bhima married Hidimbi, which secured them the protection of Rakshas. Abhimanyu, younger than Draupadi's sons, married Uttara, a Suta's daughter. They were not in the line of succession, but that cemented an alliance with Virata.

Importance of Conforming to Social Customs and Norms: The question arises whether Draupadi had a son from each of the five Pandavas. None of them must have married because there is no mention. They were all killed as the Mahabharata War drew to a close. It left the Pandavas with the child of Abhimanyu and Uttara to succeed them.

Draupadi's sons were brought up by her brother as members of the Drupad's household. Yet they were not married. Is this because they were socially isolated? It appears no Kshatriya ruler wanted to give his daughter in marriage to the children of the Pandavas. Did they avoid the Pandavas because of their non adherence to Dharma? Did they fear the power of the Kauravas?

In our Society there are people who disdain rules. This can happen in a family or a community or a club. Members of a club who violate rules are suspended or removed. A family may sever relations with an errant member. The community will discourage others to establish contact or develop a relation with such a person. This was a major message on how society responds to those who do not follow norms.

Back Channel Diplomacy is not a New Idea. The Pandavas could not match the resources and support available to Hastinapur. Arjun's choice of a non-combatant Krishna over the famed Narayani Sena needs an explanation. Krishna was a brilliant strategist. He opened doors. In our times, countries use intermediaries to resolve differences and identify common grounds. A common basis allows them to enter dialogue. Krishna remained a key advisor to the Pandavas. As their emissary, he maintained a dialogue with the Kauravas. During the war, he accompanied the Pandavas and met the Kauravas in their camp.

CHAPTER 49

Krishna Arrives at Hastinapur as a Pandava Emissary

Synopsis: What happens when your agenda is hijacked?

The Pandavas asked Krishna to negotiate for them. He travelled to Hastinapur but did not accept the hospitality offered by the kingdom. Instead, he stayed with Vidura, also spending time with Bhishma, Karna and Kunti. Kauravas viewed this as an attempt to create trouble in the State.

He met Karna and told him about Kunti being his biological mother. As he was born before her marriage, she had abandoned him. Karna was therefore a Kshatriya royal, Kunti's first born and the eldest among the siblings. This entitled him to be the king. Krishna was confident that the Pandavas including Yudhisthir would welcome him with open arms as their brother, rightful heir and future King.

Karna heard Krishna and thanked him for his revelation. Karna told him that Duryodhana had embraced him unconditionally as a friend and brother, trusting him as a key member of his team. He could not compromise his loyalty and had committed his support to Duryodhana. He wished his brothers well. Dharma demanded that he side with Duryodhana, even at the cost of his life.

In his meeting with Kunti, Krishna informed her of the negotiating position her sons expected him to take. It distressed Kunti to learn that the efforts started by her were being compromised. She wanted her sons to reclaim that which rightfully belonged to her deceased husband and their father, Pandu.

She asked Krishna to convey to her sons her anger and disappointment for making her, Pandu's widow and their mother go through the humiliation of depending on the charity of others. Her message to her sons was it is more honourable to die fighting for your rights than to live a shameful life based on compromise. It was now for the Pandavas to decide. They could choose a life of shame or a life of a Kshatriya even if they had to die in a fight for winning back their rights.

Commentary

The above event brings out many issues of Dharma. It forces every character to make a choice, based on their individual circumstances, obligations and objectives. Each individual wants to fulfil his obligation of Dharma. It also warns that the right choice may be full of pitfalls.

Karna's Response and Reaction: *Krishna was not trying to help Karna find his real identity, but to weaken him. Karna had to choose between his real family and his duty to his friend. Krishna's effort to drive a wedge in the friendship between Karna and Duryodhana failed. The temptation of being the king and having Draupadi as wife did not* work. *Karna chose duty over the temptation of having a beautiful woman and of being an emperor. He preferred his duty as a friend and as a king of a vassal state. Both Karna and Kunti will prove that they compromised their biological connection in favour of their relationships.*

For the Management Student: *This event provides the substance for a case study. It shows how to slice and dissect an opponent and to deal with each member or strength to achieve the best outcome for one's aim.*

Art of Diplomacy and Negotiating Positions: *The Pandavas sent Drupad's very experienced emissary to the Court of Hastinapur. On their behalf, he made no demands. Instead, he sought the blessings of the elders in Hastinapur. He told them about the Pandavas being in Virata after completing their final year of exile. They wanted to live in peace and harmony. The Court of Hastinapur heard the emissary and sent one of their own wishing them well and confirming their intention of peaceful co-existence. As no dispute over the completion of the period of exile was raised, the next step was to demand a return of Indraprastha.*

The Demand: *The Pandavas sent Krishna to present their demand to the Court of Hastinapur. Bhishma and Vidura, their old supporters had lost their power and influence. His promise to support the Kauravas bound Bhishma. These were conditions he had accepted for the previous partition. The citizens of Hastinapur were prospering. The influence of the Pandavas had faded.*

The Kaurava Perspective: *With no record of oppression or misrule, the Kauravas had the citizens on their side. Bhishma, Dronacharya, Ashwatthama and Karna, the greatest warriors of the time were all with the Kauravas. Therefore, the Kauravas were well protected. King Dhritarashtra had no right to return Indraprastha won by Duryodhana. Completion of the exile had won the Pandavas their right to return to Hastinapur.*

The Perspective of the Pandavas: *Without resources, they could not fund and raise an army. Bhima was brave and strong, but he could not win a war. Only Arjun had learnt the art of warfare. They did not want their allies to take over and pursue their respective personal agenda. Only King Virata joined the Pandavas out of a family obligation. The rest were there because of their agenda.*

King Virata's Perspective: *The Pandavas had killed Kichaka. When Hastinapur attacked his weakened Kingdom, the Pandavas came to their rescue. King Virata married his daughter to Abhimanyu. Marriage thus related him to the Pandavas. In the war, he provided his army. He also led a division as an ally of the Pandavas.*

King Drupad's Perspective: *Draupadi's father used his daughter. He arranged her marriage with the Pandavas. He wanted to avenge the humiliation he suffered because of the connivance of the court of Hastinapur. In the battle, he and his sons were killed. He did not live long enough to see the outcome of his revenge.*

Krishna's Perspective: *He was the greatest strategist of his times. He understood the fallacy in Kshatriya's obsession with commitment. They confused their duty with their obsession and wrongly believed it was their obligation of their Dharma. He exploited this weakness.*

The most Important Message for us All: *When Draupadi found the Pandavas ignoring their obligations to her, she sought the help of Krishna and got her matter resolved. We must not miss similar advice in the Kuru dispute. In the event of any dispute, with the family or otherwise, find resolution. When you take the dispute to a court of law, the agenda of others will enter into the equation. The lawyers and counsels make their business out of all this. Relatives with their own agenda will join or rally against the parties. Peace makers enter the equation sometimes with their own motivations. Suddenly our agenda to find a resolution becomes secondary as others step in with their own goals.*

CHAPTER 50

Krishna Presents the Pandava Claim

Synopsis: In a dispute, one must achieve moral high ground? Check the resolve and preparedness of one's opponent.

The next morning, Krishna presented himself as an emissary before the court of Hastinapur. He asked for the return of assets and kingdom of Pandavas handed over at the time of their exile. He claimed in the interest of Dharma, the Kauravas must restore the rights of the Pandavas.

Duryodhana, aware of Krishna's intense lobbying, intervened. He accused him of fomenting trouble and rejected outright the claims of the Pandavas. Krishna told the court that the Pandavas were keen to avoid a battle and were willing to accept a grant of five villages, to avert war and loss of lives.

When they analysed Krishna's proposal of the five villages, Duryodhana rejected it outright. It would have compromised the power of Hastinapur. He accused the Pandavas of breaching the terms of exile and Krishna's taking undue advantage of his status as an envoy. He threatened to have Krishna arrested and rejected the offer of a negotiated settlement. He ordered his soldiers to arrest Krishna, but he avoided them and returned to the Pandavas.

Commentary

Kaurava Perspective: A king's Dharma is to protect his territory and his subjects from external threats. Duryodhana acted in keeping with his Dharma. He refused to part with the villages as part of Hastinapur.

According to one version of the Mahabharata, the Kauravas arrested Krishna, but he used his divine powers to overpower his captors and escape. He should have used his powers to kill Jarasandha, just as he had done with his uncle Kansa and Sisupala. He could have also used them to get rid of Duryodhana for his act of Adharma.

Management Lesson: According to some versions, Krishna desired war and that is what he brought upon the two clans. He should not have met Vidura, Bhishma and Karna in private. These meetings created doubts in the mind of Duryodhana and his courtiers. Krishna accused Kauravas of Adharma. He played on one village for each of the five Pandavas, which appeared very reasonable, but he asked for them by name. A settlement must be based on mutual agreement.

The Kauravas did not trust the Pandavas; they had violated the terms of the previous division of the kingdom. Krishna knew the Kauravas would reject any offer from the Pandavas because of trust deficit. His strategy lay in achieving a moral high ground. He wanted people to accuse the Kauravas of rejecting a peaceful settlement. He wanted them to think that giving away five villages was not such a great sacrifice. The Kauravas were irresponsible, etc.

This event teaches us many things. We must avoid settling a dispute with a person who has failed in his commitments. It is important that we have the trust and loyalty of people on our team. In any dispute, we must try to seek the moral high ground.

CHAPTER 51

The Preparation for War

Synopsis: In a battle focus on attacking an opponent's strength, a strong opponent has substantial resources to guard his weakness.

The Kauravas rejected the offer of settlement. Krishna returned to the Pandava camp. They served notice to fight and win back their rights. Both sides began preparations for war in an area called Kurukshetra; a region within the land of the Kurus. Soon the largest armies would assemble there.

All Kshatriyas and their tribal supporters sided with either groups, based on marital and political alliances or past differences, or their views on Dharma. Some had chosen sides to settle scores. Takshaka aligned with Kauravas to avenge the loss of his family at the hands of Arjun. Rakshas were arrayed on both sides too, for various reasons. King Rukmi of Vidarbha offered his support to both sides, but which each rejected. Balarama went on a pilgrimage, and Vidura did not take part.

Pandavas' war council comprised Krishna, Virata, Drupad and his sons with a strategy to target individual opponents. They asked Shikhandi to focus on Bhishma, set up Dhristadumya against Dronacharya, Arjun against Karna. They assigned Bhima to target the Kaurava princes. Sahadev was up against Shakuni. They assigned Krishna to be Arjun's charioteer. This motivated the warriors to give their best, each also fighting to win his personal battle. The Pandavas would win every battle and finally the war.

Eighteen divisions fought in the war, seven on the side of the Pandavas and eleven on the Kaurava side. The heavily outnumbered Pandavas were expected to suffer defeat. Bhishma and Dhristadumya led the rival armies. In the Pandava camp, the divisions were placed under the command of Virata, Drupad, Bhima, Shikhandi, Dhristadumya, Satyaki and Chekitana.

The children of the Pandavas did not have significant roles. Ghatotkacha with his group of Rakshas joined the Pandavas.

Commentary

Moral High Ground and Sympathy: The Pandavas had eliminated some powerful partners of the Kauravas, but lacked combat experience. Having realized that the Pandavas could not match the combined strength of the Kaurava, Krishna resorted to espionage. He visited Hastinapur to sow seeds of doubt and suspicion in the minds of key Kaurava leaders. He tried to get Karna to change sides. His compromise formula appeared reasonable but was impossible to implement.

Their Strategy was to Target Opponent's Strengths: Pandavas feared Karna as their only real opponent, who could match their best. Krishna resorted to all the strategems to make him change sides, even offering him the crown and Draupadi, besides telling him that the Pandavas were his younger brothers. Karna remained steadfast in his loyalty towards Duryodhana; despite being tempted with wealth, power and sex, even if he wavered emotionally.

CHAPTER 52

Kunti meets Karna

Synopsis: Can a woman be so insensitive to another? Wife or mother, a woman's dilemma?

When Krishna failed to convince Karna, Kunti met Karna by the river when he was offering his morning prayers. Kunti told him she was his biological mother and urged him to switch over sides and lead the Pandavas instead. As her child it entitled him to be the future King, the eldest of all the Pandava siblings and co-husband of Draupadi. Karna asked Kunti about why she had abandoned him at birth? If she had recognized him at the passing out parade why did she not own him right away? What kept her away in the years since?

Karna remained unmoved by Kunti's emotional pleas. How could he turn back the clock at this stage of life? He told her he was profoundly grateful for the favours and honours bestowed on him by Duryodhana, which he valued above everything else. He had accepted the life as a Suta and married into the community, forming a deep sense of belonging and attachment with his foster brothers

246 Mahabharata: Relevance and Application in Contemporary Thought

and relatives. How could he qualify as a Kshatriya with a very different upbringing as a Suta?

Kunti said she dreaded the loss of her sons in war. Karna promised her that she would still be left with five sons. He promised to fight to the finish with Arjun. Only one would survive, but she would still have five sons.

Commentary

Perspective from the Principles of Dharma: It reveals the immense internal conflict faced by a mother in this chapter. Both Kunti and Krishna realized that Karna, her illegitimate son, presented a major threat to the life of the Pandavas. Arjun was at least an able match to Karna. But a motivated Karna could still defeat Arjun. Kunti did not want the Pandavas to discover that Karna was her eldest child. She feared their not taking up arms against Karna, but following his directions as their eldest sibling. Kunti and Krishna wanted Karna to change sides and join the Pandavas. or weaken him. A weak Karna would be a less potent threat to the Pandavas. Kunti had extracted a promise from Karna limiting his fatal attack to Arjun.

This episode brings out many conflicts in relationships faced by a woman.

Woman as Mother or Wife: Kunti had sent word through Krishna that she preferred her sons to be true Kshatriyas and embrace death fighting for their rights, then live at the mercy of others. She was strong enough to send her sons to the toughest battles, endangering their lives in a campaign to get back what belonged to her husband. Whilst on the one hand she wanted her sons to get back their rights even at the cost of their lives, she also manipulated Karna to spare their lives, which reflected her emotional attachment as a mother.

Kunti would own Karna, but without compromising the mission. Karna could have her as his mother, her other sons as his brothers, his brothers' wife as his wife, becoming the king once they won the right to rule. However, she had steeled herself to lose him or any of her other sons if required. This preference of her role as a wife over mother shows how she fulfils her prior obligation towards family Dharma and earlier too, when she gave up Karna on birth.

The authors are sending out a message that the bonds between a couple can be the strongest, surviving separation by death, even overcoming maternal attachments with the passage of time.

Mother and Child: *There is a biological bond between mother and son, which is strong at birth but strengthens as the emotional bond develops in the years following the birth. The Mahabharata and Shrimad Bhagwat both bring this point to the fore. Kunti's bond with the Pandavas was greater than her bond with Karna. Nakul and Sahadev were not her sons, yet this emotional bond was stronger than her birth connection with Karna. She knew Karna and Arjun were driven by ego. They were competing for recognition as the greatest archers of their time. She extracted the best deal she could from Karna; not to kill her other four sons.*

Wealth and Women used to Corrupt: *Kunti told Karna that as her eldest son, he may be the future King. Draupadi who was the common wife of all the brothers would therefore be his queen too. The concept of using women and wealth to tempt a man was used to the fullest extent here and has been ever since.*

Is a Mother-in-Law Always Insensitive? *A woman compromises the dignity and right of choice of her daughter-in-law. Kunti offered Draupadi to tempt Karna to change sides. Though this did not happen, Kunti expected a married woman to become a wife of* another. *This was not even Apad Dharma. Kunti once again showed she could stoop to any level to achieve her goal. They used Draupadi as a chess piece.*

Non-Violence over Adharma: *We expect a mother-in-law to adopt her son's wife as her daughter. This is much in the same way a son-in-law becomes the son of the family of his wife. Kunti once again showed that women were the biggest oppressors of another. She abused her position as mother and guardian of the Pandavas. The Pandavas followed her directions without question. As a mother, she used temptation to get her son Karna to change sides. She was not avoiding war; she was trying to ensure her victory.*

Krishna made the same offer to Karna. Some will say Krishna could foresee all that would happen. He knew Karna would reject the offer. Yet, the suggestion by itself is repulsive. It is Raj Dharma to avoid war. All must strive for peace. Conjugal relationships have been offered, even if these compromise the right of a woman to choose her partner. Marriages intending to form alliances and partnership that unite nations or businesses take place even to this day. Alliances that unite nations and avoid war are acts of Apad Dharma.

CHAPTER 53

The Conduct for War

Synopsis: Why the Geneva Convention must learn from the Kurukshetra Convention.

Before the beginning of war, representatives from both sides met and agreed to the rules of battle.

Battle shall begin at sunrise and cease at sunset. Only warriors evenly matched in skills and with similar weapons shall challenge and engage one another. A charioteer shall fight a charioteer. A foot soldier shall engage a foot soldier. No warrior shall attack an unarmed person. They will not attack a wounded person being carried away or a person not engaged in battle. There would be no duel where several warriors attack one warrior. If a person surrenders, the duel must end immediately. He cannot be harmed. A warrior cannot attack another who is unarmed, unconscious or from behind his back. A warrior cannot attack a woman. In a duel, the established rules for the use of weapons must be followed. Outside the time set for battle, people on one side were free to visit their relatives and friends on the other side.

Commentary

Value Rules: Long before Geneva Convention, they established rules of surrender, rights of Prisoner of War, rules relating to injured personnel, evacuation of the dead. This event focuses on following rules in order to live an orderly life. In the war, rules were not followed and we can see the results of such actions.

CHAPTER 54

Ved Vyas Grants Sanjay
Distance Vision

Synopsis: We must face the consequences of our actions?

O n the morning of the battle, the armies were preparing to face each other and waited for the battle to begin.

In Hastinapur, an anxious Dhritarashtra wanted to be kept updated of the events on the battlefield. When Ved Vyas offered to grant him remote vision, he requested that his charioteer Sanjay be given the boon, so that he could narrate to him events unfolding on the battlefield.

Commentary

Dhritarashtra's Blindness: Ved Vyas was the biological father of Dhritarashtra and Pandu. He would have made a last ditch effort to resolve the dispute within the family and avert a disastrous war. He was fulfilling his Parivarik Dharma. But his attempts to reason with Dhritarashtra failed. Ved Vyas offered to restore Dhritarashtra's vision, but he rejected it. Dhritarashtra believed he was denied the throne, but time and circumstances had corrected this.

Sanjay's Distance Vision, its Significance: *The concept of 'distance vision' described in the Mahabharat exceeds human achievement even in our times. One must therefore view this 'divine action' as a way for the narrators to include family elders in the events that would soon unfold on the battlefield. Over the days that followed, he would suffer immense pain and see his powers and rights slip away; the loss of his sons whom he loved, as the consequences of his folly. He had gone to great lengths to secure the crown for his son. He would witness the death of his sons and grandsons, the tremendous tragedy that his actions and desires had unleashed on his subjects.*

Can we call this his personal hell where every tragic loss is narrated to him in the detail as they arise? It must have been traumatic.

Relevance to our Lives: *Often we are given a chance to make amends in life. To right a wrong or to avoid conflict or confrontation that may have devastating consequences on our lives. Like Dhritarashtra, our view that we are the wronged party may blind us, as would the argument that the conflict or dispute is not our doing. By refusing to accept distance vision, Dhritarashtra thought he could avoid the consequences, yet he was curious to know about the outcome of his actions.*

CHAPTER 55

Final Act before the Start of the Battle

Synopsis: Did Krishna not convince Arjun? It is okay to pursue Artha and Kama, Dharma does not promote austerity and penance! Give me your wealth and I will give you Moksha–the dishonest call.

On the morning of the battle, Yudhisthir asked his charioteer to pull forward towards the mounts of Bhishma, Dronacharya and other Kaurava relatives. He sought the blessings of his elders, who wished him success and long life, despite being armed and ready for war. The previous night, Duryodhana had approached his mother Gandhari to seek her blessings for victory. She blessed her son and wishes victory to be on the side of Dharma.

In the Kaurava camp, Karna refused to join battle under the leadership of Bhishma, upset with both him and Dronacharya for disqualifying him from the group of best archers, the previous night, on the grounds of his being impulsive and unreliable. Another version says that Bhishma knew Karna as Kunti's son and did not want brother killing brother. He knew an adverse assessment would upset Karna and he would refuse to fight under Bhishma.

At Arjun's request, Krishna also drew the chariot between the two armies. The presence of so many of his close friends, relatives, persons he grew up with and those who had nurtured him in the opposite camp, deeply distressed him. He realised the terrible aftermath that would leave behind broken families, widows, orphans, financial, emotional and societal devastation. He felt that no pursuit of wealth or power justified the losses that the clan would suffer. He preferred to renounce his materialistic pursuits rather than being responsible for inflicting so much pain.

Two events occurred simultaneously. Yudhisthir had just been blessed by his Kaurava elders, his teachers and others. Before returning to his camp, he inquired whether any member from within the Kaurava side wished to join the Pandavas. Yuyutsu, a Kaurava kin joined the Pandavas. Arjuna, too overwhelmed by the terrible implications, refused to fight against the Kauravas. This is the high point of the Epic. Arjun told Krishna that he did not want to pursue materialistic goals that would put so many innocent lives in jeopardy. He did not want the blood of his relatives and friends on his hands. Then Krishna revealed his cosmic presence and the purpose of taking birth as a Vishnu Avatar.

The events now come to a standstill. Two armies are facing each other, and Arjun, the key fighter, is feeling despondent. In the *Bhagwad Gita*, Krishna explains to Arjun his Dharma as a Kshatriya, one which he is bound to uphold rather than being weakened by emotional attachments. The soul is immortal which wears the body like a piece of clothing and discards it at death, to take another one on re-birth. Why should Arjun be so attached to the bodies arrayed against him? He wanted him to perform his duty and also allow the men on the opposite side to do theirs. When everyone performs their actions faithfully, it will be naturally and fairly rewarding in the ultimate balance. The Bhagwat Gita has engaged the minds of the most accomplished thinkers and preachers worldwide. Its depth and diversity has not yet been fully fathomed and will continue to intrigue human minds as it has in the past.

Commentary

Why this Book? We have discovered that the 700 verses of the Bhagwat Gita are so rich in their thought and application to human life. It is then important to consider the illuminative power of the entire 100,000 verses of the Epic. These can encompass our understanding of life. Therefore, the epic unequivocally states that which is here must be somewhere, and that which is not here cannot be anywhere. We may be limited by our ability to understand the various incidents and the circumstances from its many dimensions. Yet, we can relate many events in the Epic to our contemporary lives and to draw on it for possible responses. This Epic can be our Google on Dharma, our way of life, guide our thought and actions.

We can avoid conflicts, disagreements, disputes, misunderstandings only if we can look at others from their point of view. We need a perspective beyond our own. We need to appreciate or understand the actions of others. Our emotions influence our actions. Our emotions may be influenced by our attachment or limited by our choice. We also need to realise how our actions will affect others or influence their response. None of this takes us away from doing our duty. It is only in the most unusual or exceptional circumstances we have no option. The worst option is to base our actions or inactions on our expectation or response of the other party. We must base our action on our conviction and Dharma.

Goals of Life: *It would be fallacious to believe life's goal is Dharma alone. Or that the purpose of life is always a function of choosing selflessly between Dharma and Adharma. That life is about right or wrong, reward or punishment, love or hate, heaven or hell and so on. Individuals have four goals in life. Dharma is following a righteous and moral path in our duty, obligations or purpose. Artha is the pursuit of wealth and prosperity in our duty as a householder. Kama is the fulfilment of our human and worldly desires. These help our growth and the progress of society. Moksha is the state of detachment. After a time, we must free ourselves from our insatiable needs and wants. They believe if we can achieve this, it will break the cycle of re-birth. The immortal soul will then rest in peace as it will be relieved of the unending cycle of re-birth.*

Kama and Artha must be pursued responsibly. We must follow the rules and obligations of Dharma. Each of the four sons of Ved Vyas represent one of the Four Goals of Life. We must credit him for this interesting characterisation of his sons.

Dhritarashtra embodies the character of Kama. He has all the weaknesses of a human pursuing his wants or Maya or emotions. His desire is to achieve power and acts to keep his power. In his blind attachment to his sons, he supports their every whim. This is at the cost of destruction of his entire family. Vidura embodies Dharma. His character reflects the conviction of a man steadfast in his pursuit of Dharma. He sides with Dharma even at the cost of being exiled or being removed from his position. He refused to take part in the war based on Dharma. Bhishma, Dronacharya and others went into the battle out of loyalty. Pandu embodies Artha. His character reflects the one who devotes his life to pursuit of wealth and honour for his family. He then forgoes all the material wealth and power when he cannot provide a successor. He then pursues his goal to grow his family as a householder. His fourth son, Sukhdev embodies Moksha. As a sanyasi, he devotes his life to meditation. As per the epic, he achieved Moksha.

The narrators of the Mahabharat have woven the goals of life into the profiles of its characters. They have described their lives, their choices and the outcome. This again points to how important it is to reflect on the story. We must not just read the story but try to understand the message behind it. As with all poetry, there is value to the paraphrase of the verse, to understand what the composers want to convey.

Management Lesson: *Why did they give Bhima charge of a division and not to Arjun? The five Pandavas represented five core virtues. They preferred Bhima as a leader for his valour over Arjun's skills. In management, a leader needs to lead, have courage to meet adversity, and must have a killer instinct. Arjun had developed skills as an archer but he was prone to emotions. He refused to fight and dropped his weapons and had to be coaxed into picking them up, but did he really fight even then?*

Dharma in the Conflict: *In war, opposite camps were risking the lives of other people and property of the state to realise their agenda. Some wanted to recover that which they thought belonged to them. Some were pursuing personal glory. Some were avenging their humiliation. Some were fighting out of loyalty, others were fighting out of an obligation of friendship or relationship or indebtedness. What figured in the agenda of each participant was Kama or Artha? Kama and Artha motivated the Mahabharat war. Dharma or Vidura did not take part in this conflict.*

Vidura and Yudhisthir represent Dharma, some believe the former was the father of the latter. The son led the battle in which his side resorted to acts of Adharma. It would suggest that in exceptional times, we cannot apply the normal rules of Dharma. Dharma, however cannot stand still, it must be a part in the process of evolution. This was portrayed by how the older generation remained uncommitted and the new went ahead forward. One represents the past which does not move and the other represents the future and has to progress.

Human beings have emotional needs and material desires, which can trigger significant internal conflict within us. Arjun's trauma reflects this internal challenge. He had the benefit of the wise counsel of Krishna; he relented and took up arms. The history of the battle is witness to him, not killing Dronacharya, Bhishma or his Kaurava cousins. He killed Jayadratha and Karna. These two killings were to avenge the slaying of his son Abhimanyu. This reflects his choice. Krishna revealed his divine self, in a way Arjun knew it was God's wish, yet, Arjun decided for himself. This explains how one can have the best of advice but end up ignoring it.

A careful analysis reveals that sometimes the pursuit of our wants and desires may violate our Dharma or duty. The resultant conflict can have a devastating effect on our lives similar to trauma of Dhritarashtra. It forced him to hear the details of the horrifying death of each of his sons as they were killed on the battlefield. We also know of the trauma of Kunti, her indiscretion led to the unwanted birth of Karna. She abandoned him at birth, but her attachment to him must have tormented her, more so after she recognised him at the passing out parade. Karna was around, but she could not own him as his mother. She stood conflicted between her role as a mother and a wife. She had to make a choice between her children.

Krishna as an advisor did his best. He revealed his divine self to convince Arjun that he was perfect and it could not be better. Yet he allowed Arjun to decide. Arjun took up arms, but he was not fully convinced. Krishna had to push him into action often. The epic deals with the importance of conviction. Counsel can help us resolve our internal conflict, but it will serve no purpose if it does not convince us. In an earlier event, it dealt with consent based on consensus and now it deals with conviction.

We must all pursue our goal of Artha and Kama. However, we must be responsible and follow Dharma. We can then follow Ashram Dharma to know when to relinquish our emotional and material attachments. We need the experience of desire and focus to achieve Moksha. These are disciplines we have learnt in course of our earlier goals. Artha, Kama, Dharma and Moksha share the same father and are part of the same family. This association points to their importance and inter-relationship in the evolution of man and society.

CHAPTER 56

The Great War

Synopsis: Weapons of mass destruction are a risk to humanity, the threat of a dirty bomb, war leaves no winners.

The battle started with the sound of the bugle and launch of the first arrow, continuing for ten days under the leadership of Bhishma. Fighting on behalf of Kauravas, Bhishma inflicted great damage on the Pandavas, causing great concern among the Pandava camp. But he refused to touch any of the Pandava siblings. Whilst Krishna convinced Arjuna to take up arms, he would not still engage with Bhishma. An upset Krishna nearly broke his vow as he stepped down from his chariot to attack the ageing patriarch. Arjun sought Krishna's forgiveness and urged him to return to the chariot. He promised that he would fight whole-heartedly.

In Kaurava camp, Bhishma's reluctance to attack Pandavas prolonged the battle and caused immense death and destruction, upsetting Duryodhana. He accused the family elder of being remiss as a leader. Then Bhishma vowed to kill the Pandavas the very next day and end the battle. When asked how he planned to go about it, Bhishma took out five divine arrows from his quiver and told Duryodhana that he would kill them with these. Duryodhana took possession of these arrows until the next battle. Somehow, the Pandava camp got wind of this event and sent Arjun to meet Duryodhana. It was now time for Arjuna to redeem the boon pledged by Duryodhana when Arjun (in exile) secured his release from Gandharva captivity, after he had lost to them in a battle. Accordingly, Duryodhana parted with the arrows.

Meanwhile, Yudhisthir and Krishna visited Bhishma in his tent, ostensibly to inquire about his health, but the patriarch immediately understood their intent. The Pandavas were looking for guidance to avoid devastation and bloodshed. Simply stated, they were asking Bhishma how they could stop him in a battle. He answered he would never engage with a female warrior. The Pandavas had Shikhandi in their camp but Bhishma considered him a woman. There was a lack of clarity whether they should group Shikhandi with males or females, paving the way for his participation in battle. Bhishma was bound to refuse a fight with Shikhandi believing her to be a woman. So as planned, Shikhandi attacked Bhishma the next day and managed to wound him grievously. Some versions suggest that it was Arjun shooting the arrows from behind Shikhandi. Another version has it that the Kauravas also withdrew the warriors protecting Bhishma, so that he would be killed, allowing Karna to lead against the Pandavas. Several arrows pierced his body as Bhishma fell from his chariot. He lay on a bed of arrows above the ground, ending his role as the commander-in-chief of the Kaurava army, on the tenth day of the battle. He remained in the condition for the rest of the days that the battle raged.

Duryodhana now wanted to give the charge to Karna, but many in his camp opposed the Suta's leadership. He then asked Dronacharya to head his army. Under his leadership, the battles became harsher, with Pandavas suffering heavy losses. Pandavas also violated battlefield rules with impunity, according to Kauravas. Arjuna's shooting arrows at Bhishma breached rules because a combatant could not join an ongoing duel.

Dronacharya created a fortress like formation called Chakrayuah or the gauntlet. Only the most accomplished of warriors could ever breach the Chakrayuah or fight their way out of it. In the Pandava camp only Arjun and his son Abhimanyu knew how to break through the formation, but the latter did not know how to get out of it. When Arjun was engaged in battle elsewhere, Abhimanyu wanted to display his skills. He offered to penetrate the formation and asked his band of warriors to follow behind him, confident that they could weaken the Chakrayuah from within and storm out to safety.

Abhimanyu's attack created an opening through which he entered, but those following behind were pinned down by Jayadratha's sudden attack. Kauravas rapidly closed the breach. Isolated within, Abhimanyu fought valiantly. Even highly experienced warriors like Karna, Duryodhana, Shakuni and others could not initially subdue the fiery prince. But their combined onslaught killed him.

Pandavas suffered a shattering loss, with the first casualty being reported from their own clan. They blamed themselves for not being there for Abhimanyu when he needed them the most. A heartbroken and disconsolate Arjun vowed to kill Jayadratha the very next day or sacrifice his life.

The Kaurava camp strategised on how best they could defend Jayadratha and break Arjun's vow. Even by sunset the next day, Arjun could not penetrate the defences set up for Jayadratha. However, the moon had gradually eclipsed the setting sun, which the armies mistook for actual sunset. An elated Jayadratha quit his protective cordon. He wanted to watch with glee Arjun giving up his arms and his life. Krishna aware that the eclipse would soon end, asked Arjun to bide his time. As expected, the sun soon emerged from the shadows. All realised that the battle had not ended. Jayadratha stood exposed and undefended, when Arjun engaged him and killed him, fulfilling his vow. However, another important rule of battle was violated. The rule required that a battle would only begin on sunrise and after a formal call with the sound of a bugle. The battle for that day had ended, soldiers had put down their weapons, but as the eclipse passed, Arjun killed a disarmed Jayadratha. From that day, battles would no longer end on sunset and continued through the night.

Bhima and Hidimbi's son Ghatotkacha had also joined battle, wreaking havoc on the Kaurava camp. As the battle continued past sunset, Ghatotkacha became fiercer because rakshas could see better in darkness. Extremely worried by the development, Duryodhana exhorted Karna to fight with Ghatotkacha and limit Kaurava losses. Still unable to stop Ghatotkacha, Karna fielded his most potent weapon to bring down the young rakshas at the instigation of a desperate Duryodhana. Once again, it plunged the Pandavas into grief, but Krishna felt much relieved as Arjun was now safe and would have the upper hand in a duel with Karna.

Under Dronacharya's leadership, the settled rules of battle were rendered irrelevant. As an inspiring leader and warrior, he inflicted crushing losses on the Pandava camp. It looked for ways to remove him, to halt their losses. They discovered that his only weakness was his son.

The Pandavas then wanted to kill Ashwatthama, but as he was invincible in battle, they thought of faking his death. So Bhima would kill an elephant named Ashwatthama and approach Dronacharya with the news of the killing. But would Dronacharya believe him? The only person he would ever believe was Yudhisthir. But he refused to lie. So they hatched a plan to serve their purpose and help Yudhisthir avoid lies.

The next day Bhima killed an elephant named Ashwatthama and hastened to meet Dronacharya. He did not believe Bhima, but wanted Yudhisthir to confirm the killing, knowing that he would never lie. But when Yudhisthir uttered those very words, Dronacharya went numb with shock, dropped his weapons and sat on the floor of his chariot. He did not hear Yudhisthir add under his breath that it was an elephant. Dhristadumya raced towards him and axed him to death. They used deception to kill one of the greatest warriors of that time. Even worse, the Pandavas had killed an unarmed warrior.

The battle had grown even more intense. Bhima had slaughtered many of his Kaurava clansmen. Fighting with Vikarna, Bhima wanted to spare his life, but he declined and insisted on fighting Bhima. Vikarna died. Bhima had killed most of the hundred brothers.

Karna led the Kaurava army from the sixteenth day of the war, but his leadership lasted for only two days. The

Pandavas hatched another conspiracy to get him out of the way, with the involvement of demi-gods who had fathered Arjun and Karna. Surya warned his son Karna to beware of a conspiracy involving Indra, Arjun's father, who would approach him. One morning, Indra approached Karna in a beggar's guise and asked Karna for his celestial armour. Without any hesitation, Karna gave it to him. Indra, ashamed of his behaviour and overwhelmed by such selfless generosity, granted Karna a divine arrow, which could be used only once and with which he killed Ghatotkacha.

Earlier, Kunti and Krishna had weakened Karna's resolve by telling him that he was the eldest of Pandava siblings and Kunti's son. Moreover, Kunti had extracted from Karna a promise to spare the lives of his younger siblings except for Arjun. Karna also had to reckon with Parashuram's curse, namely that he would forget the very code to activate celestial weapons.

Karna began the battle, but his prime focus was a duel with Arjun. In course of the two days he battled with his younger siblings Bhima, Yudhisthir, Nakul and Sahadev and true to his promise to Kunti, spared their lives.

Meanwhile, Bhima continued with his rampage, finally catching up with Dushashan. He assaulted Dushashan in a barbaric way, tearing his rib cage apart. He sat on his chest and drank the blood oozing from his body. He then called for Draupadi and who washed her hair in Dushashan's blood.

On the seventeenth day of the battle, Karna and Arjun were duelling when Karna's chariot stalled as its wheel got stuck in the mud. He requested Arjun to halt the fight. He dropped his weapons and got off the chariot to free the wheel. As the request was in keeping with the rules of battle, Arjun was inclined to accept this request.

Krishna intervened and asked Arjun to capitalize on the moment. He reminded him of the unfair slaughter of his son Abhimanyu. A vengeful Arjun shot an arrow at Karna, fatally injuring him. The Pandavas once again breached the rules, attacking an unarmed warrior.

After the fall of Karna, Shalya led the Kaurava army; only to die in a duel with Yudhisthir. The same day Sahadev also fought with Shakuni. Although Sahadev knew that Shakuni had manipulated the Kauravas into fighting Pandavas and to avenge the sufferings of his family and the marriage of his sister Gandhari, he believed that Shakuni was not obliged to fight or die in this battle. He offered to let him go. But Shakuni told him that as his life's mission was accomplished, he preferred dying a worthy death in battle. Thereafter Sahadev killed him. The Kauravas now had Ashwatthama and Duryodhana as their surviving warriors. This is the story of how and why our lives are like a treadmill. We set ourselves a goal and when we achieve it; we stretch our goals. This is not a stretch, but it is more like moving the goal post.

Gandhari worried about Duryodhana, after all her sons had been slain in battle, wanted to bless her only surviving son. She asked him to bathe and return before her naked, wanting to bestow upon him the boon of invincibility. But Krishna pursued him midway and mocked him for walking naked as an adult. How could he approach his mother in this condition? Embarrassed, Duryodhana quickly covered his manhood with a large leaf and walked into his mother's chamber.

When Gandhari removed her blindfold for the first time after marriage, she was very annoyed to note that he had covered his lower half. Gandhari's divine vision covered his body, which changed into a protective shield, leaving the area around his private parts unprotected. She advised him to be cautious.

Duryodhana isolated now, his army having deserted him, hid in a marshland, hoping for a truce with the Pandavas. This would end the battle, save his life and kingdom. But the Pandavas were eager to find Duryodhana before Dhritarashtra could call a truce. A group of tribals discovered his place of hiding and informed Bhima. They asked him to come out of hiding. Yudhisthir offered him a bait; he could fight any of the Pandavas and the winner would take all. Duryodhana picked his equal Bhima for a duel with a mace.

The story goes that Balarama had returned from his sojourn and was present at the duel. Both of them fought and were evenly matched. Krishna wanted to remind Bhima of his vow and pointed to his thighs. Bhima broke the rules. He smashed his opponent below the waist. Duryodhana fell paralyzed and in excruciating pain. Balarama their tutor was furious. He wanted to punish Bhima for his behaviour and could have killed Bhima in anger, but Krishna pacified his brother.

News of Duryodhana's plight reached Ashwatthama. At night, he came out of hiding to see his friend Duryodhana. He was in grief seeing his friend lying in pain and on his deathbed. In his view, the Pandavas had again used deceit. He wanted to avenge their behaviour, for the death of his father and the plight of his friend. He asked Duryodhana to appoint him as their military leader. Duryodhana declined because they had lost the war, his army had deserted him and he was waiting for his father to arrange a truce. As Ashwatthama was insistent, he made him the leader.

Ashwatthama wanted to kill the Pandavas for causing the death of Kaurava leaders by deception and fraud. Late that night he broke into the Pandava camp. In the darkness, he killed all the sleeping warriors. But alerted by Krishna, the Pandavas had already moved to a secret location outside of their camp. Krishna wanted them to avoid Dhritarashtra messengers, fearing that he would request them to end the war and spare Duryodhana. The Pandavas were bound to accept this request, wasting their entire effort and sacrifice. Ashwatthama in his fury beheaded his victims and carried this as proof of his action to his friend. When Duryodhana saw the severed heads, it dismayed him. He told Ashwatthama he had not killed the Pandavas but their sons. The fight was for succession between him and Yudhisthir, but Ashwatthama had destroyed the Kuru dynasty. He had killed the sons of Draupadi and the last hope of succession for the Kuru dynasty. He was heartbroken and passed away that night.

Thus ended the great battle of all times that lasted 18 days.

The next morning news reached the Pandavas. They rushed to their tent, to the mutilated bodies of sons and Dhristadumya. Krishna and Arjun went looking for Ashwatthama. He was hiding in the ashram of Ved Vyas. Arjun challenged him to a duel. In course of this fierce duel, both Arjun and Ashwatthama launched a Brahmastra at each other.

The Brahma-Astra was the most powerful weapons known to man, which had the power to annihilate all living beings and bring the world to an end. The simultaneous launch of this weapon from both sides alarmed the celestial world. Ved Vyas intervened and sought the recall of this weapon by both sides.

Arjun recalled his weapon. However, Ashwatthama could not as he did not know how to recall the weapon. He was advised to limit its damage by re-directing it to an uninhabited place so it could waste away its power. Instead, he directed it to the womb of a pregnant Uttara. He wanted to end the Kuru dynasty.

When Krishna realised Ashwatthama's wicked intent, he used his cosmic powers to neutralise the re-directed weapon. The Pandavas had captured Ashwatthama and wanted to kill him for wiping out their future generation. They were upset with Ashwatthama's deceit, until Ved Vyas pointed out they had also relied on deceit to win the war. The war had ended; he now had no reason to attack the Pandavas.

They decided that Ashwatthama should be punished by taking away the gem on his forehead. With a gaping that bled all the time, Krishna let him wander aimlessly for the next 3000 years.

The war had ended. There were no celebrations of victory, but gloom and grief everywhere. Both camps realised the immense damage the war had done, including horrific personal losses. The few survivors left on both sides united, with an understanding that so much had happened.

Commentary

Power of Mutual Destruction: *Brahma-Astra is the modern equivalent of a nuclear weapon. Although both sides possessed one, their leaders had volunteered to follow the principle of no first use. Despite having lost the war, Duryodhana did not ask Ashwatthama to unleash this weapon, which would have obliterated life on earth. Even today, the fear of mutual destruction deters a nuclear misadventure.*

Ashwatthama and his Dirty Bomb: *Weapons in the hands of the indiscriminate can destroy the future of mankind. The Epic states the divine intervention of Krishna saved the unborn child. The womb symbolises the earth, destroying which would end life on earth. Krishna's divine intervention sends out a message that in such crisis, God help us.*

Creators of weapons of mass destruction fear the risk of theft, their misuse or accidental use. Although Ashwatthama could launch and dispatch the Brahma-Astra, he had no knowledge on how to disarm or recall it. Think of what would happen today when the makers of a dirty bomb assemble and launch one, without the ability to abort it and prevent wholesale devastation. Krishna's divine intervention saved mankind and helped move the story forward. Today, it would wipe out humanity.

Duryodhana and the Message to all dictators: *Duryodhana knew he had lost the war. His brothers, his key fighters, were all dead. The only option left to Kauravas was to call for a truce, which Pandavas could not ignore. So they would have to spare Duryodhana's life. Kshatriya traditions would allow Duryodhana to retain Hastinapur. But Pandavas wanted to pre-empt the truce offer by killing their arch enemy. Duryodhana, as a true Kshatriya, faced defeat because of the Pandavas' deception. He never strayed from his goal. Neither did he prompt Ashwatthama to use the Brahma Astra, but defended his rights vigorously as the only heir of the Hastinapur.*

Symbolism of Ashwatthama's Curse: *People in India believe the curse of Ashwatthama is real. He is said to appear in disguise, begging for oil to apply on his open wound. Quite possibly, the Pandavas killed Ashwatthama in a fit of rage, when they chanced upon him. They may have left his slaughtered body to rot, without performing his last rites. In Indic culture, it is believed that until someone ceremonially carries out the last rites, the soul cannot disengage from the body and hovers around as a spirit or ghost.*

Knowledge is Power but Only when Complete: *Narrators have again used two examples to tell us that knowledge is Power. Abhimanyu paid with his life when he entered the Chakrayuah without knowing how to get out of that trap. Ashwatthama gained partial knowledge of using the Brahma Astra but did not know how to recall it.*

Ghatotkacha's Death is a Disturbing Truth: *When Karna killed Ghatotkacha, the Pandavas were grief-stricken. They had lost their eldest son, the next in line of succession. Krishna felt relieved that Karna had used up his most potent weapon to kill Ghatotkacha, eliminating the threat to Arjun. Had Ghatotkacha survived, Yudhisthir may have crowned him as his successor.*

Some versions suggest that Krishna also felt relieved that Ghatotkacha's death ruled out his being a claimant to the throne. A later addition to the story goes that the king is the upholder of Dharma. Ghatotkacha, brought up by his mother, lacked familiarity with the rules of Dharma. Ghatotkacha did not qualify to be a king as he was brought up as a rakshas.

Karna also made this point in his meeting with Kunti. He told her that he had been a lifelong Suta; had lived and married into the community. He had followed the rites and rituals as applicable to a Suta. Anyway, it was now too late for him to adapt to the life as a Kshatriya. He also lacked knowledge of the rites and rituals of a Kshatriya.

A Kshatriya would rather die than run away from danger, but Karna deserted the battlefield while fighting with the Gandharvas. A Kshatriya will exercise his craft and act with discretion at all times. His promise to Kunti or his giving away his celestial armour or his refusal to fight under Bhishma showed his impulsive nature. Bhishma and Dronacharya agreed that Karna may be a good archer, but could not be trusted with higher responsibility as he was prone to fits of anger.

Yudhishthir's Lie for the Greater Good: A lie led to the death of Dronacharya, but did not end there. Dhristadumya killed Dronacharya. This saved the lives of soldiers who would have been killed otherwise. Yudhisthir also known as Dharma Raj lied and can be accused of Adharma. However, it is believed non-cruelty is preferred to Truth. For a Kshatriya, any act that averts war or further loss of life is preferred. Yudhishthir's lie was Adharma at a personal level. As a King and Kshatriya, one can justify his actions. He needed to stop Dronacharya from killing people. However, no Dharma is more important than another. Every act of Adharma is punished. Yudhisthir and Dhristadumya both suffered the consequences of their actions. Ashwatthama killed Dhristadumya and all the sons of the Pandavas in their sleep. What greater punishment can a human receive than the pain of death of loved ones, more so when a father experiences the death of his sons?

Karna's Death Sentence: Denied the right to education, Karna claimed he was a Brahmin, and misled Parashuram, ultimately meriting a death sentence as a punishment. The Pandavas spent years living in the home of a Brahmin and seeking alms as a livelihood. The giving of alms is a personal religious act and a sacrifice. The Pandavas violated the trust of many people who gave in charity.

Why then did Karna have to suffer a death penalty when the Pandavas got away? Once again we must go back to the idea, that our hell is not always evident to all. None of the Pandavas emerged from the battle with a feeling of elation. Yudhisthir realised that the Crown for which he had waged war was not his. Bhima lost his son from Hidimbi. Arjun lost his son from Subhadra. All the Pandavas lost their sons from Draupadi. They won back a Kingdom engulfed in grief and suffering brought about by loss of wealth, property and family. The world still regards Karna for his loyalty and generosity. Krishna the divine one performed his last rites. The same Duryodhana who denied the Pandavas five villages had made Karna a king. He lived a life far beyond his role and place as a Suta and received an honour in death which all would want.

A Study of the Leadership Choices: *Kauravas appointed the leader of their army based on seniority. They first chose Bhishma and then Dronacharya, but these leaders were participating in the war as a duty; not out of any conviction. At their age, they lacked the energy needed for the war. The Pandavas did not treat leadership as a right based on seniority. They did not base it on age but looked beyond. They chose Dhristadumya for his experience, energy and ability. They knew he would be motivated by the prospect of victory. They could have chosen Drupad, but their choice reflected their better understanding of the role. Drupad was now old, he nursed a personal agenda. Dhristadumya did not compromise the rules of battle like Dronacharya. He encouraged all the able and worthy members of his side to give their best; Unlike Bhishma, who humiliated Karna and kept him away from battle under his leadership.*

The questions that arise from such choices are several. We must respect experience gained with age. We can leverage their experience as advisors but do not have to handover leadership. Bhishma, Dronacharya and Karna were not focused on winning the war for Duryodhana. They were doing so out of a sense of duty or obligation. A leader must be loyal and committed to the aim of the mission. The

Kauravas were short on strategy. They assumed victory because they had a larger army and great warriors on their side. The USA with its vastly superior forces has suffered a humiliating defeat at the hands of a much smaller enemy like Vietnam.

Krishna, the Non-Playing Captain: *The man who believed all is fair in love and war was the real hero. He achieved this in the Mahabharata despite being the non-playing captain. At the end of the war, the chariot he rode burnt itself out. The symbolism here is a Divine Avatar rode a Divine Chariot to fulfil his Divine Aim. He achieved victory for his cause without even lifting a weapon. Krishna recognised that his opponents mistook their false vanity or their commitment to principles as their call of Dharma.*

The chariot symbolises a vehicle he used to fulfil his aim. He needed a war, and he got one. They fought this war on the same ground calling it Kurukshetra and Dharmakshetra. This is because two battles were being fought simultaneously. The Kuru cousins were fighting to win or keep their right to succession. Krishna was fighting to change the minds and beliefs of people. His battle did not need weapons, it needed conviction and leadership. He wanted people to return to the path of Dharma. He wanted them to base their decisions, not on habits but on convictions.

Krishna wanted society to follow Dharma as a way of life. Dharma here is not about religion or its rituals, it is about duty. He offered Bhagwad Gita to Arjun as help. He wanted him to follow it, just as Society would come to follow it too, because this was the aid they lacked. He provided the Pandavas with spiritual leadership; he got them to act out of duty. He wanted them to fulfil Dharma as an obligation. He wanted them and the world to understand that Dharma is about obligations and not principles.

At the end of the battle, the Epic says all the Kshatriyas were dead. This is more symbolic. It merely meant that the role of the Kshatriya Royals was re-defined. The Kshatriyas would now only protect the Brahmins. They transferred the role of protecting Dharma from Kings to Brahmins. In this context, the Brahmin is the one who devotes himself to the study of Dharma, he offers guidance to people; he is the one responsible to society as a Dharma Raj. The end of the war ended the dual role of kings as raja and Dharma Raj. Hindu way of life would have a spiritual leader. Krishna, the non-playing Captain, proved that a Dharma Guru can provide spiritual leadership and guidance. His role does not need weapons.

Draupadi, her Wish Fulfilled and her Punishment: *Draupadi wanted war, she wanted to see the perpetrators of her humiliation punished. Her husband Bhima gave them death; in fact, Dushashan's death was inhuman. One cannot forget or forgive Draupadi for her misconduct and inhumanity. She laughed at Duryodhana, called him blind and mocked at his father's blindness too. She rejoiced at the brutal killing of Kichaka and washed her hair with the blood of a dying/dead Dushashan. At the game of dice, Dhritarashtra asked her for forgiveness and gave her three boons in consideration. She took the boon but did not forgive. She cheated and destiny punished her. The war she wanted did not end her suffering. She lost all her children. She would never feel the joy of seeing her children ascend the throne or the honour of being called queen mother.*

CHAPTER 57

Pandavas Discover their Relationship with Karna

Synopsis: Successful, yet joy eludes you, feel you missed your life, the success you cannot enjoy? Can you hide the truth? Can you avoid truth?

Karna lay dying on the battlefield. Arjun had shot an arrow at an unarmed Karna whilst he was trying to free the wheels of his chariot. He had asked Arjun to pause the duel, but Krishna intervened. The war had virtually ended. There was dejection all round in the marginalised Kaurava Camp. Their army had deserted them. Krishna visited a mortally wounded Karna lying on his deathbed. He wanted to test the resolve of this brave warrior famed for his selflessness and charity. Krishna asked him for a gift of the benefit of all his deeds of charity. It amazed Krishna when Karna with no hesitation gave over the benefits as demanded. In that one brief encounter, he stripped a dying Karna of the last of his personal treasures i.e. the benefit of his Punya. Punya is a Sanskrit word and has no equivalent in English. It does not just represent a sacrifice; it refers to deeds that are good, righteous, auspicious, pleasing, etc. This contrasts with its opposite deed called paap. Its close English equivalent is sin. Thereafter, Karna passed away.

A grieving Kunti rushed to the spot where her firstborn Karna lay in death. She could no longer hold back her grief and tears. This troubled the grieving Pandavas, who wondered why their mother shed tears for their enemy Karna. The Pandavas had suffered the loss of Abhimanyu, Ghatotkacha and other dear ones. They did not expect their mother to sympathise with the enemy who had caused them so much grief.

Kunti insisted that the Pandavas should accord to Karna a funeral befitting a kshatriya and a king. Sensing their reluctance, she confessed to them that Karna was her son and their eldest sibling. They were shocked into disbelief by her revelations. She then explained to them the circumstances of Karna's birth, whom she had abandoned out of fear of bringing disrepute to herself and her family.

Upon hearing their mother's story, the Pandavas realised this war had claimed yet another of their own. Pandavas other than Arjun now realised that Karna knew of his relationship with them. They understood why Karna had let them off in their battle. With Yudhisthir, his pain was even greater. He was distraught since they killed Karna under his leadership. He demanded why Kunti never shared this with them and waited till it was too late.

At a personal level, Yudhisthir was furious as he realised that all his efforts had come to naught. All his life he had pursued a right of succession to be a king that was never his. Yudhisthir cursed his mother that no woman on earth will henceforth be able to keep a secret. Yudhisthir always wondered why his mother Kunti, took such an interest in Karna's life or well-being, but chose not to ask her about it.

The Pandavas were grief-stricken to see their brother Karna lying dead. They accorded him a funeral befitting a member of the family. In Dharmic thought, in the absence of a father, the eldest sibling had the status of a father. In death, Karna had received the recognition he had yearned for all his life. Recognition apart, he received the highest honour in death. Krishna performed his last rites.

Commentary

Kunti, the Mother: Kunti had abandoned Karna but it could not whittle down her emotional attachment. The master story tellers bring us this guidance yet again. Ved Vyas could not remain disassociated from his biological children and grandchildren. He tried his best to make Dhritarashtra see reason. He wanted to grant his blind son distance vision so he could see the dire consequences of the war. This is a dramatic play on the idea where the father tried his best to reason with his son and make him realise the folly of his decision. This was a demonstration of his concern for the wellbeing of his son and his family. Kunti also knew the war would put the lives of her sons in jeopardy, pitting them against each other. She did all she could to restrain Karna from fighting with his own siblings. Had she acknowledged Karna as her first born, it would have averted the war, but this was not acceptable to her. The relationship between Duryodhana and Karna was as between a Royal and his loyal retinue. Karna had confessed his loyalty to Duryodhana and his obligation to him. He would have unhesitatingly surrendered his right to Duryodhana. Kunti had to choose between her sons, based on her obligations as a mother, a wife and a former queen. On

Karna's death she knew the Pandavas had won the war, fulfilling her obligation as a wife and queen, and was now at liberty to acknowledge her relationship with Karna. She ensured he received the highest of honour when Krishna conducted his last rites.

Kunti's Lie: Kunti in her moment of weakness or inquisitiveness had committed a blunder, resulting in the birth of Karna. To compound her error, she abandoned him, resuming life as if nothing had happened. She got married, Pandu could not father a child, she told him about the boon but not about her firstborn. Maybe she thought her problem was over. However, many years later, the first-born surfaced again. She could not acknowledge him because it would put her life and that of the Pandavas in jeopardy. People would not also believe her claims of the divine linkage associated with the birth of the Pandavas. People would suspect that the three Pandavas born to her and the twins born to Madri were her sons. As she had claimed these children were born to her from divine beings and not Pandu, meant she had relationships with five men. Now if Karna was also her son, it would imply that she had been in six relationships. Society would view her as lacking in morals and no one would believe her. The consequences for her and all her sons could have been devastating if the Kurus also disowned them. She had to continue to live with her lie. Over the years, Karna and the rest of her sons turned hostile to one another, they were in opposing camps. Soon, a war would break out and her son Karna would fight with her sons from Pandu. Now again, she had to live her lie because of her obligations, and it would torment her all her life. As a mother, she could not embrace her first born in public. Her lie had embraced her, it was a death embrace, and it would not leave her till time destroyed its relevance. Karna then died, she had a choice to keep her secret, but she knew not owning the truth would not release her from the torment of her lie. She owned up and faced the consequences. None other than her own son, the dutiful and obedient Yudhisthir cursed his mother. The curse had devastating consequences for not only her as a mother, but for all women.

Just one irresponsible act haunted her all her life. Despite her best efforts to avoid the truth, she was forced to acknowledge it at last, sending a subtle message to all of us. That if we decide to live a lie, we will face horrible consequences until we acknowledge the truth. Accepting the truth can often have immediate and devastating consequences, but living a lie or in hiding or as a fugitive is much worse. We may escape the consequences of our evil deeds in earthly life, but the Epic delivers the final warning: That we cannot escape the consequences of our Karma.

The Different Perspectives: *Thinkers and promoters of the Indic Faith could have deleted this cruel episode. Krishna was being heartless even as Karna lay dying. Instead of trying to ease his pain in the last moments of his life, Krishna asked him for a major sacrifice, surrendering the glory of his Punya. Dharma entitled Karna to Heaven as they had killed him in a battle. So keeping the benefit of his Punya or giving it away did not matter. Then what was then the intent of this exchange? Why did Krishna even bother to ask Karna for it? What is that larger message they wanted us to receive?*

The authors wanted us to understand the subtle workings of Dharma, Karma, Punya, Heaven and Hell.

Dharma is all about our obligations. We do not get credit for fulfilling our obligations. However, every failure is a violation. They count even a violation that helps fulfil higher obligations as a violation. In simple terms, it is like driving on the road, there is a fine for exceeding the speed limit. Driving within the speed limit is an obligation. Stealing a rich man's wealth and distributing it to the poor and hungry does not negate the offence of theft. Religious preachers want us to believe our acts of Punya will make up for our acts of Paap. Karna's several acts of Punya or Daan should have benefitted him. The only benefit we could attribute to his Daan was the recognition and honour he received on his death. His soul did not need it. He had died in battle and would go to Heaven.

This connects Dharma with our soul, whereas our acts of Punya are connected with our life and body. Krishna wanted us to realise that we will enjoy the benefits of our Punya in our life. Our Punya will extinguish on death as it identifies our actions as living beings with a body. When we perform an act of Punya, we experience momentary bliss. In the long term, Punya will benefit us whereas Paap will cause suffering. The benefit and consequences of both will end on death as it identifies these with our body. The Abrahamic School equates sacrifice with Punya. It claims such acts save a sinner but does not claim it offsets a sin. Our acts of Paap and Punya can even survive the body, because people may remember it long after we are gone.

Dharma is an obligation and an expectation. A soul achieves Moksha through fulfilment of Dharma. Only Dharma can provide the soul eternal bliss. The outcome of Dharma will implicate our Soul. Extending this logic further, our acts of Adharma will attach to our souls and we will suffer its consequences as Karma. According to Indic thought, Karma generates our circumstances in our future lives.

Religions and proponents of Dharma, talk about Heaven and Hell. They obviously cannot provide evidence of its existence. Fear of punishment has been the primary driver that ensures we follow a path of Dharma. Krishna's taking away from Karna the benefit of his good deeds on his deathbed is to guide us that in our life we shall always reap what we sow. Just as with Karna, we will have to face the consequences of our actions in our life-time. Heaven and Hell are therefore only an illustration of Reward and Punishment.

Looking specifically at Karna's life, he realises both his Heaven and Hell on earth. His Hell was seeing his dearest friend die in vain and the pain inflicted by the death of his children. His unfair end in battle as a punishment for the underhand means he adopted to learn his war craft. It credited his heaven for his many good acts. He achieved Heaven when none other than Krishna performed his last rites. Kunti accepted him privately and then publicly. His brothers expressed grief, and the world remembers and recognises him for his loyalty and his integrity. Despite having sided with the Kauravas, he remained the least maligned amongst them all.

According to the Mahabharata, it is our duty to act out of our obligations of Dharma. Therefore, we must always do what we must do or are obliged to or expected to do. We cannot replace duty with an act of generosity, charity or penance. Therefore, our acts of charity or penance or sacrifice cannot replace our acts of Adharma. There is no escape from the consequences of Adharma. The many characterisations within the Mahabharat prove beyond doubt that there is no escape. We must face the consequences of our acts. In this context, Krishna's last interaction with Karna becomes relevant because it draws us to our Dharma.

In the life of all the major characters, circumstances change. Life is never always good or consistently bad. Characters go through their period of highs and lows. Our own actions, inactions or reactions trigger such conditions. At other times, we cannot explain these changes and attribute it to Destiny.

They used the life of Karna to explain the subtle difference between Dharma and Good Karma. His acts of charity are examples of Good Karma. This was an attempt to explain the difference between Good Karma or Punya and Dharma. In the life story of Karna, his acts of charity did not offset, erase or remove the consequences of his act of Adharma. The world acknowledged his acts of Charity, his generosity, his loyalty to his mentor, etc. But for his act of Adharma to his tutor, he suffered the consequences and paid with his life.

Humanity can acknowledge our acts of charity and these can even survive in collective memories. However, it is our acts of Adharma which decide our Hell and Heaven. It is not enough for our good deeds to exceed our bad, for it to reward us a place in Heaven.

Hindus believe bathing in the Ganga at its confluence or at other specified locations can wash away our sins. This must then violate our Intelligence. We visit Holy Shrines as our way of thanking God. This may be in the expectation of some positive events in our life or for seeking Divine Blessings for some positive outcome or for seeking repentance for our past Adharma. We can view visits to difficult-to-reach Holy Shrines such as those in the mountains, confluence of holy rivers as acts of penance. It tests a person's commitment to abstain from acts and deeds, which would ultimately lead to Adharma.

Nowadays, technology has mitigated the risks of travel. However, 2000 years ago they would expose a person to challenges and risks travelling on foot or horseback or bullock cart. They would face the risk of weather, terrain, predators, natural calamities, etc. These unknown hardships and hazards, travel with no access to credit cards, hotels etc. could feel like a punishment. He would return as a transformed man to society and family. Islam recognises and respects all those who returned home after a visit to the Holy Shrines of Mecca and Medina. As would the Hindus regard a man returning from a visit to Char Dham and other holy shrines.

We must recognise the risks, time and consequences of travel when such ideas surfaced initially. Even then a visit to a holy shrine or bathing in a holy river cannot save us from the consequences of paap or Adharma. Yet this experience would be transformational and therefore society may look up to him and give him another chance. It is this second chance that our religious texts call a fresh start or as if he has washed all sins. Through his long journey to the holy shrine he has renounced his place in society. He would have suffered unbeknown to us; he would have encountered life-changing experiences. He has already experienced his Heaven or Hell on this earth. Such a visit reinforces the existence of unpredictability and uncertainty that surrounds our lives. However, there is no assurance that such a visit will always lead to fulfilment and we call this unpredictability Destiny.

Confessions, Sacrifices, Holy Deeds or Pujas, Acts of Charity and Effect on Future Karma and Past Karma: *A confession is a recognition of a wrong done intentionally or otherwise. A wrong act is wrong, the intention is entirely irrelevant. Intentions can alter the perspective of other people, but it cannot alter the consequences based on Dharma. Therefore, the person must suffer the consequences. Confessions help improve introspection and can bring positive change.*

Sacrifices can be in the form of fasting, oaths, self-inflicted pain or hardship. It is often a step beyond introspection or a way to re-enforce our resolve, but nothing beyond.

Acts of worship or prayer or visits to Holy Shrine is an emotional aid and helps our resolve. It helps us to talk ourselves into a state of resolve over an act based on deep introspection.

Acts of charity is not a Robin Hood tax, you cannot steal from one and offset it by giving to another based on your perception of whose need is greater. Acts of charity with selfless intent help the needy with emotional and or material support. The Karna Event says it all. They will remember the giver for his acts during his lifetime and maybe even beyond, yet the giver will have to still suffer for his Adharma.

Dharma is our duty to do all that we should do, so there can be no positive credits. Some of us are born in abject poverty, others are born blind, yet we all have an equal obligation despite being placed unequally. How is it fair that despite our unequal circumstances, they compel us to walk the same path of Dharma?

Karna was born to a Princess and abandoned at birth. He grew up as a child in an ordinary home of a charioteer. They deny Vyas his mother's love and he grows up outside the Royal household. Bhishma, the firstborn and a worthy successor to his royal father has to not only stand down as the crown prince but also remain celibate. Dhritarashtra the first born was born blind and passed over as first choice for the crown. As the son of a Dasi mother, Vidura was ignored though he was born first and considered the most eligible. Dronacharya discriminated against Eklavya and denied him an education. When he gained it by deceit, he took away his thumb so he could never be the ace archer he was.

The Mahabharat is an essay of characters who suffered or experienced an unfair start or lived an unfair life. Yet they got no concessions from Dharma and had to suffer the consequences of their failings. All that this suggests is that one cannot avoid the obligation of Dharma or its consequences.

The Mahabharata often uses our past life to explain the circumstances of our present life. Krishna in the Bhagwad Gita is clear. It attaches our identity in our present life to our body and that on death the soul will leave the body to journey into another body. So how does one explain unfair beginning? Why are some born so rich and others so poor and some born fit and others differently abled? Yet we can never convincingly answer why some should have a life filled with more denial than others. Dhritarashtra's blindness, Pandu's impotence, Shikhandi's third gender, Gandhari's self-imposed blindness or Karna's abandonment does not reduce their obligations of Dharma, relative to their fellow human beings.

Karna's Life beyond Kunti's Silence and Yudhishthir's Anger: She concealed the secret of Karna's birth from the Pandavas and the Kauravas. Many apart from Kunti knew of Karna's birth and could have averted war if they had revealed this early on. Is it then possible that Karna was a character inserted to highlight the failings of our society or how we discriminate based on birth, of our biases, our customs, etc. Kunti-Bhoj adopted Kunti. They put the newborn baby in an earthen vessel and left it to float away. A childless charioteer who served King Dhritarashtra discovered this earthen vessel with Karna upstream. Karna's life is a study of society's bias for inherited status versus deserved status. It highlights the prejudices based on caste, right of legacy based on patriarchal principles which probably even continues today. Karna and Vidura were two deserving individuals. Society denied them their rightful place based on a bias. Karna is an example of a person belonging to a weaker section of Society. Contrary to popular belief, they could not manipulate or tempt him and he did not lack conviction.

Yudhishthir's Anger and its Relevance: We may spend a lifetime pursuing a goal and after attaining it, we realise it was just not worth it. Facing the rival camp on the battlefield, Arjun raised similar concerns. What would he do with a kingdom which demanded the sacrifices of many of his loved ones? When Yudhisthir realized *that he had a brother's blood on his hands, he felt cheated by a hollow victory but lost everything. Pandavas fought under his leadership, whereas it was Karna's right to lead them as the eldest sibling. As a winner, he presided over a citizenry mourning the death of its male members. He had lost all his cousins, his relatives, his children and now he was guilty of fratricide. In our contemporary world, a leader must also take moral responsibility for his decisions.*

As a son, his outburst was the only recorded act of rudeness or defiance towards his mother. Yudhisthir always wondered why his mother Kunti took more than a passing interest in Karna's life or his wellbeing. Yet, he never bothered to ask her about it. We must recognise this behaviour as being in denial or escapist. Truth is often bitter; we prefer to be in denial in order to escape from the turmoil that the discovery of the truth would entail. It did not justify Yudhishthir's curse or anger based on his failings. It was a warning on how secrecy can affect outcomes and our decisions.

Parents shield children from the harsh realities of the world, as they are not mature enough to grasp their implications. However, once they have grown up, parents must treat their children as mature adults and exchange views. Kunti demanded that it was the Dharma of her children to regain the lost kingdom. She expected them to prefer an honourable death to cowardice, in pursuit of their goals. Kunti owed it to Karna, Pandu and the Pandavas to reveal Karna's truth, which would have altered the course of history. It would have saved Yudhisthir the trouble of leading the Pandavas into battle. The responsibility would have then devolved on Karna, as the eldest sibling. Without Karna, Duryodhana would have compromised and settled the issue. He had given Karna a whole kingdom, then would he not have settled the claim for five more villages.

CHAPTER 58

Pandavas Return to Hastinapur

Synopsis: In war, there are no winners.

The victorious Pandavas now returned to Hastinapur, only to find the city enveloped in a pall of gloom, mourning the loss of its loved ones. Krishna accompanied the Pandavas when they met Dhritarashtra and Gandhari at the royal palace, to offer his guidance and support.

How could Dhritarashtra, as a grieving father, forget or forgive Bhima for the brutal assault on his sons? Apprehending that he might injure or kill Bhima, Krishna had his life-sized replica prepared for the meeting. When Dhritarashtra embraced what he believed was Bhima, he crushed it. Having realized his folly; he broke down and sought their forgiveness. When they met an inconsolable Gandhari, she held Krishna squarely responsible for the hostility and the deaths of her children and countless innocents. In a fit of indignation, she cursed him with a painful death and the extermination of Yadavas in the 36ᵗʰyear. Krishna accepted Gandhari's curse.

The Kuru Dynasty was left with only the children of Pandu to succeed Dhritarashtra. He stepped down as king and handed over the crown to Yudhisthir. He wanted to leave Hastinapur, but Yudhisthir persuaded him to stay as a family elder and guide. As peace had returned, the Pandavas and Dhritarashtra together conducted a final ceremony called tarpan for the peace and release of the souls on their onward journey They conducted this ceremony on the banks of the river. According to the Epic, the souls of the men killed in battle came and accepted the offering, visible through a divine vision. All the widows followed their dead husbands except Uttara because she was pregnant.

Commentary

The Anger of Grieving Parents: Gandhari bore witness to the growing dispute between the cousins that led to the war. She knew of the attempt to burn the Pandavas alive in Varnavat, the humiliation of Draupadi, the confiscation of their kingdom and the exile of the Pandavas, and the refusal to return the kingdom at the end of the exile. Duryodhana had rejected Krishna's request for five villages in settlement of the Pandava claim. Gandhari still blamed Krishna for manipulating the events. She knew he could have avoided the war but did not, causing the death of her sons. We cannot fault Gandhari's intelligence, as we know Krishna manipulated the Draupadi Swayamwar so that Drupad could marry his daughter to the Pandavas. Krishna orchestrated the assassination of Jarasandha and master-minded the Rajsuya Yagna. Krishna planned the strategy that enabled the Pandavas to organize an army of seven divisions. It was Krishna who guided the Pandavas at every stage of the battle. He helped the Pandavas overcome their hesitation in killing the most formidable Kauravas. As a heart-broken mother, she viewed the events from an emotional perspective. She blamed and cursed Krishna for the death of all her sons. Dhritarashtra limited his anger to Bhima. She showed the emotional bond that exists between a mother and child.

Kunti and Gandhari, the Mothers Compared: The authors of the Mahabharat have illustrated the relationship between a mother and her children.

Kunti has six children, five of whom she pushes into a battle to recover the status and rights that belonged to her family. She had abandoned her sixth to avoid shame and disrepute. Unlike Kunti, Gandhari is blind to the faults of her children. She refrains from guiding them, has never seen any of them except Duryodhana in the last days of the war, but still suffers the pain of their loss. She blames and curses Krishna.

All Soldiers Killed in Battle go to Heaven: The epic uses one big broad brush and states that after a ritual funeral the souls of all the slain soldiers ascended to heaven. The reason provided is that they fulfilled their Kshatriya Dharma and so deserved Heaven. They introduced the message of Dharma over Life or Dharma always as a follow up to Kunti's message. She told the Pandavas to take up arms to secure the rights even at the cost of their lives.

In Islam, there is a similar concept in the principles of Jihad. This broad brush of death on Holy Duty being a guaranteed ticket to Heaven debunks the concept of Heaven and Hell in afterlife. When a dacoit and rapist joins the army and dies in battle, he will go straight to heaven. This will sound as unacceptable as a dip in the Ganges or elsewhere that can wash off all our sins.

War, Destruction and its Aftermath: The War ended, but the destruction continued. Mahabharat is a narrative on Dharma. It states that whenever Dharma is eclipsed and Adharma rises, an

Avatar shall descend on Earth to return us to the path of righteousness. The Holy War is against evil, temptation, greed and injustice. When there is a battle between good and evil, it provides temporary gains to good. This is because evil shall soon rise again and another Krishna will have to take birth to destroy evil and establish dharma. This continuing cycle of war against evil shows how easy it is for a man to succumb to evil.

War against evil can bring momentary triumph for good. Whereas, fighting and overcoming evil within us can provide gains that are more enduring. Such gains come without causing hurt, grief or death. Wars lead to death and widowhood. It denies ageing parents of their support in old age. We orphan young children. Broken homes take away the much needed emotional and economic security essential for a secure upbringing and childhood. Although the war had ended with the death of Duryodhana, the destruction continued in the form of curses and revenge killings.

Victory in war or any form of conflict does not bring closure. Negative emotions, anger and hurt survive war, as does the desire for revenge. Parikshit, the unborn son of Uttara, survived the deadly attack from the Brahma Astra. Yet years later, he was a victim of revenge killing by Takshaka, the leader of Nagas who survived the destruction of the forest on which the Pandavas built their capital. Gandhari's curse destroyed the entire race of Yadavas. A valiant Krishna died a quiet death.

Conflicts between nations, religious groups, communities, families and individuals plague our society today. These jeopardise peace and harmony. Often these conflicts bring with them hardship and economic doom. The intolerance among diverse doctrines endanger our lives. We live in fear from the next attack. It takes away our right to live the life of our choice.

The Mahabharat is not just about a fight for succession between two groups of cousins. It deals with the struggle between cultures, races, communities, families and individuals. It shows how the lack of mutual respect and accommodation can lead to loss of lives and revenge killings. In the words of Buddha, hatred does not cease with hatred. The brutal terrorist attack on the twin towers in the USA generated a global outrage against the terrorists. The response that followed was a military response. Their aim was the destruction of the infrastructure and organisation of the terrorists. However, the collateral damage destroyed members of innocent families. It brought immense personal pain. These mindless assaults affected innocent lives and brought negativity into the lives of their families. Instead of driving people away from violence, it blinded and angered people into seeking revenge. Today, the world is lot more dangerous than ever before. They intended the characterisation in the Mahabharata to highlight that we must not judge people as good or bad. We cannot say the Kauravas were bad, or the Pandavas were good. Krishna knew Gandhari was right when she accused him of the death of her sons. However, centuries later, we continue to make the same mistake. We continue to profile people based on our perception of good. This flaw in our judgement has led to the isolation of people by religion, colour or race. As a result, we bring negativity into our behaviour and sow the seeds of conflict. We must focus on destroying evil, not people. Gandhari punished Krishna because she thought the war and destruction could have been prevented had Krishna tried, and her sons would have been alive. The narrative that follows at the end of the Epic Battle shows that just no one was a winner. There was a loss, suffering and despair all round and at the individual level there were no winners.

This loss, suffering and despair also affected the Pandavas. They had lost their sons from Draupadi, Bhima's son from Hidimbi and Arjun's son from Subhadra. They had lost their brother Karna from Kunti. Men earn wealth to secure the future of their family. Pandavas defeated the Kauravas but had no descendants to share this success with. They had won the war, but their personal losses made success meaningless. They had won the war using unfair means, the consequences of their Karma were unavoidable. Even Krishna suffered the consequences of his Karma. The only survivor was a son, Babruvahana, born to Arjun and Chitrangada, as he remained in Manipur. He did not take part in the Mahabharat War. Arjun's son Iravan from Ulupi died in the War. The Kuru Dynasty of Shantanu was once again left with no successor. They killed all the grandchildren of Pandu and Dhritarashtra in the battle. The only survivors were the Pandavas, Vidura and Dhritarashtra and his son Yuyutsu. The biggest learning from this war was that in war there are no real winners.

CHAPTER 59

Yudhisthir is Now King

Synopsis: Mahabharata has two versions of Gita. According to Krishna, Bhagwad Gita was meant for wartime. He desired we follow Anugita during peace time. Do sons always connect with their father through their mother?

The war had ended, and they crowned Yudhisthir King. At his urging, Gandhari and Dhritarashtra continued to live with them. Yudhisthir enjoyed the wisdom and advice of both Vidura and Dhritarashtra in ruling and healing the wounds of the citizens. After some time, Krishna returned to Hastinapur. He advised Yudhisthir to conduct an Ashvamedha Yagna. Hastinapur was still recovering from the effects of war. Its treasury was in dire straits. Yudhisthir initially hesitant to deplete his treasury, agreed to perform the Yagna after much persuasion. The ceremony was organized by kings to impose their sovereignty. They set a horse to roam for a year, during which they assign a group of warriors to protect it. When the horse enters another kingdom, the warriors must ensure its free movement. At the end of the year, they guide the horse back to its origin. The convention is that the kingdoms where the horse has roamed acknowledge the supremacy of the king who has released the horse for the Yagna. They would hold a ceremony and sacrifice this horse and declare the king a sovereign.

Bhima and Arjun along with other warriors were assigned to protect the horse. In course of the year, the horse entered Manipur. The ruler of Manipur, Babruvahana happened to be the son of Arjun and Chitrangada. He prevented the entry of the horse. Arjun tried to reason with his son, as there was no enmity between the two states. Babruvahana refused to allow the horse free access to Manipur. Arjun let Bhima and other warriors resolve the matter. The dispute escalated into a battle in which he defeated Bhima and Karna's sole surviving son. Arjun in a fit of rage vowed to kill Babruvahana or immolate himself if defeated. Babruvahana killed Arjun in the battle that followed.

Word of Arjun's death soon reached Chitrangada, and she rushed out to revive her husband. At the urging of his mother Chitrangada, Babruvahana got from Ulupi, another of Arjun's wives, a gem to revive Arjun. He then used the gem to revive Arjun and Karna's son and allowed the horse to continue its journey. At the end of the year, they guided the horse back to Hastinapur and completed the Yagna.

Several years after the war, Krishna and Arjun were together again. Arjun confessed that he could not recall the Bhagwad Gita, which upset and disappointed Krishna, for his lack of attention and being heedless of the divine message. As Arjun kept on pleading for a second chance, Krishna told him that the divine message was no longer relevant under the changed circumstances. He had delivered the Bhagwad Gita in the context of a war, whereas there was peace all round now. He then delivered another divine message called Anugita.

Commentary

Yudhisthir and his Materialism: *After the Rajsuya Yagna, the Pandavas now wanted to perform Ashvamedha Yagna. Vyas later told them they had fulfilled their role and mission and now needed to renounce the world. The Pandavas had lost their grown-up sons in the war. They needed to hold on to power till Parikshit had grown up. However, there was no reason to ignite the possibility of war and bloodshed to prove their supremacy yet again.*

Nearly all the Kshatriyas had died in the great battle, so where was the challenge to their supremacy?

Bhagwat Gita and Anugita: *Krishna refused to repeat the Bhagwad Gita, on the grounds that it was no longer relevant in a peaceful world. By presenting it as a request from Arjun, the authors show their mastery over story telling. We must showcase the teachings of the Bhagwad Gita for its depth, diversity and rich content to the world. Yet no thought or guidance is timeless or worthy of universal application. Our thoughts must evolve with time. The only constant is our need to live a life of Dharma and our goal to achieve Moksha.*

Karna's Son was not Considered for Succession: *Karna as Kunti's son was a half brother of the Pandavas. His son had survived the war at Kurukshetra but was not considered for succession by the Pandavas. At one stage, Krishna and Kunti had offered Karna the right to be future King. Karna's son had survived the war but was* not even in the reckoning. *This clarifies the patriarchal rules of succession followed by the Aryans.*

The Father and Son Relationship—was it Hatred vs. Ego:
There is another dimension to the relationship between a parent and a child. Kunti compromised her son Karna for a higher goal. However, Arjun was ready to lose his son to ensure he remained unbeatable. As a joint family, every Pandava had a parental responsibility to every child born to any Pandava.

CHAPTER 60

Dhritarashtra Leaves Hastinapur

Synopsis: Legacies are always so welcome, we all like an inheritance, but in life minuses will always come with the pluses. We all must give back to our parents, better late than never.

Dhritarashtra and Gandhari continued to live with the Pandavas. Draupadi dutifully served both Kunti and Gandhari as the daughter-in-law of the house. Yudhisthir was grateful to Dhritarashtra and Vidura for their advice. However, Bhima was often rude and looked for ways to insult and humiliate Dhritarashtra. After about fifteen years, an old, weakened and emotionally disturbed Dhritarashtra sought to renounce the world. Despite initial hesitation, Yudhishthir accepted Dhritarashtra's desire to renounce the world.

Kunti also expressed her desire to join the family elders and spend her last years serving them. It shocked Yudhisthir when he heard his mother's request. Yudhisthir pleaded with his mother to stay back, he told her it was now time for her to enjoy the privileges and prestige of a queen mother. Kunti told her children that she was born a princess, had married a king and enjoyed the status of a queen. She was glad that her children had at her urging won back the Kingdom. This victory was for them to enjoy, she had no interest in their wealth or in enjoying the status of a queen mother. In her mind there was no enmity between her and the elder brother of her husband and his wife. She wanted her sons not to stand in the way of fulfilling her Dharma. Her Dharma was to look after her parent like relatives.

Dhritarashtra along with Gandhari, Vidura, Sanjay and Kunti left for *sanyas*. The senior Kurus spent their time in the forest engaged in penance and meditation. Yudhisthir also set up a secret camp in the forest for the service of the elders. He wanted his staff to ensure that they met the needs of the Kuru elders, and they encountered no difficulty in the forest. The Pandavas would also often visit them. Kunti spent her time serving the elder Kurus. In the meantime, Vidura isolated himself and engaged in deep penance and fasting. On one visit, Dhritarashtra informed Yudhisthir to stop all future visits. It concerned him that these visits were a distraction. He wanted to renounce all material and emotional attachments. Yudhisthir realised his elders wanted to enter the final stages of the Ashram Dharma. He accepted their request with deep sorrow. As it was their last meeting, he went out looking for Vidura to pay his final respects. He found a naked Vidura in a disheveled, under-nourished and meditative stance. After much persuasion, Vidura recognized him and embraced him and breathed his last. Some days later, a fire engulfed the forest. Dhritarashtra, Gandhari and Kunti realised that their time to renounce the world had come. As a final act, the three Kuru elders walked hand in hand into the fire.

Commentary

When the Time is Up: Dhritarashtra continued to live with the Pandavas and acted as Yudhishthir's advisor, but it helped him realize his time was up. From a business management perspective, a CEO must hand over charge and move on. When they still continue as advisors or chairman emeritus, the business fails to move on. It is not unusual for the former CEO to manipulate the events for "more of the same thing" or "old wine in a new bottle." In most instances, this hurts the business and affects the performance of the new CEO. Applying the analogy of flying a kite, they invest the new CEO with the responsibility of flying and manoeuvering the kite in a sky filled with other kites, jostling to achieve supremacy. If the former CEO stands behind his successor and insists on controlling the bobbin that releases the abrasive string attached to the kite, it can handicap the new CEO. All the elders leaving together symbolize a total transition.

The same applies to elders who insist on controlling the family. More so when the next generation may be old and have children of their own. It would be very frustrating to have all the responsibility and no authority. Elders must respect the rules of transition and allow the next generation the right to run their affairs. There is a difference between an advice and a direction. The former may or not be heeded, whereas the latter is a command.

Kunti's Perspective: From Kunti's perspective, she had achieved her life's goal, she wanted to fight for restoration of her husband's right in favour of her sons. She showed that we must focus on our differences but not let our differences hurt our relationships.

Many amongst us are like Kunti. We often postpone our obligations to serve our parents or elders in pursuit of our life goals. Mahabharata, through Kunti, provides us with a subtle reminder to fulfil this obligation before it is too late. We must recognise and provide this when it is needed the most. In the forest, a blind and aged Dhritarashtra and Gandhari would suffer unknown hardships without their customary support. They also needed emotional support. Kunti could provide this to them. The subtle message is that with age, our parents need support and respect.

Dhritarashtra Ends Further Visit by Yudhisthir: *It is hard to give up our attachments. We may feel tempted to re-engage. It is like giving up smoking; we need to stop smoking altogether; we have to suffer the pain from the withdrawal of the chemical addiction. Dhritarashtra wanted to end all future meetings to have a complete severance of ties. Dhritarashtra ensured that both sides could transition to their respective next stages, this was a release of mutual obligations. Our Dharma suggests that we should begin a process of detachment from all material things and our emotional attachments in the final stages of our life.*

From a management perspective, this represents the handover phase. A former CEO may be available to his successor, but, at some point, this engagement must end. It is irrelevant who calls for such disengagement. It must be mutual and complete.

Yudhisthir and Vidura, the Death Embrace: *There is great significance in the symbolic death embrace. This is a symbolic transfer of the responsibility of the Kula and its Parampara. It requires the son to accept this transfer. He accepts his father's material and spiritual wealth and is enriched. He not only inherits the material wealth but also the traditions, responsibilities, name and the social obligations that come with it.*

There is also a larger message. All human beings will leave behind a legacy which in some combination will be a burden, a responsibility, an obligation or wealth. The body may die, but the legacy of our actions will burden and/or benefit the next generation.

CHAPTER 61

The Curse of Gandhari Takes Effect

Synopsis: No mortal can avoid the consequences of their action, not even Krishna. Recognize your peak and learn to walk into the sunset.

All was going well for the 35 years after the war. The Yadavas at Dwarka flourished as never before. They spent more time drinking indiscriminately or indulging in debauchery and adultery, often showing scant regard for elders and teachers. The growing Adharma in the community worried Krishna, who feared it would endanger their future. They did not heed his pleas to mend their ways. The community gradually split up into groups, thanks to internal rifts. Krishna realised the curse of Gandhari was now taking effect.

One day, a fight broke out over some dispute between the rival camps, which triggered mass killings. A worried Krishna requested Arjun's help to save the old and the women. Arjun arrived with his army only to learn that

Krishna had been killed by an arrow. As Arjuna was leaving with the survivors for Hastinapur, a storm struck Dwarka, sinking it. Recent excavations confirm that the submerged city could be ancient Dwarka.

On the way back, bandits attacked Arjuna's entourage, and abducted some Yadava womenfolk. It distressed Arjun that he could not protect people who depended on him for safety and security. This was his second defeat. He sought the advice of Ved Vyas, who told them to take sanyas, having served their purpose.

Commentary

Krishna's Curse and Destruction of the Yadavas: The Yadavas had fled from Mathura to Dwarka to avoid the attacks by Jarasandha. After the death of Jarasandha, Krishna should have focussed on governing and guiding the Yadavas. Instead, he took the centre-stage in a feud between the Kuru cousins over the right of succession. The Bhagwad Gita clarifies his role in the fight. While how he approached the situation he faced is justified, in hindsight, how we wish that the war was avoided. Buddha, another Vishnu Avatar, taught us the need for compassion for all living beings. He had famously said: "Hatred does not cease by Hatred." No mortal being can avoid the consequences of his actions. We could credit Krishna in his human avatar for identifying our obligation of duty in exceptional circumstances. Krishna understood and applied the principles of Apad-Dharma. His actions focussed on a higher cause and outcome, yet at an individual level they were often wrong. He had to suffer the consequences. The curse and ultimate death of Krishna sets at rest this point.

Arjun's Failure: Our life is like a graph that begins from a low point and reaches its peak, and then begins to go down, which is final and certain, as exemplified by the life of Jarasandha. Both Bhima and Arjun faced failure once past their prime. This is a message for all of us. After reaching the peak, we must be prepared to walk into the sunset.

The best analogy would be of an aircraft. Upon take off, our goal is to gain the maximum permissible height. When the fuel reaches a critical level, we must guide the aircraft safely to touchdown. Any attempt to overreach will lead to a crash. There is an important lesson for all of us. We must know our limits and try to land our aircraft before the fuel runs out. We must also avoid trying to breach the limits of height which can send us crashing. From the perspective of Ashram Dharma, the equivalent would be the transition through the various phases. Even the Pandavas needed to be advised of the need to transition to the next phase showing how difficult it is for us to realise that our time is up.

How could the Culture of the Yadavas Degenerate? *The wisdom and presence of Krishna and Balarama could not prevent the deterioration of culture of the Yadava clan. Arjuna, a direct recipient of Krishna's celestial message did not engage in a deathly duel with Bhishma, Dronacharya or any of his Kaurava cousins. Dhritarashtra also could have called for a cessation of battle, but did nothing. An advisor can only advise, but he cannot enforce. Krishna was a Kshatriya with the character of a Brahmin. He had knowledge, he could guide and advise, but the responsibility of enforcement of Dharma rested with the King. Krishna was not a leader of men. These people would often hesitate, he could persuade but not direct. This was the subtle difference between him and Duryodhana. Duryodhana asked Karna to use his best weapon and Karna* *immediately did so, even though he wanted to use it on Arjun. Krishna used persuasion on Arjun but could not compel him against his will.*

The Mahabharata and the many learned thinkers who added to it ensured that we understood the divinity of Krishna. They wanted us to understand a very important difference; the power of conviction. Krishna allowed each individual to decide and follow the path of their choice. This is a very significant message for parents, teachers, lawmakers and society. We must provide guidance, but every individual must be free to choose his path. Krishna in his mortal avatar allowed Arjun to exercise his choice. Yet in our times we see preachers of many faiths imposing their views, often demanding unquestioned compliance.

However, society has rules to checkmate negative choices to avoid the risk of annihilation. The destruction of the Yadavas highlights this need for enforcement. Dhritarashtra had the best of advisors, yet the Kauravas destroyed themselves. The advisors to the Yadavas were even better, yet they destroyed themselves. Whilst conviction is important, execution is the key and society must counteract negative choice to avoid destruction. Several years after the war, Arjun requested Krishna to repeat the Bhagwad Gita, but Krishna narrated to him Anugita. He explained to him that his earlier message was no longer relevant. People were now living in peace and therefore Anugita is appropriate.

CHAPTER 62

Parikshit is the New King of Hastinapur

Synopsis: Legacy represents both assets and liabilities.

The Pandavas renounced the world, after crowning Parikshit as the next King of Hastinapur and appointing Yuyutsu as his advisor. They also appointed Vajra, Krishna's great grandson, as the king of Indraprastha, but offered no formal position to Karna's son. As a responsible ruler, Parikshit brought peace and prosperity, but only to be killed a few years later by Takshaka, a descendent of the family Arjun had slaughtered. Thus ended the story with an act of revenge; a dispute between a right and an entitlement, punctuated with mindless violence and brutal deaths. Every participant had his own agenda, yet, there were no winners.

Commentary

History had repeated itself. They made the Dasi putra of Dhritarashtra, Yuyutsu an advisor. Was Vajra's appointment as

*king an acknowledgement of Krishna's contribution to the victory of
the Pandavas? How and why would the Pandavas hand over a
family legacy to Krishna's family? Why was Karna's surviving son
not crowned despite being the eldest in line? What should we make
of the offers made by Krishna and Kunti to Karna? Was that offer
made to tempt Karna? It is understandable that they applied the
rules of succession based on patriarchy, but how did Vajra qualify?
The enmity between Takshaka and the Pandavas continued. The next
generation completed the unfinished business of revenge. Our
legacies cover both assets and liabilities.*

*Mahabharat delivered its final lesson on Karma. We shall realize
our Heaven and Hell in this life. We will also realize the outcome
from our Karma in this world. If not by us, they will transition to
our survivors as a legacy.*

CHAPTER 63

The Pandavas' Last Journey

Synopsis: It is not easy to give up your emotional attachments and material comforts. The process of disengagement is revealed.

After crowning Parikshit and appointing Yuyutsu as his counsel, Pandavas left Hastinapur for the Himalayas as their final destination. Firstly, the Pandavas headed to the South and reached the sea. Agni appeared and asked Arjun to hand over his bow. He informed Arjun that the bow had served its purpose and he would no longer need it. After handing over the bow, the Pandavas proceeded south-west. They reached the coast where Dwarka was situated. There they saw it submerged in the sea. Thereafter, the Pandavas headed to the Himalayas and began their ascent towards Heaven. On their way, a dog befriended them and followed them on their journey.

An exhausted Draupadi was the first to succumb to her death. Bhima turned to Yudhisthir and asked him why was Draupadi not able to complete her journey. Yudhisthir told Bhima that she suffered from the vice of partiality. He said she was partial towards Arjun. The next among the

Pandavas to fall was Sahadev, and his failing was his immense pride in his wisdom and foresight. Soon thereafter, Nakul fell because he suffered from a pride that he was the handsomest of men. The Pandavas continued their journey and Arjun fell. Once again Yudhisthir explained to Bhima that Arjun's failing was his pride, that he was the world's best archer. Now Yudhisthir, Bhima and the dog continued their journey. Along the way, Bhima fell out of exhaustion. Aware that he could not continue his journey he asked Yudhisthir why he had fallen? Yudhisthir told Bhima he suffered from a vice of gluttony; he ate without discretion, ignoring the needs of others present.

A lone Yudhisthir and the dog now continued. On their journey to heaven, Indra met them in his chariot. Indra invited him to ride on his chariot to heaven but refused to allow the dog to join them. Yudhisthir refused to leave the dog, at which point the dog transformed itself into its celestial self. It was God Dharmaraj (or Yama).

When Yudhisthir reached heaven, he noticed all the people who had sinned in their lives, like Duryodhana and his other Kaurava cousins were enjoying the bliss of Heaven. He enquired about his brothers, wife and other people who he believed had lived a life of Dharma and deserved heaven. They then led Yudhisthir to Hell, where he found these people suffering. A shocked and upset Yudhisthir wanted to join these people in their suffering in Hell. It upset him that Duryodhana was enjoying bliss in Heaven, whereas his brothers were suffering.

Sage Narada appeared before Yudhisthir. He advised him that upon death, we must leave behind all our likes, dislikes, friendships, enmity, etc. Upon death we must surrender all our attachments. It was appropriate for

Duryodhana and others to be in heaven because they had died in battle while discharging their dharma.

Yudhishthir's insistence on staying with his brothers and wife pleased the Gods, and they forthwith removed the illusion of Hell. Yudhisthir could then see his brothers, his wife and many virtuous people he knew on earth all enjoying the bliss of heaven.

Thus ended the Mahabharata.

Commentary

Krishna's Message: Krishna described death as part of a cycle for the soul when it discards one body and clothes itself in another. In between this transition it enjoys the bliss of Heaven and the sufferings of Hell. This cycle of re-birth continues until the soul achieves moksha, and then it returns and becomes once again a part of the Param Atma.

On earth, the soul wears a body until it leaves behind the body upon death. We cannot visit heaven or hell in the human form. This must have been the intended message.

The Order of the End—Different Perspectives: It is interesting to follow the order in which the Pandavas and Draupadi die. In Indic thought, after marriage the spirit of the husband and wife unite. We can therefore take this union to understand the sequence of the end.

In our life, the first to fall is our emotional attachment. We experience our deepest, strongest and longest emotional union in our marriage. In our journey to the end this is the first union to break, and it breaks because one amongst the two will first die. It also says when we sever our emotional commitment to life, our will to live is the most compromised.

Amongst the Pandavas, the first to die is Sahadev. This is the death of our foresight, our perspective and our ability to see the future. We often see many elderly people completely oblivious of the consequences of their deeds, taking undue risks, challenging themselves to do things which can endanger their life. The withdrawal symptom of life is now at a new level. It might appear that we are challenging death every day, as if eager to die. We then see the death of Nakul the handsome one, as our emotional engagement and attachments in our life wanes. We lose interest in our personal wellbeing, looks, and engagement at a social level. Dying from within, we appear eager to embrace death and thus we lose our sense of purpose and direction and our Arjun dies. This now reflects on our body and its strength gives away. Bhima is our sense of physical wellbeing. When we impact it, we are about to die. When our brain or Yudhisthir's finds no support from our emotional and physical side; it stops working and we die.

The authors have provided guidance on why human life or our will to live represented by Bhima depends on our emotional wellbeing. Draupadi is the symbol of relationship, emotional engagement and wellbeing. Yes, so often we see people recovering from a challenging sickness or accident, and we credit this recovery to their will to live. When Draupadi passes away, Bhima loses his will to live.

The Pandavas and the Order of Death—a Perspective: *The authors of the Epic provide us with another perspective and a message. In our life, all the five attributes are important, but only Dharma can lead us to Moksha. By allowing Yudhisthir to reach heaven, the authors wanted us to understand that commitment to Dharma stands taller than Bhima's determination or Arjun's focus. Also, when we take all the five attributes together, our moksha or the release of our soul from the cycle of deaths and re-births is possible if we focus and devote ourselves to Dharma. We can only achieve moksha when we follow Dharma.*

Symbolism from their Last Journey: *When a person dies, death forces him to leave behind his material and emotional attachments. Ashram Dharma recognises and prepares us for an orderly end. In Hindu Thought, they call this 'tyag' or surrender of our 'moh maya' i.e. our desires and attachment before we meet our end.*

The handing over of the bow is the surrender of our materialistic side. The last journey to Dwarka was the surrender of emotional attachments. When the Pandavas reach Dwarka, they discover that it lies submerged in the sea, which implies ending emotional and material attachments. In life, we hoard our assets viz. cash, jewellery, houses, investments etc. because it secures our well being. However, a person on his deathbed will no longer have an attachment to the wealth he knows he cannot spend before he dies. The surrender of the bow was the surrender of means for their life. They then headed to Dwarka and they knew it was submerged. This journey was a pilgrimage to the shrine of Krishna. He had provided them with the methods. They owed all they got to Krishna and to his guidance. After having given up their means, they paid homage to the provider of the methods in their life and finally with motivation they commenced their last journey and surrendered their life. Shakti was the last to leave them. The circle of life was completed. Shakti gives us birth and will be with us till the last.

CHAPTER 64

Rewards and Punishment versus Heaven and Hell

Synopsis: Did Mahabharata bust the myth of Heaven and Hell? Religions use fear for immediate results, but conviction was the intended but inconvenient path.

Yudhisthir reached heaven, where he beheld Duryodhana amongst others in astonishment. The subsequent narrative spells out the reasons. One message is for human beings who need the crutch of heaven or hell to stay on the narrow path of Dharma and another for those who need no crutch and understand that we reap as we sow in this life alone and not in afterlife. They equate Yudhisthir with Dharma. The symbolism here is that only through a life led under Dharma can one realise heaven or moksha.

Yudhisthir's meeting Duryodhana in Heaven is symbolic and explores the idea of Heaven and Hell in our afterlife. The battle of Kurukshetra was not a battle of right versus wrong or good versus bad. It was a battle between two sides, where each believed theirs was the righteous path. Each stood by their principles even at the risk of their lives, their family ties and happiness. Each side paid a price of misery whether in victory or defeat or in death or in life thereafter.

In the Bhagwad Gita, Krishna reveals to Arjun that death is only of the body because the soul lives on. When the soul achieves enlightenment, it achieves a higher state and then it unifies with the Supreme Soul or the Param-Atma.

The Epic associates the identity of a dead Yudhisthir and Duryodhana with their body and not with their souls. This linking of their souls with their discarded bodies in Heaven or Hell should help us realise that all is here and now. Generations of thinkers have talked about how death ends all discrimination. How our mortal remains revert to dust. They often describe our journey of life as one 'from dust to dust'.

When Yudhisthir saw Duryodhana in Heaven, he cried foul. They told him in death we leave behind all our passions, possessions and attachments. We should accept it is the death of all our desires, aspirations, emotions, attachments, possessions and associations. We are all reduced to a state of total detachment, death is a state of Nothingness.

We can only experience our Heaven and Hell in our mortal state and not in our afterlife because it is a state of nothingness. This is a message for those of us who live our life each day, disregarding the consequences of punishment as it awaits us only in our afterlife.

The concept of Heaven or Hell is a common thread running through every school of religious thought. They intend this message to aid and persuade us to follow a righteous path in our daily life. The fear of horrible suffering and punishments acts as a deterrent against evil. The bliss of Heaven, howsoever described, is an incentive to encourage righteous behaviour.

Rules were often set by religious leaders as in the Abrahamic Schools to our present day laws as established in our Civil and Criminal Codes. The principles set out in the Practice of Dharma are based on 'Do', whereas subsequent rules are based on 'do not do.' The application and enforcement of Civil Codes, Rights and Criminal Codes stand independent of the concepts of Sin, God, Heaven and Hell, Religious Diktats, etc.

Mahabharat deals with Heaven and Hell. However, it provides countless examples of how humans face the outcome of their actions in their current lives. This offers to the more sophisticated amongst us, an alternative view without debunking Heaven and Hell as being that place where the soul ends up in their afterlife.

A rich man may take millions from his bankers using the cover of his business. He siphons off all the money defrauding his workers, bankers and creditors and continues to live in ultra luxury. To the common man, a fraudster is rewarded, but unbeknown to the outsider, the rich man may be ill or his actions might affect the lives and prospects of his children or his siblings may reject him or society may ostracise him. However, to a man struggling to feed his family, he may see the fraudster as enjoying the choicest of foods, it may be another matter that he may be suffering from stomach cancer and has no appetite.

People can evidently see our success, our happiness unlike our pain which is personal. This is the message the

Epic provides when Yudhisthir could see Duryodhana enjoying in Heaven, but failed to recall the Hell he had already suffered.

Mahabharat provides countless examples, amongst which are

Bhishma's Hell on Earth: *Bhishma abducted three princesses Amba, Ambika and Ambalika to marry them to his brother. Amba's lover abandoned her, and when Bhishma refused to marry her, she committed suicide. They depict Amba as Shikhandi in her next life, and she punishes Bhishma by injuring him in battle. An injured Bhishma suffers and watches how the very Crown he had sworn to protect with his life was defeated. Thus designed in the characterisation and life story of Bhishma is an example of how he was punished with failure for his misdeeds during his lifetime itself.*

Dronacharya's Hell on Earth: *After receiving guru dakshina, his role as tutor of the Kuru Princes had ended. Yet he was compelled out of loyalty to side with the Kauravas in the war. He was a broken man who died knowing he had lost his son in battle. A teacher who never practised what he preached. He could have enjoyed a life of plenty, but preferred subservience as a courtier. They killed a heart broken Dronacharya so that his soul travelled straight to heaven, however; he suffered his hell on earth itself.*

Dhritarashtra's Weakness and his Punishment: *Dhritarashtra obsessed with keeping iron control over the Kingdom, denied the Pandavas their right. Despite his various orchestrations, defeat in war forced him to yield power to the Pandavas and live a life of humiliation at the palace under their rule. Besides all this, his hell was the 'loss of all his sons.' For a Kshatriya, a life after defeat is most dishonourable because they prefer an honourable death in battle. His hell was the loss of his crown, his sons and their children.*

Queen Gandhari's Hell on Earth: *In her blindfold, she rejected her marriage, and her Dharma as a queen, as a mother and as a wife. It is hell for even the one who is wronged and forced to marry against her wishes? Authors of the Mahabharat would ascribe her marriage with Dhritarashtra to her Karma, but that gives her no licence to ignore Dharma. She grieves for her children; she takes off her blindfold hoping she can save Duryodhana's life; she sacrifices the benefit of her lifelong penance, but in vain. Gandhari suffers the agony of seeing her daughter as a widow. If this is not Hell, what is?*

Queen Kunti's Hell on Earth: *For a mother to see her children facing one another in battle and being selective about them, only to witness their pre-mature death is hell personified. She suffered the humiliation of seeing her husband prefer Madri to her. Throughout her life, she faced hardships with no support from her parent's house whilst she fought for the rights of her children. Kunti abandoned Karna at birth. However, when she acknowledged this relationship, her own son cursed her. Kunti could not avoid or hide her indiscretion.*

The authors here also deal with how lies or untruth will always be discovered and that the guilty will always suffer in silence. Sooner or later, the truth will surface.

The Suffering of Duryodhana: *He witnessed the death of his brothers, his children, his friends, lost his wealth and kingdom and in fact saw the end of the Kuru Dynasty itself when Ashwatthama displayed the dismembered heads of Pandavas' children. Duryodhana paid the price for his actions in his lifetime itself.*

The Suffering of Yudhisthir: *He lost his children, although he won the war and got the right to rule, he discovered that this right was never his. He set up the murder of his teacher by lying, allowing*

Dhrishtadyumna to kill an unarmed Dronacharya, who in turn was killed by Ashwatthama in his sleep.

Drupad's Hell on Earth: *He brought death and sorrow for his children in his desire to avenge his humiliation. As a man, he suffered and met his death on the battlefield, fighting not for a cause but for revenge. Life is full of stories of how parents sacrifice their life for the welfare of their children, yet, Drupad is one who wrecked the lives of his children to avenge his humiliation.*

Draupadi's Hell on Earth: *Laughing at and humiliating Duryodhana, urging Krishna to not allow her husbands to give up on avenging her humiliation, not tying her hair until she could bathe it in Dushashan's blood are instances of her Adharma. She got her revenge but lost all her children; she pined for Arjun's affection but was forced to accept that Arjun preferred Subhadra. Staked over a game of dice, she was humiliated and abused, whilst her husbands watched passively instead of coming to her rescue. Such was her hell.*

Krishna's Hell on Earth: *Krishna's profile and character in the Mahabharat is distinct from his Divine Profile as a Vishnu Avatar. In the Mahabharat, he uses deception and cunning to avenge his humiliation. He is cursed by Gandhari and dies seeing the destruction of his clan and Dwarka. He is unable, despite his immense knowledge and power of persuasion, to convince members of his own tribe or to convince his dearest friend Arjun. Krishna won the Kurukshetra war for the Pandavas, yet he died as a failed leader.*

CHAPTER 65

The Concept of Second Chance

Synopsis: Life gives us a second chance we must recognise and seize it.

The Mahabharat is full of examples of a second chance, we all deserve and get a second chance; this is a principle of human justice and fairness.

King Shantanu and his Second Chance: Ganga, his first wife, left him for breaking his oath to her. In his subsequent marriage, he ensures he keeps his promise despite endangering the succession of his dynasty.

Satyawati and Her Second Chance to Retract a Wrong: It is because of her that Bhishma was compelled to take a vow of celibacy that also jeopardised the Kuru Dynasty. She offered to release Bhishma from his vows, but he refused.

Bhishma and his Second Chance: His queen mother wanted to release him from the vow of celibacy, and his mindless action of abduction resulted in his obligation to marry Amba. There would have been no Mahabharat, the violence and death that followed.

Dhritarashtra and his Second Chance: *Denied the right to the crown despite being first in line, he wore the crown after Pandu's abdication. He, as the father to both his sons and the sons of a deceased Pandu, needed to appoint the ablest of them all to be his successor. Often wealth is hoarded to secure the lives of future generations, despite such attempts being unsuccessful or counter productive.*

Karna and his Second Chance: *Kunti and Krishna told Karna why he should change sides prior to the war. He acted on his perspective of Dharma. Had Karna changed sides, war would have been averted and, Duryodhana and Karna may have come to a settlement. They would have avoided death and destruction. The story would have ended.*

It is unfair to speculate that Karna would have handed over his kingdom to Duryodhana as an act of charity or obligation. As one well versed in the Rules of Dharma, he would have known Raj Dharma was a bigger obligation than his Swadharma or his Dharma as a friend. Karna was proficient in matters of Dharma could have sided with the Pandavas. He chose a prior obligation.

Pandavas and their Second Chance: *They lost all they owned in a Game of Dice, when asked to return for another game, they could have refused, but did not. One amongst them was appointed crown prince but was removed, they got a Kingdom through a division, but wanted more.*

Kunti and her Second Chance: *She abandoned Karna, then destiny got them together at an event, she could have righted a wrong,* *acknowledged that Karna was her son, but she did not. She suffered the trauma of seeing her sons battling one another.*

Draupadi and her Second Chance: *In Indraprastha, Draupadi had insulted both Duryodhana and Dhritarashtra. As her treatment at the Game of Dice was unbecoming of the Kauravas, Dhritarashtra sought her forgiveness and gave her three boons in consideration. When the Pandavas were recalled for another round of Dice, she did not stop her husbands from repeating their folly.*

Yudhisthir and his Second Chance: *They made Yudhisthir crown prince and then gave him a kingdom carved out of Hastinapur. But, he gambled the second time and lost everything.*

Krishna and his Second Chance: *As Ranchhod, it sullied his reputation, forcing him to move with his tribe to distant Dwarka. This happened when he intervened and killed Kansa. Life gave him a second chance on relocation to Dwarka to look after and guide his tribe to prosperity. Instead, he meddled in the feud between the two factions of Kurus. Dwarka sank, his tribe faced extinction and he died a lonely death.*

Dronacharya and his Second Chance: *Impoverished and unable to meet his responsibilities as a grihastha, he found employment as a royal tutor. He could have retired in peace, but instead he hung on to his job and suffered the consequences.*

Gandhari and her Second Chance: *Her blindfold was symbolic of her rejection of her marriage, but when she had children, she could have had taken it off and mothered her children. Life gave her an opportunity, but she squandered it. When she took off her blindfold, it was too late.*

CHAPTER 66

Mahabharata—Study of Relationships

Father and Children: The Epic places father and son skillfully at different stages and circumstances. This placement helps us to appreciate the finer nuances of their relationship. Babruvahana, Ghatotkacha and Shantanu grew up under the sole care of their mothers.

Bhishma grew up under the sole care of his mother. His parents had separated. After completion of his education, his mother handed over his custody to his father. Pleased with his education and upbringing, he immediately made him crown prince. In a single parent environment, he missed the bonding and joy of a united family. He did not experience the power of the shared dreams of his parent for building a future for themselves and their children. He then lived a celibate life, never having the opportunity to experience the sensitivity of bonding in a marriage and family. Shantanu his father also had no experience as one. He wanted a son as his successor; he had got one. But when another woman attracted him, he forgot his obligations as a father. Neither father nor son shared a relationship. When

Arjun called him father as a child, he corrected him. It is not about the real relationship he shared with Arjun, but about an emotion he did not grasp or experience. An innocent Arjun saw in him a father, but an inexperienced Bhishma did not want to live up to the expectation of the innocent Arjun.

Often parents expect that their children will treat them well because they brought them up well. Yet the same parents might not be conducting themselves well with their own parents. These parents of impressionable children miss an important perspective. How as parents we treat our children will condition them for parenting. They will pick those aspects of our behaviour which they like and will try to change those aspects they dislike. Children judge our behaviour towards them but learn and replicate our behaviour towards others.

Ghatotkacha's father left him as soon as he was born. The authors demonized his life by suggesting he grew into adulthood as soon as he was born. He then re-appears in the Epic to fight for the Pandavas. Hidimbi, his mother, continued to love his father Bhima. This emotional connection was reflected in his upbringing. Ghatotkacha respected and admired his father. When Bhima wanted him to join the family fight, he did so whole-heartedly. He fought and died in battle. Ghatotkacha had never experienced family bonding, yet he sensed the positivity of the emotional attachment between his parents.

A son was born to Arjun and Chitrangada, whom they named Babruvahana. It happened to be a loveless marriage. Babruvahana grew up sensing this deep divide. He did not join the war at Kurukshetra. Despite being the only surviving son of a Pandava; they did not consider him for succession. When the horse crossed into Manipur, Babruvahana prevented its entry.

We then have the examples of Dhritarashtra, Pandu and Vidura born out of Niyoga, who grew up in a palace without the influence of a father. These princes grew up under the influence of their respective mothers. Pandu died young, Vidura lived a life as a Suta, and Dhritarashtra lacked the guidance and influence of a father. When Arjun was young he once called Bhishma 'father,' who insisted that 'he was not his father but his grandfather.' The message here is that none can take the place of a father because only a father will teach you the Parampara of his Family. Bhishma lacked this education; otherwise he would not have pledged away his right to the crown. They crowned his father king because of his competence and not because he was first in line or because he was the favoured one. It was this very parampara that Dhritarashtra lacked and consequently caused a war.

Then, we have fathers like Dhritarashtra and Dronacharya, they lived their missed childhood and lives through their sons. Blinded by their egos or ambitions, they wanted their sons to be victorious at any cost. A father like Dronacharya can go to any extent to provide for his children, even if it implies a lifetime of bondage. Often fathers want to live their lives through their sons. Then there are fathers like Drupad who manipulate their children to fulfil their agenda. These children live life as robots. A legacy is like a river, we must add more to it to be perennial and not dry up. They killed Drupad and all his sons in battle. His daughter Draupadi, born a princess, lives a pitiable life in exile. They killed her children in the war; she suffered from a personal humiliation and much more. Ashwatthama though crowned king and an accomplished archer has to beg for the opportunity to lead the Kauravas and then destroys the reputation of his illustrious family. Duryodhana pursues the legacy he believes was his, but ends up not only losing whatever he got through a family division, he also lost the war and all members of his father's branch of the Kuru Family.

Then there is the father and son relationship between Abhimanyu and Arjun. Abhimanyu grew up in the home of his maternal grandparents as his father spent most of his years in exile. Arjun had fathered sons from each of his four wives yet, Abhimanyu was his dear one. Fathers who lost their sons in battle would have grieved in private for their son as would have befitted a Kshatriya. However, Arjun's attachment to his son went deeper. He killed Jayadratha, his relative, only because he held him responsible for his son's death. He would not have killed Karna had Krishna not reminded him that he had a hand in Abhimanyu's death. The father in Arjun grieves for Abhimanyu.

The Epic does not just depict the relationship between a father and son as manipulative or selfish. Dronacharya depicts the emotional side where the father is so grief stricken that he gives up his life. Dhritarashtra forever yearns that his sons can regain and keep the legacy denied to him. There is Satyawati's father, who wants to ensure the best for his daughter. He compels Bhishma to forego the position of crown prince and remain a life-long celibate. There is also Shantanu who ends his marriage to save his son's life and then accepts his son's sacrifice of his future rights and celibacy so he can wed a woman of his choice.

Kunti's father too gave her away to his childless friend, and begets a child out of wedlock. They abandoned this child to protect her integrity. King Drupad manipulates his daughter to marry the Pandavas, so he can exact revenge for his humiliation by the Kurus.

Mother and Children: A mother has a powerful bearing on the personality and emotional state of her child. Their emotional bond is also particularly strong, whether born of her or nurtured by her. In the Mahabharata, the mother has been invested with the responsibility of a child's upbringing. Even though Karna and Kunti shared a connect, he could not ditch Duryodhana out of a sense of duty and obligation. Nor did he disappoint his biological mother because of their divine connect.

Kunti and Radha in the Mahabharat brought up children not born of them as their own, unlike Dhritarashtra. Although he considers both the Pandavas and Kauravas as his children, he cannot overlook the reality of Kauravas being his direct offsprings. Karna loves his foster mother. We also know him as Radheya, meaning the son of Radha. Kunti was often harsh with her own sons, but loved Madri's sons. There is no evidence she ever discriminated between her and Madri's sons.

Motherhood is not only about an emotional bond, but also comes with a divine connect that binds both the mother and child, according to the authors of the Epic. Kunti gives Karna away at birth, but later when she discovers him again, she continues to pine for him. They could not agree to make their relationship public but still maintain a bond.

Karna her elder son, promises not to kill any of her sons other than Arjuna. Arjuna kills Karna and her secret could have been sealed forever. But, despite all the humiliation, she owns up Karna and wanted the world to know and remember that he was her son.

In the Epic, a father may have disowned or denied his son. No mother has ever done so. Gandhari takes off her blindfold to protect and save the life of her son Duryodhana. Kunti could have kept her secret, but she could not let her son die as a Suta.

The intuitive link between mother and child is such that her children can pick up her emotional state. When the mother feels challenged or unhappy in a marital relationship, the children grow up resenting their father. Babruvahana and Ghatotkacha reflect the two sides of this argument. Duryodhana or any of his brothers do not share a bond with either parent. They grew up as virtual orphans with no real care or support from either parent. Their parents were blind and unable to provide direction. The mother has a dominant role in developing the emotional side of the child. She grooms them and gives them their Sanskar. These are several small yet significant lessons that a child learns as he grows up. Her influence in every aspect of their life, their response, their perspective, their character is all influenced by the mother. She devotes her time in preparing her child to face the world. Several lessons that a child picks up from its infancy are sanskar; the knowledge imparted by parents apart from education. We see Kunti as a constant guide to her children whereas Gandhari remains aloof. Kunti chides her grown-up sons for being passive about their rights. She insists that it is more honorable to die fighting for their rights than to live on charity. Before the war, when Duryodhana seeks Gandhari's blessing, she states: "May victory be on the side of Dharma," which only bears out that she never offered guidance to her children.

The Mother is a protector and she will go to any extent to the save her children. Gandhari gives up her lifelong blindfold to provide Duryodhana with a celestial armour that would protect him from Bhima's attack. Even Ganga and Satyawati were good mothers who ensured that they fulfilled their duty as they should. Whilst acknowledging these positives, the Epic proves once again that nobody is always right, and none is perfect. Ganga drowns her children at birth and Kunti abandons her child at birth.

Sibling Relationship: Siblings respected hierarchy, Duryodhana held sway over all his brothers. They never questioned his authority. The Pandava siblings also never challenged Yudhisthir's decisions. It was not as if they obeyed this authority without question. Yudhisthir and Duryodhana were both questioned by their younger siblings for their Adharma during the Game of Dice. An upset Bhima in a fit of anger wanted to assault Yudhisthir, but was pacified by Arjun. They state that going against the will or decision of an elder brother is Adharma. But the Epic teaches us we must side with Dharma and standup against Adharma. Vidura in his position as advisor often voiced his dissent. On one occasion, they banished him from Hastinapur, but they soon called him back. The relationship between Krishna and his elder brother Balarama was far more open and the brothers would disagree, and Krishna could convince his brother to agree. A structure where the eldest leads and the junior follows ensures order and discipline. There were no coups or power struggles between brothers. Rigid structures can give rise to Adharma, so the authors scripted several exceptions.

The other aspect of sibling relationship is that of brother and sister. In the Epic, brothers often fought for the rights of their married sister. They were involved with bringing up their sister's children. They would not leave a girl child once married, at the mercy of her husband or his family. The girl's family remained engaged and protected her rights and that of her husband. Often a bride's family would join forces with the groom's family. Draupadi's marriage to the Pandavas provided enough cause to Drupad to join the war. Jarasandha attacked the Yadavas multiple times forcing them to flee to Dwarka. Marriage related the Panchal, Virata and Yadava to the Pandavas. They commanded most of the divisions of the Pandava Army.

A study of sibling relationship cannot be complete without reference to Hidimbi, and her brother Hidimba, who objected to the former's marriage with Bhima. He staked his life to protect his sister's ethnicity and legacy.

Uncles and Nephews: Krishna brought up his nephew Abhimanyu. Draupadi's children grew up under the watchful eyes of her brother. Contrast this with Shakuni, who may have abused a similar relationship. He manipulated his nephews unto a path of self-destructive confrontation and conspiracy. Another perspective, however, is that Shakuni as a good strategist avoided conflict and bloodshed. He guided his nephews to take back Khandavprastha. Shalya fought on the side of the Kauravas. One cannot believe a king set out to join the

Pandavas in battle joined the other side. Dhritarashtra overlooked the manipulations and conspiracies that denied the Pandavas their right. Then there is Bhishma, who acted as Regent whilst his nephews came of age. We cannot ignore the example of how Krishna fought and killed his uncle Kansa or how the Pandavas killed their uncle Shalya.

Tutor and Student: Dronacharya, Parashuram and Krishna are the tutors in the Epic. As Brahmins, both Dronacharya and Parashuram fulfill their Varna but show a strong bias. Dronacharya refuses to teach a suta Karna. He wants to be the foremost tutor, so he demands the sacrifice of Eklavya's thumb. This enables him to establish Arjun as the foremost archer. A responsible tutor would focus on bringing up the weakest in the class. Instead, he focuses on making Arjun the best in archery. Dronacharya was training a group of young royals as his private army to settle scores with Drupad. Parashuram also showed his bias, but he was training the trainers.

Teaching can be in the form of imparting Knowledge or knowledge sharing. Imparting is a top-down exercise, whereas knowledge sharing is less formal and not forced down. Krishna did not impart knowledge to Arjun in the form of Bhagwad Gita. He did not force him to follow it, this was clear from the events that follow.

CHAPTER 67

Pandavas—Were They Five or One

In the Ramayana, Ravana had mastered the knowledge of the six Shastras and the four Vedas. They presented him in plays with ten heads, representing his mastery of the subject. In the Mahabharata, the challenge was how to present the five attributes in a single person. Each had to be highlighted to the fullest. Sometimes, they had to be presented concurrently and at other times it required them to interact with each other. To achieve this aim, they presented the Pandavas as five persons. They created a back story for Draupadi in her previous life to support this. Also, Draupadi's boon was realized by Pandu's desire, which Kunti's boon facilitated. Whilst there is no intention to re-write an Epic revered by so many, it helps us visualise aspects that are not obvious but relevant to our lives.

When Pandu and his wives moved to the forest, they were childless. Kunti was not yet aware if her firstborn was alive or not, so would have adopted Niyoga to get a child. Kunti knew she had children from four different Demi-gods and was also married to Pandu, ending up with five relationships. Although the birth of Karna was a secret, she refused to get further children through her boon. She therefore transferred the boon to Madri, who then became the mother of Nakul and Sahadev. A woman with the knowledge and understanding of social customs and stigmas would not have forced Draupadi to marry five men. Drupad would not have allowed her to marry five men.

They enacted the Epic as a play. The Pandavas represented the five most desired attributes in a man, whereas the Kauravas represent innumerable desires or shortcomings. They then created Karna, who combined all the attributes unique to each of the five Pandavas. The Mahabharata used this to illustrate the finer aspects of Dharma, social practices, biases, Sanskar and Kula. The story of Kunti and Madri and their children deal with the role and relationship of women and child.

So what did they intend to achieve by representing the Pandavas as five instead of one? The five Pandavas portrayed in the Epic represent the five attributes desired in a husband by Draupadi in her previous life. Because of her insistence, they fulfilled her wish, but only on the condition she married five men. The message here was that no one can be perfect. It would require five men to meet Draupadi's expectation. When she finds one, he is unacceptable because of his Suta origins.

The five Pandavas are like the five fingers in our hand. The thumb is the strongest and represents Bhima. The trigger finger represents our dedication or focus and represents Arjun. The middle finger that stands tallest in our hand represents Dharma, i.e. Yudhisthir. The ring finger or the finger that draws humans to each other stands for attraction and is Nakul. Finally, we have intuitive discretion, our inner voice or our conscience and this is our little finger and Sahadev represents this. Our little finger needs elaboration because it makes our heart race when we do wrong. It is our in-built warning system.

The concept of Five Pandavas also stands tall in our lives. The starting point of all human engagement is Desire or temptation, and this is Nakul represented by our ring finger. When we desire, we attempt to visualise the consequences or implications i.e. foresight or discretion comes into play and this is our little finger or Sahadev. Tempted, our tall finger takes over and looks at our obligations of Dharma and this is our Yudhisthir. When approved by the eldest, we engage Arjun or our trigger finger to our goal i.e. dedication. And to reach our goal or fulfil our needs we must draw on our determination represented by Bhima or the thumb. These 5Ds are critical to our objectives, whether in life or work. The Mahabharata cautions us with our 5Ds. To recognise and understand these cautions, we need to relate to the entire epic and not just to the Pandavas.

Desire: Shantanu's desire for Ganga and then Satyawati set in motion the events that affected his destiny and of the future generations. Dhritarashtra divided the kingdom, both Yudhisthir and Duryodhana got a share. It satisfied neither. Duryodhana wanted to take back Pandavas' share of the kingdom. It led not only to his death but also the loss of his share of the Kingdom. The mind must not get clouded by desire and must learn to master its weakness.

Discretion: Kunti's indiscretion with the mantra granted by Sage Durvasa led to the birth of Karna. Without Karna by his side, Duryodhana would not have gone to war with the Pandavas. Bhishma's indiscriminate abduction of the three princesses led to his ultimate death. Without the rebirth of Amba, Shikhandi would not have had cause to kill Bhishma. Bhishma's indiscriminate action forcing Amba, unsuccessfully, to marry into the Kuru household, ultimatly, led to Shikhandi's birth. Discretion is critical to our success.

Dharma: Yudhisthir and Vidura are Dharma personified. Vidura is one who could do no wrong, unlike Yudhisthir who had an emotional side to him. Dharma represents our obligation, our duties, our role and responsibility. This side of our personality must not show emotion. This idea is fallacious, and Yudhisthir had wants and weaknesses too. He wanted to contribute to the Pandava struggle to recover the kingdom that belonged to his father. His foolish wager lost the kingdom, respect of Draupadi and of his loyal brothers. When we are swayed by our emotions, Dharma will falter.

Determination: Bhima shows his many soft sides. He is devoted to Draupadi and his brothers, yet, a brutal streak in him surfaces with Dushashan. Bhima was brutal to a fault, but he had the determination, he took difficult vows and fulfilled them. They acknowledged Bhima's determination and leadership as he was the only Pandava given the charge of leading a Division. Drupad's long-term focus and his desire to avenge his humiliation show his single-minded determination. When emotions influence our actions, our determination can be excessive to a fault.

Dedication: Krishna narrated the Bhagwad Gita to Arjun. He picked up his weapon to fight but was not committed to his goal. Krishna could not convince him. Conviction is critical to dedication. This does not mean Arjun lacked dedication. Through his dedication, he gained incremental skills that made him the best Archer of his time, the only one with the knowledge of piercing and exiting the Chakrayuah and use of the Brahma Astra. Yet it was not Arjun who won the war, he killed no warrior of consequence except to settle scores. The conduct of Eklavya is a classic case study on Dedication. Denied access to training, he created an earthen replica of his tutor. He used this imagery to self learn the skills he watched the tutor impart to the royal princes. Dedication requires focus and conviction.

Although each of the five Pandavas had attributes that were best in their class, the authors wanted us to understand that it is impossible to get all in their best measure in a single person. It is just as all the five fingers in our hand can never be equal. The authors therefore used the Pandavas' last journey towards Heaven to develop a ranking. The ability to discern represented by Sahadev is an intuitive attribute and enjoyed the lowest relative rank. It is therefore the first attribute to end its life journey, and its twin Nakul or desire followed. Thereafter, our dedication or conviction which is our strength of mind gives way and therefore Arjun leaves. It is only our Dharma or our goodness that can stand tallest and reach Heaven whilst Bhima or determination falls short.

The Pandavas and Karna: Knitted deep into this symbolism is the creation of a character called Karna. He had all that Draupadi desired in a man. Yet, she had to marry five men to get it.

Karna was a mirror visualisation or MAYA or illusion intended to enable us to grasp the finer aspects of Dharma. In a society for Dharma to sustain, the leader of the Society must follow it. He must have the Sanskar and Parampara of a leader, for these his Kula is critical. When Ghatotkacha dies in battle, the Pandavas grieved, but Krishna was unmoved. His death meant the next in line to be King would be of pure Arya origin and would have the Sanskar, Parampara and Kula to be King and upholder of Dharma.

CHAPTER 68

Spousal Relationship in the Mahabharata

Each of the five Pandavas represented one trait, but together they had the personality and ability a woman seeks in an ideal husband. In the Epic, a character was created for each attribute and this uniqueness was exemplified and amplified. They also created Karna, and he had all the attributes. Draupadi refused to consider Karna because of his family background. In arranged marriages, Kula is an essential and critical part of the search and match process. Draupadi's Swayamwar was not just about finding her a groom; it was about what a girl should look for in a groom. Often parents do not have this discussion with their children. This is a message the Epic provides on parenting. We often hear about how young couples introduce their partner of choice to their parents, hoping to get their approval. They are often shocked when their parents do not approve of their choice. In most cases, there would have been no prior discussion of what parents expect in the partner of their child. So how can we understand what our parents are looking for in our partner beyond our perception of what is right for us?

This answer is provided through the course of this Epic by Krishna. He points to the importance of Sanskar and Kula in a marriage. In a marriage, the consent of the partners is also of utmost importance. In his view, when two persons love each other, nothing else matters.

As per the Epic, so-called Aryans believed a woman lacked virtue if she had relationships with five or more men. In the Epic, Draupadi married five men and lived with them at the same time. The epic used a back story and divine help to justify this. This helped overcome any social stigma. Whenever the epic introduces divine help, the event has thoughts, ideas and messages which need deeper analysis. As such ideas can touch our lives in multiple ways, it is important for us to recognise these signals and look for the guidance provided.

They set up Draupadi's Swayamwar in a manner that excluded all but the best of archers. They ended up with just three real contenders. Draupadi rejected Karna's participation, Ashwatthama did not take part, and Arjun took part and won. Arjun's victory and marriage to Draupadi would not have served Drupad's purpose. Draupadi's marriage to a prince third in line to the throne would not justify his joining a battle against the Kauravas. This might be a clue that maybe there was only one Pandava and this splitting up into five was to provide a detailed characterization of a woman's expectation from the man in her life.

Whilst Draupadi married the five Pandavas, she was to live with each for a year at a time. At the beginning of every year, they transformed her into a maiden because of a divine blessing. This was a fine play on a man's expectations. Every male expects his wife to be a maiden. However, in reality it was not possible for any Pandava who was not first in line to ignore her prior co-habitation with his other siblings.

Relationship between Yudhisthir and Draupadi: There was no evidence of mutual attraction or 'love' in their relationship. Yudhisthir without hesitation staked his wife, although she also belonged to his brothers. When Draupadi was being accosted by Kichaka, he chose not to act. They partnered in their quest to take back control and rule over Hastinapur. Draupadi's marriage and her role as the spouse of Yudhisthir appeared limited to being his chief queen. Their relationship focused on the public side of spousal relationship. Yudhisthir wanted Draupadi's love and attention. However, there is little he did to get her love. He ended up losing her respect and trust. He bet her as an object in a game of dice. How could a woman love a man she did not trust? They based their relationship on shared responsibilities and obligations as between a king and queen. Their inter-actions revolved around Dharma and they reflect it in their relationship.

Relationship between Bhima and Draupadi: Bhima's relationship with his wives provides contrasting examples of his behavior. Hidimbi married Bhima because she loved him. He married her so that the Pandavas could live peacefully in the forests inhabited by local tribes. Bhima abandoned her and their son Ghatotkacha on his birth. He visited her only when he needed their son to join forces in the War. When the warring sides were rallying support and building up their armies, the Kauravas got the support of Nagas led by Takshaka and Rakshas tribes seeking revenge against the Pandavas for slaying Bakasura. To counter this, Bhima re-established his relationship with Hidimbi and their son and his group to join battle with the Pandavas. It would appear Bhima was not committed to his marriage.

Conversely, Bhima was attracted to Draupadi. He was forever willing to do anything for her. When Dushashan accosted her and dragged her into the royal court, he swore not only to kill him but all the Kauravas. He was the only Pandava sibling to challenge and condemn Yudhisthir for wagering Draupadi in the game of dice. His love for Draupadi was not reciprocated. Again, when Jayadratha abducted her and was taking her away, it was Bhima who led the rescue. He would have killed him, but Draupadi intervened as she did not want to widow the Kaurava Princess.

Bhima also married the princess of Kashi. Yet his love for Draupadi was the driving force in their marriage. When Draupadi collapsed on her final journey, Yudhisthir said she did not love her husbands equally, but favoured Arjun and moved on. Only Bhima wanted to support her, which shows how much he cared for her. This relationship focuses on the emotional side of spousal relationships.

Relationship between Arjun and Draupadi: It was Arjun's archery skills that won him Draupadi. Unlike Bhima, who was prone to fits of anger, Arjun was focused and a good listener. He was the only Pandava to understand the power of Krishna and the one to whom Krishna narrated the Bhagwad Gita.

Arjun had won her, yet Kunti forced him to share her with his brothers. After their marriage, they decided that

Draupadi would establish a conjugal relationship based on an order of seniority. Arjun attracted Draupadi and they reflect this in Yudhisthir's comment about her partiality towards Arjun.

The relationship between Draupadi and her three husbands are examples of the different dimensions in a spousal relationship. It showcases a woman's love for her husband and the sacrifices she can make to keep him happy. This is reflected in Draupadi's behavior with Arjun. A man's love for his wife and the things he can do for her is shown by Bhima. The relationship between a man and his wife is driven by a bond of service. Love may or may not exist but the relationship thrives because of shared obligations as with Yudhisthir and Draupadi. In spousal relationships, we will often have to take the path of love, shared obligations and compromise. This is the message that is intended. In such relationships, there is an expectation from a partner. Draupadi shows us how to deal with it.

Kunti fights to recover the rights of her late husband. Spousal relationship does not end with death or separation. Ganga performed her duty as a mother in bringing up the child. She then hands over her child to her former husband. Mutual consent can only sustain relationships. No party must feel compelled to remain in a relationship. It also recognises pre-nuptial agreements. This is the agreement that Satyawati got. In every relationship, there is a responsibility, a right and an expectation. A disappointment can cause a partial or a total break. Hindu thought does not have an opinion on this. Every person is free to decide. It is customary for Hindus to think marriages are made in Heaven or it is ordained by some divine forces and lasts for seven lives. They intend these thoughts or ideas to encourage a couple to work to make a success of their marriage. It would be wrong to compel a couple to stay in a relationship against their wishes. Finally, the frequent offers to Draupadi to walk out of her marriage and marry another, is a sign of an existing practice. There was no bar on a wedded woman to leave her husband and take another. A woman could marry again.

CHAPTER 69

A Look at the Life Stories of the Departed Souls

The epic depicts the story of its principal characters. We discover the events or circumstances that turn their lives into a struggle. Why did their lives end with a feeling of failure or regret? Some unique factors affect the lives of each of the characters, which influence their personality, perspectives on Dharma and their actions.

Bhishma: His Achievements and Failures

Key Influence: His vow of celibacy and commitment to serve Hastinapur influenced his life, decisions and his end.

A character painted so noble and virtuous that he forgoes his right of succession and willingly embraces celibacy, which took precedence over every other obligation. He had promised to let his siblings ascend the throne, but they died and left no successors, rendering his vows redundant. He refused to fulfil his obligation to marry a woman.

Bhishma often faced a choice of fulfilling a vow or his Dharma, but he always preferred to follow his vow. His biggest failure was his undertaking to serve and protect the crown. He had dedicated his life to the service of Hastinapur, but he watched it virtually collapse in a fight to the finish.

Bhishma may have been a virtuous man, but he had scant regard or respect for women. He abducted Amba, Ambalika and Ambika so his brother Vichitravirya could marry them. He allowed a sage to impregnate Ambika and Ambalika the widows of his deceased brother. He forced Gandhari to marry a blind Dhritarashtra, and then he paid a bride price for Madri to marry an impotent Pandu. At the Game of Dice, he did not intervene when Draupadi was staked as a bet. He did not stop the Kauravas from dragging her into the court or her attempted disrobing.

Instead, he relapsed into silence, thinking about the rights a husband has over his wife. Bhishma must squarely take the blame for the torture and brutality unleashed on women.

His actions may have focused on a greater good, yet they were wrong. The princesses who married his brother ended up being widows. The marriage did not yield a successor to the throne. Gandhari refused to accept Dhritarashtra as her husband. Madri's irresistible charm led to the death of Pandu. Bhishma's silence led to the death and destruction of the Kauravas.

As the eldest son of Shantanu, he surrendered his right to the crown so that his father could marry again. His father sacrificed his marriage to save him from certain death. As his son, he reciprocated by promising to remain celibate and aiding his father's re-marriage. This marriage ensured his father's return to the path of Dharma that was blocked when his first wife left him. Yet again, the Mahabharata provides us with an amazing message. A widowed or divorced person if young enough must marry again so that he or she can resume normal life under the umbrella of Dharma. This is also an integral part of our Samaj Dharma.

A man cannot steal to feed his dependents and fulfil his personal obligation because he commits an offence against his community. It is this conflict Bhishma often struggles with throughout his life. Bhishma justifies his action as a fulfilment of Parivarik Dharma when he kidnaps brides for his half brother or forces a woman to marry a blind Dhritarashtra. Bhishma gives precedence to his personal vows over his obligations of Dharma. He refuses to perform Niyoga on his widowed sister-in-laws claiming he preferred to honour his personal vow. Adopting the same stand, he refused to marry Amba, choosing his personal vow over Dharma.

Hindu marriages require the consent of the bride's father and the bride. He forced these marriages to provide for succession and stability to Hastinapur. He thought he was fulfilling a higher obligation to the State, even though he violated the rights of a woman.

As a grandfather, he ensured all his grandchildren the best of training and education, but provided no personal guidance. As a senior male member, he could have guided the young Kurus. Although it was okay to have a favourite one, he did not heed to the rest. He noticed all kinds of pettiness between Kauravas and Pandavas but did nothing, and these became deep-rooted. He showed his bias for the children of Pandu, and this conflict between duty and love led to the defeat of the Kauravas.

We then have instances of Bhishma's avoidance, silence and misguidance. When asked for advice on choosing the person to honour first at the Rajsuya Yagna, he created trouble for Yudhisthir as the Kauravas saw this as a rejection of their supremacy. Had he advised Yudhisthir to honour a Kuru elder, there would have been no resentment. When Draupadi questioned her husband's independence to wager her, he remained silent. He did not object to Shakuni's plan to a game of dice. He watched in silence as Yudhisthir wagered his kingdom, his brothers, himself and Draupadi. He insisted on keeping his vow of celibacy instead of providing succession to the Kuru Lineage.

Ashram Dharma applies to all individuals, and Bhishma arranged his father's re-marriage and return to Ashram Dharma. However, as an individual he did not follow the same Dharma. Had he done so, he would have experienced human relationships in all its dimensions. A man's relationship with a woman starts from his mother and then leads on to sisters, lovers, wives and daughters. The relationship between Krishna and Draupadi also expands to a platonic friendship. Bhishma had only experienced the love of a mother.

When Duryodhana respectfully asked him to lead the Kaurava army, he should have declined in favour of someone younger. He was already at a stage where he was more suited to the role of an advisor.

His father gifted Bhishma with life so he could live as long as he desired. A message that the Epic provides is that a man comfortable and secure in his current situation may never desire to move on in life.

His Varna Dharma as leader of the Kaurava army was to ensure the defeat of the enemy. He refused to target and kill the Pandavas in the war. A humiliated Karna refused to fight under his leadership. It was his duty as a leader to carry all members of his team. He compromised his side when he told the Pandavas he would not fight against a third gender.

He did not tell his warring grandchildren that Karna was Kunti's son. If he had, it could have stopped the war and prevented the death of millions of soldiers.

Bhishma could have done a lot to avoid the war, and won our praise and sympathy, but his life ended watching the House of Kurus fall apart. He lay helpless on a bed of arrows aware of the Adharma, loss of lives and the tragedy that unfolded.

The purpose and intent behind his characterization becomes clear when Krishna requested Bhishma to share his administrative experience with Yudhisthir. Bhishma lacked a humane side, but he was a master of the rules of governance. He shared this with Yudhisthir before his death. Governance needs a clinical perspective for it to be fair to all. We must tax income but cannot base taxes on capacity to pay. Shooting to kill is an offence and must attract a punishment. A king has to uphold Dharma and like Bhishma he must fulfil this vow in preference to all his obligations, even if these arise in his personal life. A king must at look at his larger responsibility.

They say life always gives you another chance. Bhishma had several opportunities to look beyond his vows. His is an example of how we fail when we tie ourselves into impossible knots called principles. We must face situations as they arise, not limit our responses because of our vows. It is said all is fair in love and war, then should a Kshatriya always engage in battle in keeping with their traditions?

What if the opponent is not a Kshatriya or does not respond in Kshatriya tradition?

Dhritarashtra split up the kingdom between his sons and the Pandavas on the condition that Bhishma would swear allegiance to the Kauravas. The Kuru dynasty had ended with the division, and therefore his vows had become redundant. It released him from all prior obligations. Bhishma like many others in his time had mistaken his habit for Dharma.

Dronacharya: His Achievements and Failures

Key Influence: Dronacharya's struggle with poverty and consequent insecurity influenced his future behaviour. He thought his loyalty was his Dharma.

The tutor of the Kuru princes was a Brahmin trained by the best in the art of war and the use of weapons. He wanted to show how his students were the best trained and most accomplished.

Under his leadership, the Kauravas violated the rules of battle. Why did he or other Kaurava warriors including Karna not avenge the deaths of their princes by attacking the Pandavas? Why under Dronacharya's watch, Karna not engage Arjun, nor did the unbeatable Ashwatthama engage Bhima? Did he lack strategy? Was he a self-serving traitor?

Was the guru of all the valiant warriors torn between his emotional attachments and duty? Is this message reinforced in the depiction of his death? Hearing about the loss of his son, he went numb with grief, dropped his weapons and allowed himself to be killed. Dronacharya's life is a classic characterisation of so many of us, who achieve professional heights but crash as miserable failures. His life is a lesson of how most of us end up as abject failures in our lives.

Mahabharat adopts a 'cradle to a coffin' narrative, providing abundant examples of personal failings. It points to the misery that we suffer as these are triggered by Adharma.

He died a broken man in the belief that he had lost his son, a prime example of a teacher who did not practice what he preached. He could have moved to Northern Panchal and enjoyed his guru dakshina, without getting involved in a vicious war. Like so many of us, he worked all his life, never stopping to enjoy the fruits of toil. It is an illustration of how our lives are on a treadmill; we continue to collect trophies and milestones, never pausing to enjoy what we have. His characterisation teaches us that excessive focus on the treadmill of materialism ensures failures.

Dronacharya refuses to train Karna on the grounds that his mandate is limited to the royals. He brutally punishes Eklavya for learning the art of archery clandestinely. His punishment and those given by Parashuram to Karna convey the principles and right of ownership of intellectual property, which must be gained with the consent of the owner. It is at the discretion of the holder of intellectual property with whom he should share his specialized skills. He can punish violators and prevent them from using his Knowledge.

However, Dronacharya discriminates on the basis of birth or possible future occupation, when he should have imparted these skills selflessly as a Brahmin. Dronacharya as his guru dakshina had king Drupad captured, freeing him only after taking away half of his kingdom of Panchal. A vanquished King is not hurt and nor is his kingdom taken away. Dronacharya lacked the knowledge and understanding of how Kshatriyas behave and ended up violating the rules of war.

Bhima claimed he had killed Ashwatthama. Dronacharya sought confirmation from Yudhisthir, based on his perception that Yudhisthir would not lie. As his mind was emotionally biased, he did not corroborate Yudhisthir's statement and fell for his half-truth.

Dronacharya lacked the etiquettes and tradition of a Kshatriya. As a result, we ended up viewing the Kaurava army and its key warriors as violators of Dharma. He did not imbibe the Sanskar of the Kshatriya and nor did his son. His son murdered the children of Pandavas in their sleep. He publicly grieved his son's death in battle, a weakness not befitting a commander and a Kshatriya.

A Guru must have both knowledge and Sanskar. They cast Dronacharya opposite Balarama so we can understand this.

Karna: His Achievements and Failures

Key Influence: Suffers from the burden of indebtedness, often over-reaches for recognition.

Karna was born to Kunti before her marriage and she abandoned him at birth. A childless charioteer to King Dhritarashtra found this abandoned child by the banks of the river. He took the child home, and they brought him up in Hastinapur. Kunti, before her marriage to Pandu, lived along the same river, but further downstream. In a strange coincidence, the three characters come together again in Hastinapur. Bhishma and Krishna know Karna is the child Kunti abandoned at birth.

Karna faced discrimination because of the background of his foster parents. He had to fight against the prejudices of society. He had to struggle to get his education. When denied training by Dronacharya, he used deceit to gain it from Parashuram. He was an accomplished archer; they denied him the right to show his skills because of his social status. Duryodhana made Karna a king, yet society regarded him as a loyal courtier of Duryodhana. The Kshatriyas never accepted him as one. He married a Suta being one himself by sanskar, even though he was a Kshatriya by birth. Despite being a king, Draupadi did not let him take part in her swayamwar. Mahabharata contains many instances of social discrimination and individual suffering. Over time, social stigmas have increased manifold and so has human suffering.

Sanskar comes not with birth but with upbringing and exposure. He had fled from battle; he was emotional and could be distracted from his goals. He had also told Kunti about his lack of exposure to a Kshatriya's Sanskar.

Kunti, Krishna and the gods conspired to weaken him. They took away his weapons, his armour and his emotional resolve. On the battlefield, whilst unarmed, Arjuna killed him. Krishna sought and got from him the benefit of all his generosity and good deeds, depriving him of his karma. A soul denied and devoid of its karma would on re-birth never enjoy the bliss or enjoy its karma. No soul would have suffered such utter degradation in life or death.

Here was a man who owned all the attributes which made each of the Pandavas distinctive, born of the same mother, yet could not achieve his full potential. He dedicates his life to Duryodhana, which he construed as his Dharma. It is yet another example of how emotional attachment can lead one into the path of Adharma.

Karna had the skills and expertise to win the war for Duryodhana. Kunti manipulated him into making a promise not to kill any of her sons other than Arjun. Lord Indra exploited his generosity, and he took away his celestial armour. Surya his father had forewarned him of this plot, but his generosity got the better of him. Karna gave up his armour and compromised his invincibility in battle. At Duryodhana's command, he used his most potent weapon on Ghatotkacha. Karna wanted people to know him as a man of charity. He compromised his own life, the victory in battle for Duryodhana which he could have got and on his deathbed, he even gave away the benefit of his Karma. We often admire people for their goodness, but with Karna his goodness became a weakness. In life, we must learn to say no. Karna in his life never looked beyond himself. He yearned to know the truth of his birth; he wanted to be the best archer; he wanted people to remember his charity. Brought up as a Suta, it conditioned him to serve a Kshatriya. His loyalty to Duryodhana was not just his indebtedness to him but reflected his Sanskar, which made him devote himself to the service of a royal.

They regarded Karna as someone willing to stake his very life for his friend Duryodhana, who unwittingly suffered huge losses because of Karna's mindless acts of charity. His bid to exhibit his magnanimity drove his views on charity. A loyal friend would not hide the truth of his ties with the Pandavas, he would not promise not to kill some of his enemies; he should not give away his armour.

The Mahabharata created a Karna with all the attributes of the five Pandavas combined, but in Draupadi's view, he lacked the Kula of a royal. They use this to convey the importance of Sanskar and explain the importance of being a part rather than being able to play the part. The Karna Factor (KF) affects many of us in similar ways. We may find we cannot adjust with a crowd as we do not share the same ethos. At other times, we do not wish to be with certain types of people. Society looked at Karna as an imposter. No other character in the Mahabharat disobeyed his father or rejected his Jati. Karna a Suta in real life wanted to be a Kshatriya.

Karna's life and experiences reflect the many failings of our society, which does not address these issues. His experience touches our contemporary lives and we remain intrigued by his struggles and the prejudices he suffered because of his birth.

Shakuni: His Achievements and Failures

Key influence: A master of strategy who devoted his life to secure and protect the interest of the Kauravas.

Shakuni wanted to secure the rights of his nephews to keep control over the Kingdom. If he had an evil mind, Vidura and Bhishma could have isolated or rendered him ineffective. He was an astute politician. He planned the Game of Dice but did not take part in the humiliation of Draupadi. Draupadi's ill treatment was not part of this plan, and Shakuni had no hand in it.

He fought on the side of Kauravas and showed his Dharma as a Kshatriya. Though some believe he was evil and focused on the destruction of the Kuru race, his enmity was with Bhishma. He however showed great respect for Krishna. Shakuni was a devotee of Shiva. Krishna was the mind behind the Pandava campaign to regain their lost Kingdom. Shakuni was the brains behind the defence launched by the Kauravas. They demonised Shakuni for his actions targeting the Pandavas or trapping King Shalya to support the Kauravas.

Shakuni did not act against the interest of the Kauravas. Even if he was part of the conspiracy to remove the Pandavas, it was for protecting the rights of the Kauravas. Bhishma, Vidura and Dronacharya often acted in their self interest or were in a conflict of interest. They were openly sympathetic to the Pandavas. Karna was loyal to his friend Duryodhana, but he did not support their cause. His desire to prove he was a better archer than Arjun drove him. Krishna had his interests too. He tempted the Pandavas into a Rajsuya Yagna and used them to kill Jarasandha.

Another version said, Shakuni hated the Kurus for the atrocities on his family and his sister. He manipulated his Kaurava nephews and set them up against their cousins. They accuse him of sowing suspicion and enmity between the Kauravas and Pandavas. It was his artful manipulation that pushed the Kauravas into battle with the Pandavas. The Pandavas believed Shakuni had manipulated Duryodhana into entering war. His mission accomplished, he could have returned to his Kingdom, and he did not have to take part in the war. Sahadev who duelled with Shakuni even offered to let him go. Shakuni preferred to fight and die in battle. As a Kshatriya killed in battle, he would go straight to heaven. He said he wanted to die looking at Krishna, the God Incarnate. He had achieved his life's goal and wanted to take responsibility for his actions that led to countless deaths and destruction of families. In our own life, once we have achieved our goal we must learn to stop, we must take a 'Shakuni Call.'

Shakuni's goal was to destroy the 'Kuru Dynasty' and he devoted himself whole-heartedly to his goal and achieved it. He used deceit and carried the burden of many sins and paid for his life but goes to Heaven. In our lives, we set out to achieve goals and once done, we set ourselves more goals and we are busy running on a treadmill. Often we extend time, maybe we add speed until suddenly we die. 'Shakuni Call' is an important message for us; get off the treadmill before it throws us off.

Some suggest that for the wager, he carved his dice out of the bones of his father. He would throw the dice and magically draw the numbers he desired, suggesting he was a dark personality. Shakuni was avenging the death and destruction of his family. Other would suggest he was protecting the interest of his nephews. His sister had married an incompetent and blind man. In his view, Bhishma and Vidura, the powers behind the throne were sympathetic to the Pandavas, so he took on the role of protecting the Kaurava interest.

At the time when he chose death in battle, he had achieved his life goal but in an alternative scenario, he had failed as a protector. In both scenarios, the time was right for him to get off the treadmill. Shakuni's character demonstrates that we must not blindly trust our relatives as they might have an agenda of their own. Although regarded as a negative character, it might surprise many of us that there is a temple devoted to Shakuni in Southern India.

We must take our 'Shakuni Call' and realise when it is time to move on. Bhishma, Dronacharya, Jarasandha and

Arjun are examples who believed they were invincible despite their advancing years. Kunti's makes a 'Shakuni Call' appropriately by directing her sons to seek Draupadi's guidance. She again takes a well-timed call of Sanyas, unlike Satyawati and her daughter-in-laws.

Ashwatthama: His Achievements and Failures
Key Influence: ended up destroying his legacy in seeking recognition.

He, like his father, made friends with royals as students. Drupad insulted Dronacharya for trying to re-engage as a friend. Ashwatthama got to know Duryodhana as a student, but he never attempted to seek equal status with him even after he became King of Northern Panchal. We can contrast the experience of both father and son and their childhood friendship with the royals. They made Ashwatthama a king despite being the son of a Brahmin, once again showing how Hastinapur disregarded the practice of discrimination based on birth. Ashwatthama was a trained warrior. Duryodhana did not want to make him the commander of his Army because by Sanskar he was a Brahmin. Karna had Kshatriya roots, this Duryodhana did not know. Even as a Suta, Karna was qualified to lead an army as a service to the crown.

Being born with a celestial gem on his forehead invested Ashwatthama with invincibility, according to Bhishma. Regarded as a Shiva incarnate, he happened to be the only archer other than Arjuna capable of using the Brahma Astra, besides being one blessed with eternal life. It is likely that a warrior of his capability could have defeated the likes of Dhrishtadyumna and Shikhandi. The Epic demonises Ashwatthama for his cowardly acts. It is possible they inserted the use of the Brahma Astra to demonise Ashwatthama. With the death of all the Kauravas and their children, he killed the sons of Pandavas, Dhrishtadyumna in cold blood and directed his Brahma Astra to kill an unborn child. Krishna used his divine power to save this unborn child and the future king of Kuru Dynasty. The Pandavas captured him, pulled out his gem and left him bleeding to wander for eternity. This could mean they killed him but did not cremate his body. His soul would have therefore wandered around the earth, unrecognised and detested by all living beings. They call a wandering soul a ghost. Hindus cremate their dead. The fire turns the body into ashes and returns it to nature. The soul begins its journey to the netherworld. If the last rites are not performed, then it does not detach from the body.

Dhritarashtra: His Achievements and Failures

Key Influence: Suffers at the hands of destiny, he cannot rise out of self pity and his love for his children blinds him.

Born blind, they passed him over in favour of his younger brother Pandu. Was her tying a blindfold a poetic way of presenting her as a wife who never sided with, supported or accepted her husband? Did he seize the Kingdom from his younger brother and send him on exile to never return? Was it this guilt that drove him to allow a widowed Kunti to return with her five young children to his palace? Was it the same guilt that made him appoint Yudhisthir as a crown prince and to offer him half a kingdom?

Dhritarashtra's character was of someone who suffered at the hands of destiny; one who felt so wronged that he could never rise beyond his self pity. He felt no wrong was greater than the wrongs he suffered. He was one who never thought beyond himself, insecure and weak.

As a king, he appeared to be weak and submissive. However, he and his sons were running a parallel government. Although it would appear scandalous, we must complement the authors for introducing this covert side of government which exists even today. He and his sons planned the assassination of the Pandavas. He silenced Bhishma and got his support in favour of the Kauravas in exchange for giving the Pandavas control over Khandavprastha. The invitation to the Game of Dice was an initiative of this inner state. It was a non-violent way of getting rid of the Pandavas.

Dhritarashtra felt they denied his rights to him and then destiny righted this wrong. He believed his sons must succeed him. He was unwilling to share any part of his Kingdom with the sons of Pandu. He later relented when the Pandavas gained the support of the Panchal and Yadavas.

Gandhari could have been his eyes and ears. He expected her to be his partner in Dharma and Karma, but she refused. The Kauravas and Pandavas received the same education, but there was a key difference. Kunti as a mother provided parental guidance, i.e. Sanskar. The blinded state of their parents denied the Kauravas their Sanskar. Draupadi's ill treatment and humiliation shows the lack of Sanskar or parental guidance in the Kauravas.

Dhritarashtra could have got guidance from his family's Itihas and Parampara in matters of succession. They crowned Shantanu in preference to his elder brother.

Bhishma who had passed over his right in favour of his brothers could have taken the throne, saying he had fulfilled his promise when his brothers died.

Circumstances had convinced Dhritarashtra that destiny would never deal him a good hand. Yet, he was the only one to have children since King Shantanu. He reigned over Hastinapur, despite being passed over. He was a direct recipient of most revered divine message called the Bhagwad Gita. He was privileged to have able, devoted guides and advisors in Bhishma and Vidura. Sanjay narrated the entire Bhagwad Gita to Dhritarashtra, but to no effect. The best tutor can impart knowledge, but without conviction it cannot impart wisdom.

A very subtle message yet again, it is hurtful if one is born differently abled, but our loss must not so blind us we cannot appreciate when life favours us more than others.

Duryodhana: His Achievements and Failure

Key Influence: Painted the villain of the Epic, dies trying to protect what he believed belonged to him and his branch of the Kurus.

Duryodhana rejected the claims of the Pandavas because compromises were leading to further damage to the rights of the Kauravas. He had tried to protect his rights by removing the Pandavas and sending them to Varnavat. Many people in Hastinapur were sympathetic to the Pandavas. Rather than imprison these sympathisers, he sought to eliminate the root cause, i.e. the Pandavas. He failed because some Pandava sympathisers compromised the plan.

After division, the Pandavas had to rule under the supremacy of Hastinapur, they ignored the terms agreed and performed a Rajsuya Yagna. When Duryodhana learnt that Ashwatthama had killed all the surviving children of the Pandavas, he was heart-broken. He was not just unhappy, but heart broken as Ashwatthama had destroyed the Kuru Dynasty. Duryodhana was only fighting for what he thought was his right. When the war was all but lost, they asked him to pick a Pandava to fight with. The winner would be declared as having won the war. As a true Kshatriya, he picked Bhima his equal.

Duryodhana was fighting for his rights, but he did not realise his key Generals, Bhishma, Dronacharya and Karna were not fighting for his cause but out of loyalty and obligation. Duryodhana did not lack strategy; he lacked the commitment of his team. There is a lesson we can take. A good leader must have the support of a committed team to succeed. Strategy, commitment and execution are the keys to success, being big, strong and resourceful is not enough.

Jarasandha: His Achievements and Failures

Key Influence: An egoistic reigning Samrat who disregarded his Ashram Dharma.

As expected of a father and reigning Samrat, he went after the Yadavas for widowing his daughters. A principled man, they manipulated him into combat with one not his equal. His principles turned out to be his weakness. We must re-invent our perceptions and principles in life with age. We must act our age as the saying goes. Leaders of our society and family recognise it is lonely at the top. People bolster a leader's ego, praise his ideas and prowess, even if they pay him tributes, they privately resent him.

Krishna, Bhima and Arjun exploited Jarasandha's false sense of prowess. He was no longer their equal; he was one whose time had passed. Jarasandha, a legendary wrestler and past his prime, could not match a much younger Bhima. He was the father-in-law of Krishna's uncle and therefore fairly advanced in age.

Krishna and the Yadavas fled to Dwarka owing to Jarasandha's relentless attacks on the clan. During a battle, Krishna fled, and they called him 'Ranchhod,' or the one who flees the battlefield. This personal affront motivated him against Jarasandha. There were no more battles between Jarasandha and Yadavas once they had settled in Dwarka. It would appear that this was Krishna settling old scores. He used the Pandavas to make it appear as if the removal of Jarasandha was their agenda.

The Epic uses Samrat Jarasandha's character to convey many important messages. Positions and titles are not permanent because there will always rise a challenger and the old will have to make way for the new. A leader must not be authoritarian; his role is to provide direction and vision of the future. He must not oppress and hold the weak in 'a death embrace.' A leader must plan his succession and complete transition before his time is up to avoid being forcibly removed. As a powerful father, he merely taught the interfering Yadavas a lesson. Kansa removed his father Ugrasen, Krishna killed Kansa and returned Ugrasen to the throne. Soon thereafter, Ugrasen seceded in favour of Krishna's father. This story is about a fight for succession between a son and a son-in-law. It violates the principles of Patriarchy and Succession. After marriage, a girl becomes a part of her husband's Kula, we convert her rights into a Stree Dhan and give it to her. However, where the King has no surviving male heirs, his son-in-law may succeed him. We must protect a leader from intruders. Krishna, Arjun and Bhima gain access to him disguised as Brahmins. This cautions leaders to guard against assassins and fraudsters.

Vidura: His Achievements and Failures

Key Influence: Destined to serve the King, this humble advisor was the harbinger of change, a supporter of Pandavas.

The widowed queens had tricked Ved Vyas into performing Niyoga on a palace maid. They brought up the child born as a royal and brother of Pandu and Dhritarashtra. As a Suta, rules did not entitle him to be King. A fearless advisor to Dhritarashtra, he was an authority on Dharma. Members of the court knew he was a supporter of the Pandavas. As an emissary, he brought back the Pandavas to Hastinapur and also carried the invite for the Pandavas to the Game of Dice. He had often come to the rescue of the Pandavas, including forewarning them of the risks in Varnavat. When the Pandavas went into exile, Kunti stayed in his home. Krishna also stayed with him when he called on the Hastinapur as a peace emissary. A principled man, he did not take part in the Epic War. When Dhritarashtra and Gandhari proceeded to the forest, he along with Kunti accompanied them.

As with most events, they have conveyed a message in the relationship between the two stalwarts of Dharma. This is a message of change and transition. Vidura or Dharma in his times was subservient to the King. He was at the king's beck and call. They ignored him and once even banished him from the Kingdom. The change in Dharma's position and importance is fathered by Vidura. His son Yudhisthir became the king and upholder of Dharma. In the times that followed, the role of king and Dharma was segregated. Both Gautama Buddha and Mahavir renounced their royal status to devote their life in the pursuit and practice of Dharma. They even established their own Bhakti movements.

King Shantanu: His Achievements and Failures

Key Influence: The story of a man who wanted, but took no responsibility, Parampara, Itihas of the Kula are legacies that father must handover to his children.

A royal abandoned by his first wife, marries again with a pre-nuptial promise that replaces his crown prince with a yet-to-be born son. Through his characterisation, they introduce us to the ideas of pre-nuptial agreements and divorce. They returned him to the cycle of re-birth because his celestial mind succumbed to temptation. We can achieve Moksha through the determination of mind. It subtly suggests that Atma in after life and re-birth are concepts that will motivate us to follow Dharma in our lifetime. The epic warns us of the power and influence of temptation.

A father through his actions creates Itihas and adds to the legacy of Parampara in his Kula. It is his duty to educate and pass on this knowledge to his sons. We must therefore act with responsibility because our actions can have far-reaching consequences. It may affect many generations that follow us. Bhishma would not have given his right to the Crown or made a promise to remain celibate if he knew the right to appoint a successor was a king's obligation based on suitability. Kuru family had an established Parampara on succession. Bhishma did not have the benefit of the Itihas and Parampara of his Kula as he was born in a single parent home with no inputs from the father. Shantanu had a duty to educate his son on the history of the family. We know of Shantanu's character and his weakness for women, which must have made him overlook Bhishma's Adharma and blesses him with 'life at will.' The blessing was in fact a curse. According to a backstory, both father and son were celestial beings serving their punishment on earth. Their souls wanted to achieve Moksha and reach a higher plane at the earliest. Also, as we all know, no human will desire death in the normal course.

In the Epic, there are many instances when people do not have the benefit of Parampara of their Kula. Bhishma grew up without the influence of his father. His next generation also lacked the influence of their father. The sons of Pandu also did not have the benefit of his inputs because of his early demise. It denied the sons of Dhritarashtra input of both parents, and even Parikshit's father died before he was born. Each of them would have responded to events differently if they had the knowledge of the Parampara and Itihas of their Kula.

CHAPTER 70

Friendship in the Mahabharata

Friends are an important part of our lives, and they often influence our lives. We value this relationship, at times, we feel closer to our friends than to our siblings and other relatives. Mahabharata accords to friendship the pride of place. They join Krishna and Arjun in such a relationship. The Epic provides guidance on the principles and values of friendship. It portrays the many dimensions of friendship that arise at various points of our lives. We must not confuse friendship with duty and obligation. It requires no consideration or give and take. Friendship is the outcome of shared utility, goodness and pleasure. The Epic also explores the subtle distinction between bonding, friendship and soul mates.

Drupad and Dronacharya: With Drupad and Dronacharya, their relationship was based on the innocence of childhood. Theirs was a classic example of how childhood friendships often fade away. As the young friends grew up, each moved on to take up his own responsibility. Soon social and economic status that never mattered in their childhood surfaced. This is a familiar experience with all of us, we discriminate. We look at our differences and then we look around for people with whom we have lots in common. This is not about materialism, having much in common makes us comfortable.

Drupad rejected Dronacharya's demand; he refused to honour his childhood promise. In his view, he lacked the maturity to understand the implication of promises made as a minor. He viewed their friendship as a childhood bond; it was over once they left the Ashram. Drupad rejected the idea that they were friends because a friendship can only be amongst equals.

We bond with people at work, at the club, at points of time in our lives when common interests, mutual needs and circumstances bring us together. Then we move on and this bonding ends. Soon the exchange of birthday messages, season's greetings stop. Facebook and the likes provide reminders and so we may remain friends on Facebook. However, the events or circumstances that created the bond have now passed and we are not friends.

When we meet our friends from our childhood, after the gap of many years, we often struggle to recreate that chemistry. This is because our life and circumstances have changed. We wish to end the chance encounter soon with a promise to meet again, but never do. The bonding from sharing the same bench in school, sharing of lunch and playing together ended. This would be a natural end or because one of us moved to a different location or a different school or a different class. This points to a bonding that was circumstantial or conditional. Yes, people move on in life, because of re-location, a change of circumstances and sometimes because our social or financial circumstances act as a practical wedge and draws us apart. The friendship of Dronacharya and Drupad deals with the concept of bonding that was, but no longer is.

Karna and Duryodhana: This is a coming of age friendship. Duryodhana was quick to recognise that Karna could be a valuable member of his team who could take on Arjun. He befriended him and used all that was within his means to gain his loyalty. Karna's loyalty to Duryodhana cost him his life. Duryodhana trusted him more than his own siblings, and he based his decision to fight the Pandavas on the commitment and capability of Karna. It is clear here that the friendship started based on utility; then flowered based on goodness on both sides.

This friendship was not between equals. The friends did not see each other's families as equals. Their families formed no relationship based on marriage. This was often the case between the families of two friends. This is the one difference between their friendship and the one between Krishna and Arjun. Krishna asked the latter to abduct his sister Subhadra and marry her. There can be a friendship between two individuals of unequal status based on mutual utility. Such a relationship can turn into a friendship if there is an acceptance of status quo. Both parties know and accept that all things amongst them cannot be equal. It is this demand for equality by Dronacharya which Drupad rejected. They point to this demand when Drupad was asked to give his childhood friend half the Kingdom. Duryodhana needed Karna as he was a match against the archery of Arjun. Karna was grateful for the generosity and goodness of Duryodhana.

It based their relationship on mutual trust and acceptance of each other. There was mutual respect. In the most important decision of his life, Karna sided with Duryodhana and sacrificed his life at the altar of his friendship.

Krishna and Draupadi: Mutual trust, respect and equality, all existed in this relationship. Krishna did not expect or desire anything from Draupadi. He was not seeking the attention of the most beautiful woman of her time. Draupadi often called on Krishna to come to her rescue, and he did. Whilst Krishna did many things for Draupadi, she never reciprocated. When Draupadi found herself cornered or in the most hopeless of circumstances, Krishna was her saviour. Theirs was a bond that united their hearts and souls, it was selfless. The highlight of this bond was that Draupadi could share her grief with Krishna. After the exile was over, the Pandavas were seeking a peaceful resolution of their demand with the Kauravas. They had forgotten her humiliation; it was Krishna who understood Draupadi's ordeal and assured her that the guilty would not go unpunished. This kind of friendship is a fulfilling relationship and the only way we can may understand them is to cast them as soul mates.

The authors provided two subtle messages. Two of the most desirable persons of the opposite gender of their time can be friends and share a platonic relationship. Second, a friend is someone who understands you, whom you can confide in and one who can come to aid whenever you want them. You can depend on this friend even more than on your partner. The relationship of soul mates is the highest form of bonding. Its definition places it beyond the realm of any categorization, with a seemingly divine connect. It is hard to explain but easy to feel. We often meet someone and develop an instant liking for such a person. Sometimes, it is love at first sight and flowers into a lifelong relationship. At other times sex or marriage may not enter the relationship and yet the bond may be stronger.

Arjun and Krishna: The relationship between Krishna and Arjun in the Mahabharat was that of friends. Krishna would bow and seek the blessing of Yudhisthir and Bhima as they were both elder to him. Krishna and Arjun are two persons equal in age and similar in status. They were both Princes, related as cousins, shared many life experiences together. Krishna asked Arjun's help after the war to rescue the widows from abduction. Krishna made it clear that he considered Arjun his equal by asking him to marry his sister. Over the entire narrative, it based their friendship on mutual utility and shared pleasure.

Krishna agreed to be Arjun's charioteer, even though this was a lesser role. King Shalya was unhappy to be the charioteer to Karna. Krishna as his charioteer exercised great restraint and never overshadowed Arjun. Despite revealing his Divine Self to Arjun during the Bhagwad Gita, he did not force his views on Arjun. He did not demand that Arjun must follow his directions. Arjun took to battle, but he did not kill a single Kaurava or his guru or Bhishma. Krishna, his friend, offered him space. He worked his own agenda without imposing his will on his friend. On occasions when Krishna could not restrain himself and wanted to break his vow, Arjun would beg him to reconsider and would promise to improve. They show their care or goodness for each other too.

Arjun valued Krishna and preferred him over the entire Narayani Sena. He chose Krishna despite knowing he would not take up arms in battle. It also reflects Krishna's confidence in Arjun, he was confident Arjun would choose him and not the Narayani Sena. His choice reflects the complete understanding that can only exist in a true friendship. They shared a bond that went way beyond trust. Krishna offered himself knowing well that Arjun would pick him no matter how attractive the alternative choices were. Krishna was a Vishnu Avatar who took birth on earth with a mission. His purpose on earth depended on Arjun making the right choice. Arjun did not know of this mission, yet Krishna knew he could trust Arjun to choose him.

When Duryodhana went to war, he assumed that Karna would join him, there was no need to convince him. Karna disregarded Krishna and Kunti's offer to be the future king as the eldest Pandava. They could not tempt him with the right to have a beautiful Draupadi as his chief wife. Instead, he stayed with Duryodhana, even if it meant embracing death.

The friendship of Krishna with Draupadi and Arjun started at a mature age and lasted for a lifetime. There was mutual respect, trust, equality, selflessness and a bond in their relationship. Mahabharata teaches us we must engage in this relationship with maturity. Friends must accept their differences and be able to grant space to each other. Krishna accepted that though Arjun took up arms in battle, he killed no Kauravas or his guru. Duryodhana accepted that Karna was not his equal, yet they could depend on each other. Krishna and Draupadi shared a bond that was selfless.

Karna and Duryodhana shared an unequal relationship. Some would think they were not friends, and Karna was a courtier to a King. Karna would often stand up and express a dissenting view, and this would be accepted by Duryodhana. Dushashan resented the special position and trust that Karna enjoyed. Often in an unequal friendship, the weaker party is looked upon as a leech or a hanger-on because we believe friendship must be among equals. So why do people still go after unequal friendships? Often a person's strength attracts others, and often his strength can fulfil the needs of those who surround him. In his subconscious mind, he is also looking for someone who can fulfil his needs. There can be friendship when the relationship between two people is fulfilling. However, with a courtier, there is no shared bond, but a consideration for a shared agenda defines their relationship.

CHAPTER 71

Yudhisthir Moment in our Lives

Yudhisthir the Dharma Raj, could do no wrong. He knew the answers to all the questions. The Epic placed him on a high pedestal, yet he lied. Dronacharya believed Yudhisthir and paid with his life. That was his Yudhisthir moment (YMs).

Experts on Dharma would justify Yudhisthir's lies because absence of cruelty is the highest form of Dharma. The early death of Dronacharya, a ruthless warrior, prevented further loss of lives. Yet, we cannot ignore the fact that Yudhisthir lied. No one is devoid of a personal agenda and is always truthful. It is unfair to place any human on such a pedestal. Zero defect is an impossibility in reality.

The issue highlighted here is Trust. Yes, repeatedly in our life we have our YMs. We have friends letting us down, partners cheating on us, these experiences can be shattering and destroy us emotionally, financially or socially.

Hindu Shastras provide a guidance on The Concept of Truth.

In the Epic, every thought or idea central to our lives is often explained through events to help us grasp that there many dimensions to truth. When it appears to be different to people based on perspective, experience or thought, it is called relative truth. Relative truth is that which one can see or visualise often based on the circumstances that surround the moment and therefore that can be defined as the truth for that moment of time.

Indic thought suggests that truth is of two types. Relative and Absolute Truth. (Source: hinduwebsite.com)

Truth is something that can be proved either with logic or with facts. It can be a relative truth or absolute. The challenge is never with Absolute Truth. It is self-existent, permanent. They need neither application of mind nor senses for they are, as the term suggests, absolute.

The issues arise when we are dealing with relative truth. These might even be half-truths or even falsehoods that appear to be true. This is because of the fallacies and limitation of the human mind and intellect. A person under emotional stress also suffers from limitation of human mind. Relative truth needs to be examined from various standpoints and perspectives. Therefore, the conclusions may be conditional, contextual, temporary or relational. Hindu thought has established standards. It bases truth on direct knowledge or testimony or inference. Of these, direct knowledge is obviously the most reliable, followed by a testimony which is useful as a method of corroboration.

It bases direct knowledge on what we perceive or experience. Though this may often be reliable, yet we should not always take our experience for granted as our defective perception or biases may influence us and therefore what we may see may not be true and what we do not see may not be false. We may see or experience something we do not recognise or have experienced before or know anything about, hence we may miss the truth.

Therefore, direct experience may be helpful. However, we need to be careful about the conclusion and observations we draw from it. These may be limited by our experience, biases or prejudices. However, when direct experience is supported or validated by expert knowledge, we can accept our conclusions to be more reliable and accurate. Yet, there may be issues that still need to be resolved or gaps in our knowledge that may need to be filled.

Direct knowledge is the best way to arrive at the truth, although we may have to combine it with inference. In effect, direct knowledge with expert knowledge is the most reliable source of truth, they follow this by direct knowledge combined with inference and the third form is testimony.

Absolute truth has the following characteristics. Truth must be universal. It must be the same everywhere. Truth must be indestructible. It cannot be falsified or destroyed. Truth must be constant. It cannot change. Truth must be independent. It must not depend on anything. Truth must be the cause or source, but not the effect.

Our minds cannot grasp absolute truth as we may have a million standpoints or opinions, and these impacts our ability to grasp truth.

Dronacharya was a doting father. The wellbeing of his son Ashwatthama clouded his mind. When we are worried about someone we care for, our minds often fear the worst. When our loved ones do not return home on time or do not respond to our phone calls, re-assurances do not work, it is only when that person returns or responds to our call do we feel relieved, until then, our mind conjures up the most negative of thoughts and emotions.

When Bhima and Yudhisthir said his son was dead, Dronacharya went into a state of shock and Dhrishtadyumna took this advantage to kill him. Dronacharya depended on Yudhisthir's testimony based on his perception that Yudhisthir would not lie. As it biased his mind, he was emotionally overwhelmed and did not further corroborate Yudhisthir's statement. He fell for his half-truth.

Yudhishthir bet his wife Draupadi in a game of chance, with little regard to the fact she was the common wife of his brothers too. He staked his kingdom in a personal game of chance, contrary to his responsibility as a King. Although he suspected that Karna was his brother, but instead of dealing with his suspicion, he waited for someone to reveal it.

It was Yudhishthir's responsibility to ensure the proper fulfilment of Dharma.

As intended every character in each event in the Epic plays a unique role to provide us with a better understanding of people, dharma and lesson in our lives. We cannot ignore Yudhishthir was the only Pandava to reach Heaven. However, this must not be taken to mean that he was always in the right. He was an upholder of Dharma and that is why he deserved Heaven.

Ganga trusted Shantanu and married him based on a promise. She expected that Shantanu would trust her judgement and not question her actions. Their relationship ended not because they breached this promise, but because it lost the trust between the husband and wife.

Eklavya trusted and respected Dronacharya, his teacher, yet, his guru asked him for his thumb as dakshina. Duryodhana trusted Karna, yet, he gave away his celestial armour, promised Kunti not to kill her sons except Arjun. This was treason. Even Kunti kept secret the crucial information of Karna's birth until his death. Through these subtle examples covering many relationships, the authors warn us not to take trust lightly.

Our YMs are not just about others and their acts of deception, it can also be self-inflicted. Yudhisthir suspected all along that there was something special between his mother and Karna. He waited for truth to be revealed.

CHAPTER 72

Relationships and Hurt in the Mahabharata

Relationships are the key to our emotional well-being. When not dealt with, it can often cause hurt. The Mahabharata does not just tell us how to deal with relationships. It provides guidance on the emotional management of relationships. Relationships are like a drawbridge that facilitates the flow of emotions from one island to another. This definition allows us to visualise it. There is no need to quantify or scale it. Every individual is like an island and is connected by bridges to other islands at the same time or at different times. The concept of a drawbridge is important because it defines the nature and type of relationships we experience.

We can scale relationships into four broad types. The deepest form is anytime, never mind types. In this type, there are no restrictions of time or circumstances. We experience anytime, never mind type relationships as parents with our young children or with our siblings when we were young. This is when the bridges are never drawn up, so emotions flowed, unrestrained and unconstrained.

Then as we grow up, we draw up our bridges to make time for study, interests, other relationships, friends, etc. Free flowing exchange drops to the next stage when me times are excluded. We are now available at most times, but we exclude me times. This example is easy to understand: we need time to be with a friend or go to the gym or study.

As barriers enter our relationships, we agree to interact only at mutually convenient times. This happens as we get busy with our lives, we need more time for ourselves. We look for mutual convenience but are always available in emergencies. This means we draw up our bridges whenever we need time for ourselves. Our emotions cannot flow as freely as before.

Finally, we get deeper into our own lives and our exchanges are limited to mutually convenient times only. At this stage, our bridges are open to traffic at a mutually agreed time only.

Relationship with friends and family can start along this scale. This scale is defined by the time our bridges remain open for emotions to flow. Strangely, yet often on this scale, family relationships move down the scale whereas friendships often move up the scale. Mahabharata maps this unique phenomenon.

Mahabharata also provides us with another guidance on relationship. Whenever we approach relationships with an expectation or a sense of entitlement, it exposes us to the possibility of hurt. This is the principal take away from the experiences of its characters.

Ganga and Shantanu based their marriage on trust. She expected Shantanu to trust her and never question her because any question would end their relationship. Shantanu questioned her, and this ended their marriage.

Dhritarashtra expected his wife Gandhari to be his eyes and support in their marriage, but she rejected him with a blindfold. As King he could have ordered her to take off her blindfold, but instead of forcing his will, he offered his love and care in the expectation she would change. Gandhari did not change, and this hurt Dhritarashtra. When children were born, she was keen to see her children but was a prisoner of her blindfold decision. Dhritarashtra could have commanded her to take off her blindfold, but by now his hurt had turned to anger, so he stayed quiet and let her suffer instead.

To fulfil the demands of her husband, Kunti submitted herself to Niyoga thrice. She also shared the boon with Madri. She expected that Pandu would not engage in sexual intercourse and confront death. Pandu suffered from a curse of death if he ever resorted to sex. The future wellbeing of her children and herself depended on Pandu staying alive. Pandu died whilst fornicating with his younger wife, Madri. Kunti suffered the consequences as his widow. She had to seek the safety and support of Hastinapur to bring up the children.

To protect her reputation, Kunti abandoned Karna at birth. But when she offered to accept him as part of a deal, he turned her away.

Princess Amba declared her love for King Shalwa and was returned to him. Out of a sense of vanity and principle he refused to marry her claiming he had lost her in the fight with Bhishma. Amba ended her life in misery as nobody would marry her.

Dronacharya visited King Drupad expecting a childhood promise entitling him to one half of his Kingdom. Drupad promised it to him when they were students. It distressed him when Drupad rejected his claim of friendship and refused to give him anything.

Eklavya expected his performance to please his Guru Dronacharya, and he would bless him. He wanted to please his Guru and offered to give him the Dakshina he desired. Dronacharya demanded his thumb as his Guru Dakshina.

Parashuram and Karna shared a close relationship. He gave Karna access to the most advanced weapons. It disappointed him when he discovered that Karna had misled and cheated him.

Draupadi was partial to Arjun, yet he humiliated her by bringing Subhadra to share their home against their agreement. The Pandavas could marry other women, but they would not stay in the home where Draupadi lived. He then went on to not only ignore her but their son too.

Draupadi stood by her husbands and looked after them in exile. She expected that her husbands would fight to avenge her humiliation. She had to seek Krishna's help to ensure that they had not forgotten her humiliation.

Duryodhana depended on Karna to win the war for him. Karna gave away his armour, promised not to kill any Pandava other than Arjun. He did not disclose the secret of his relationship with Kunti. His principal motivation in life was to prove he was a better archer than Arjun. No man deceived Duryodhana as much as Karna.

Ashwatthama another person he befriended to counter the Pandavas brought him grief and shame. He like Karna put himself and his emotions before their friendship.

Blinded by his need to avenge his father's death, he destroyed the next generation of Kurus. He virtually ended the dynasty.

Duryodhana's friendship with Karna and Ashwatthama served a purpose. Each of them had their own agenda, and these were not aligned to his. This not only set them apart but also reinforces an important message—beware of the friends you keep.

Balarama taught both Bhima and Duryodhana to fight with a mace. He was very disappointed with Bhima for violating the rules in his fight. He wanted to kill him for unfairly causing Duryodhana a grievous injury during their mace fight. The relationship between a teacher and a student does not end with the completion of the education. A teacher expects a student will follow his education and make him proud. When Bhima broke the rules, it was not just his failing but the failing of his tutor too. It hurt Balarama's pride as he expected his students to follow the rules he had imparted.

Kunti as a mother of Kshatriyas and the wife of a King was disappointed when Pandavas offered to abandon their fight for Hastinapur. She regarded their offer to settle for five villages as her failure as a parent. They expect a Kshatriya to protect his rights, and if he is a royal, they expect him to protect the rights of those under his protection. The offer for settlement meant they were surrendering their rights. In her view, her children should rather embrace death than live a life of cowards.

In relationships, we can experience hurt because of many factors, as Mahabharata points out. These can be a loss of trust, cheating, suppression of truth, lies, stealing, misconduct, rejection, abandonment, illicit relationship, humiliation, broken promises, loss of assets or rights, conflicting agenda, etc. In the Mahabharata, the only relationship that encounters no hurt is the relationship of soul mates such as between Krishna and Draupadi. The argument could be that both Krishna and Draupadi were divine avatars and therefore experience this exception.

Mahabharata not only provides instances of hurt in several types of relationships, it also offers us instances of how relationships slide up and down the scale.

There are two classic examples of a slide down in relationship between siblings and a slide up in a relationship with friends.

We have the example between Duryodhana, his brother Dushashan and Karna. When the brothers were growing up, they closely bonded and conspired together to deal with the brutality of Bhima. When Duryodhana met Karna, the relationships changed. Dushashan viewed Karna as a courtier and hanger-on, yet the latter would often dissent or give a contrary view at meetings. Dushashan would always support the views of Duryodhana. Duryodhana trusted Karna. He would listen to him, and often concur with him. They enjoyed any-time access and trusted each other completely. He agreed to go to war because he depended on Karna more than his own brothers.

We then have the example of Yudhisthir, Arjun and Krishna. Kunti wanted her sons to respect and abide by the directions of their elder brother. In Hindu thought, they regard the eldest brother as a father figure. They base this on the idea, that on the death of the father, the eldest son takes responsibility as the guardian of the family.

Throughout the initial years, Arjun respected and obeyed his elder brother and in course of these years his friendship with Krishna grew stronger. It was not only friendship but trust too. He picked a non-combatant Krishna over the offer of the famed Narayani Sena. He took up weapons on the advice of Krishna. When Arjun was not committing himself whole-heartedly to fight, Krishna stepped down to take up the battle. This was against his vow. Arjun sought Krishna's forgiveness, promised to do more and begged him to return to the chariot. On the 17th day of the battle, in an argument, Yudhisthir accused Arjun of being a coward and not fighting hard enough. An angry Arjun took up his bow and aimed an arrow at Yudhisthir. Arjun was oath bound to shoot an arrow once strung to the bow. Yudhisthir faced certain death, but Krishna intervened, and Arjun relented. Contrast the reaction of Arjun to the accusations of Krishna and Yudhisthir. When Krishna accuses Arjun of not doing enough, he begs forgiveness and promises to do more, but when accused by his elder brother, he wanted to kill him.

CHAPTER 73

Bhima – The Ideal Husband

It is fascinating that whilst the authors of the Epic had focused on how a woman should choose her husband, towards the end, in their own masterful way, Draupadi picks on one of the Pandavas as her ideal husband.

Draupadi, based on her life experience, urges Bhima to be the firstborn in their next life so they can live a peaceful and happy life. Hindus believe they make marriages in heaven and that it joins a husband and wife in this relationship for seven lives. It is with this belief Draupadi may have wished that Bhima should be born as the eldest in their next life, so that as man and wife they can all live a peaceful and happy life.

Why was Bhima the husband that Draupadi wanted in her next life? Through Bhima, the authors of the Epic provide guidance on that ideal husband.

Bhima left Hidimba after their son was born and returned several years later to get the support of his son for the war, yet Bhima retained Hidimba's love and respect.

At the Game of Dice, Bhima stood up for Draupadi and insulted Yudhisthir for his reckless conduct. He vowed to avenge Draupadi's humiliation and carried it out without guilt or remorse. Arjun was all guns roaring to avenge his son's death in battle, but avenging Draupadi's humiliation was not on his mind when confronting the Kauravas in battle.

Bhima tried to ease Draupadi's pain and suffering during their long period of exile. He would bring her flowers and do his best to bring her relief. Bhima wanted to kill Jayadratha for abducting Draupadi. As a husband, he not only protected her person but would punish anyone who violated her dignity. When Kichaka was accosting Draupadi, Bhima killed him. Bhima kept his promise of avenging her humiliation by killing every Kaurava. He brutally killed Dushashan.

On their final journey, Draupadi fell first, the Pandavas carried on, Bhima fell too, but out of concern for Draupadi he dragged himself towards Draupadi. Though physically spent, he asked if he could be of any help to her and if she wanted anything. She replied asking him to be born the eldest in their next life, so they could all live happily, in peace and security.

Bhima had won over Draupadi's heart with his undying attention and commitment. On her deathbed, Draupadi wanted him, not Arjun and not Karna as others believed.

In one master stroke, the authors not only provide the ultimate guidance to a woman on which amongst the five virtues would serve her best, but also extend this guidance to a man on the way to a woman's heart.

Why could Yudhisthir not recognise that Draupadi shared a deeper emotional bond with Bhima and not with Arjun?

Yudhisthir lacked emotional connect and could never understand women. He staked Draupadi, ignoring her right to dignity and self- esteem. Which man would stake his wife?

Arjun attracted Draupadi, he had won her at her Swayamwar and like his friend Krishna, he was also popular with women. Yet, he married three other women and even forced Draupadi to allow Subhadra to live in their common home. He was also biased in favour of Abhimanyu, often ignoring his son from Draupadi.

Her relationship with Yudhisthir lacked emotional warmth. They were a dutiful couple who together performed all social and religious functions. Draupadi could never forgive him for staking her and violating her dignity as a woman. Their relationship lacked trust and mutual respect.

Bhima, when he was breathing his last, sapped of his strength, still dragged himself to Draupadi to ask her if he could be of any help. Draupadi could trust Bhima, he cared for her; he stood up for her; he was her shield; he comforted her and did small things to please her and bring her some joy in her tough life in exile. He loved her unconditionally, despite her obvious infatuation for Arjun. Shakespeare several centuries later summarized it well in Twelfth Night "Love sought is good, but giv'n unsought is better."

In her final moments, Draupadi desired that in her next life she would prefer Bhima to be born as the eldest, because then they could live a happy, secure and peaceful life.

CHAPTER 74

Krishna in the Mahabharata

Krishna's role in the Mahabharata serves a purpose. As a Vishnu avatar, his purpose on earth was to restore the faith of society in Dharma. He wanted to rid the society of the misinterpretations of Dharma. Society gave the kings the responsibility of protecting and ensuring Dharma. However, some kings mistook vanity or their ego for Dharma. He appears in the Epic to convey the finer points of Dharma and provide valued guidance at other times. Krishna shows to us the importance of each of us having one like him in our lives. Worldwide, people need guidance on a variety of subjects, anyone who fulfils this role as a guide is a Krishna. The creation of Krishna is the biggest gift to humanity. Krishna is a concept of Hindu Thought; that allowed us all to accept that we all need a guide in our lives.

He first appears at the Draupadi Swayamwar. Krishna introduced the idea and importance of Kula in a marriage. Again at his intervention, Subhadra married Arjun and not Duryodhana. Although both were part of the same Kula, he preferred Arjun over Duryodhana. This was because of his upbringing. This upbringing in Hindu thought is referred to as Sanskar. Krishna himself married Rukmini. Her brother fixed her marriage with Sisupala, but she wanted to marry Krishna. Krishna led the way with this example. In his view, a girl must be free to marry the one she chooses.

At Khandavprastha, he and Arjun clear a dense forest for setting up their Capital. As Aryan civilisation was growing, they needed land for settlement and agriculture and to be close to a water source. The razing of forests was crucial for their growth and development. However, razing of forests caused dislocation of natives. It also resulted in the loss of lives, insurgency, revenge killings, etc. At his intervention, they spared Mayasura's life and asked him to build a palace with stones. The Asura used poisoned arrows and then used anti-dotes to revive the wounded attackers. The Aryans could learn many new skills from other communities, and we must not miss this point.

All knew the division of empire was unfair to the Pandavas. They did not get an equal share and had to acknowledge the supremacy of Hastinapur. Krishna appeared again to help them gain independence. He wanted them to hold a Rajsuya Yagna. Progress, independence and growth are a natural path of progression in life. We achieve human progression under the guidance of our parents or mentors. As we progress, we seek and get our independence. It then allows us to achieve growth on our own count.

At the Rajsuya Yagna, they accorded Krishna the highest honour instead of choosing one of the family elders. It would appear they were not showing respect to their elders. However, it symbolises the cutting of the umbilical cord. In life, as we grow up and gain confidence, we desire to move on and achieve growth independently. In our initial stages, we accept and operate under the guidance of our family. However, once we gain confidence, we look to base it on our own creativity. In this endeavour, we may look upon and take the guidance of an outsider who we call a mentor. The Epic suggests that we must show respect to our elders, but for any role, capability and potential must be preferred over age and experience. In such transitions, we may often prefer the wisdom of our mentors over that of family elders. We do so because they often share our vision. Elders offer wisdom based on their experience, this is valuable but as times and circumstances change their experience may not appear relevant. Many a family misunderstanding arises because elders may not realise that their wards do not want to do more of the same thing. Sometimes, because of the change in times and circumstances, the old ways may not achieve the results they now desire. This idea sits well with the concept of Yug Dharma. It requires us to change with the times.

Family or business partitions, break-ups or parting of ways by mutual consent can leave emotional scars and a trust deficit. That which is broken can be fixed but can never be the same. This is because there is hurt and where there is hurt there is anger and treachery, revenge or at least negativity. That is why Krishna would not have allowed the Pandavas to accept the invite to the Game of Dice.

When Krishna appears at the call of a desperate Draupadi during a proposed visit by Sage Durvasa, he resolves her challenge. We can achieve results when we act with conviction and commitment. When both Arjun and Duryodhana come to him for his support, he offers them either his powerful army or himself in a non-combatant role. He left the choice to them. A well-crafted strategy can beat a stronger and resourceful opponent.

Krishna stopped the dithering Pandavas from taking half measures. Why accept five villages in charity when you are entitled to the entire kingdom. During negotiations Krishna claimed the Pandavas were on the side of Dharma whereas the Kauravas were committing Adharma. Duryodhana rejected Krishna's moral judgement and compromise offer. They blamed him for the consequent war. He got for the Pandavas, the moral high ground. He gained sympathy and support for their cause. He could get Kunti to reprimand her sons and set them on the right path. Krishna knew Kunti could resolve the confusion in the minds of her sons. Krishna could get results without having to lead and win the argument.

Krishna offered Jarasandha the option to duel with Arjun the archer or Bhima the wrestler. In his vanity, Jarasandha chose Bhima and consequent death. Krishna's mission on earth was to bring about change. He realised that kings would often confuse vanity and their personal ego with Dharma. On the last day of the war, Yudhisthir asked Duryodhana to duel with any Pandava and the winner would take all. This gamble was unlike Krishna's offer. Krishna taught us the difference between taking a calculated risk and a gamble.

Arjun agreed to join battle only after Krishna revealed his divine self. Yet he killed none of his Kuru relatives except those he held responsible for the death of his son. Krishna could not convince the Yadava clan to stop wasting their life over alcohol and misconduct. We cannot impose Dharma using fear or persuasion, it requires conviction. Krishna takes part in the war, he provides critical inputs, manipulates individuals to either weaken their resolve or get them to act. These masterful interventions point to the value of emotional engagement with people.

He remains cautious even after the war because enmity must end in spirit too. Both Ashwatthama and Dhritarashtra did not let go. Dhritarashtra wanted to avenge the death of his sons by killing Bhima. Ashwatthama wanted to kill the Pandavas to avenge his father's death.

Krishna died a lonely death shot by an arrow on his heels. Alone are we all be born and so shall we be when we die.

CHAPTER 75

The Objectives of Our Epics – A Perspective

We can compare Mahabharata with another epic called the Ramayana and we will find many similarities. In this Epic, Ram, a Vishnu avatar, descends on this earth along with his consort Sita. He is engaged in rescuing his wife from Ravana her abductor. In the Mahabharata, there is no mention of Krishna's consort Radha but only a reference to his senior wife Rukmini. In Southern India, there are temples dedicated to Draupadi where she is worshipped as a Shakti avatar. Hindus lost this knowledge because foreign invaders undermined the worship of female deities. In the Epic, there are no instances of the miracles of Krishna. He is not a cowherd as in other religious books. Krishna in the Epic is a leader of men, who commands respect in both camps. Like all men, he loses his influence and position as a leader. His followers no longer listen to him and he dies a lonely death.

The Mahabharata stands taller as an epic. Krishna, a Vishnu avatar collaborates with Draupadi, an avatar of goddess Shakti. She is the consort of God Shiva. This would have been the basis of their relationship in the Epic. Goddess Shakti has often rescued the universe from oppression and evil. Hindus worship her in the form of Durga, Amba and Kali. In the Epic, they both descend on earth to restore Dharma. This is the first time that an avatar of Shakti and Vishnu were needed for the purpose.

As a result, the events in the Mahabharata were bigger, grander and more complex. Draupadi's Swayamwar was more complex than Sita's. They only expected Ram to lift the bow of Shiva. Arjun not only had to lift the bow, he had to string it and hit the target. Whilst both spent time in exile, the exile of the Pandavas included a year to be spent incognito. Whilst both Sita and Draupadi were abducted in their exile and rescued, Draupadi had to face several hardships. The war in Mahabharata was bigger and caused great misery and loss of lives. Draupadi suffered more personal pain and agony, this included the loss of her sons. Sita had to suffer because of her husband's reaction to a member from his subjects who suspected her of an illicit relationship. Ramayana needed Vishnu and his consort to descend on this earth. The Mahabharata needed Vishnu and the consort of Shiva known for her ability to destroy evil to descend on earth. Ramayana focused on what made a person an ideal son, brother, husband and King. The Mahabharata frames its characters in situations pointing out what we must do and the consequences when we do not. It is an *Itihas* and deals with dharma, sanskar, kula and parampara. At the end of the Mahabharata, the so-called Aryans enter a new Era.

In the Mahabharata, both Vishnu and Shiva through his consort Shakti work together to revive Dharma, which ended all discussions of a rift or divide between them. In the Epic, Krishna removes all those who stand against him or obstruct his efforts in his goal of restoring Dharma. Some amongst them are worshippers of Shiva. However, he is always available to Draupadi and responds to her every call. This is a message to all that there are no differences between him and Shiva. This unity is now integral to Hindu thought. According to the structure of the Hindu Trinity, each serves a purpose and thus conflict is avoided. The structure is open-ended and allows faiths like Jainism, Buddhism amongst others to exist peacefully with it although they may differ in ideas and thoughts.

This is in contrast to the inter-religious differences and intra-religious divides that Abrahamic religions face. This is not about religious tolerance; it arises from its structure. Indic thought allows every individual to accept any guru of their choice as their Krishna. As Hindus are not in a monastic structure, people have the freedom to pursue and propagate as they choose. This sets Hindus apart from other faiths in this world.

Interestingly, at the end of the Mahabharata, we were told that it is the beginning of Kaliyuga. They also tell us when that ends the world as we know it will also end. Yuga means an era.

Mahabharata provides guidance to us on the principles of Dharma, and it uses easy-to-understand examples. It deals with the goals of Artha, Kama and Moksha. It shows the values of upbringing in the form of Sanskar, kula and Parampara. Finally, it promotes diversity at the highest level. As a result, it unites all Hindus despite their choice of a spiritual path or leader. This places Hindu thought where the world accepts and values its Spiritual Wealth, Values and Tolerance. Tolerance promotes diversity. A rule-based system can be repressive, at least to those who differ in their views. The world ignored this contribution and instead chose a path which separates people based on faith. Krishna and Draupadi together left us with a better and tolerant tomorrow. The peace and prosperity attracted the world to our doors. They arrived to plunder the wealth because prosperity is only possible when there is peace.

This artful inclusion of so many thoughts and perspectives on Dharma required the creation of many characters with larger-than-life profiles. The narrative can violate our belief, as it may not always be real and rational. Yet when we reflect beyond these excesses, we discover the Mahabharata provides us with many valuable messages. These remain relevant to our lives and thoughts.

For generations people did not read the Mahabharata, because of a superstitious belief that it could expose the reader's household to strife, rifts and sufferings similar to those experienced by the Kurus. However, without disputing this belief, we cannot ignore its rich content. There is a possibility we may in fact enjoy its readings and learn from it. It is the world's largest poem, which has contributions from so many proponents over centuries. Obviously, it has not just been read, but many have contributed to it and made it richer. The contents are a compilation of thoughts and experiences aggregated by several individuals over their lifetimes. The experiences of several lives cannot be easily understood by one in a lifetime. However, if we read it, it can support and enrich our life. We experience many emotions whilst watching a movie and often empathise with the main characters. The magnum opus that is Mahabharata has several key characters. No one is wholly positive or negative. They are real, and larger than life at other times, but placed in circumstances or situations we could empathise with, learn from or be inspired with.

In Vedic times, Kshatriyas dominated society. They were protectors and upholders of Dharma. In the Ramayana, Vishnu takes birth as Ram, he was a Kshatriya and a King. Dhaumya was a priest and was engaged in preserving the sacrificial fire for the Pandavas. He performed yagna and sacrifices, educated and offered advice to people. Brahmins were advisors, whereas the King was responsible for upholding Dharma. In the war, they killed all the Kshatriyas. This was once again symbolic. It marked a new era in leadership. It now limited the responsibility of a King to running the country. They expanded the role and responsibility of Brahmins to upholding of Dharma. This is the new era that is often referred to in the Epic. It heralded the transformation of Society and allocated the leadership of the faith to those who were involved in the study of their faith. This change in role and responsibility was probably a response to the challenges it faced from monastic religions.

The Vedic gods descended on this earth in the form of humans. They took birth because of Kunti's boon. Indra was born as Arjun, Yama was Yudhisthir, and Vayu was Bhima. They all accepted the leadership of Vishnu born as Krishna on earth. Surya in his earthly form was Karna, and he refused to join the Pandavas and support Krishna. Karna was a dissident and Arjun killed him in the battle. We all know this was on the advice of Krishna. As no human could conduct the last rites of a God, Krishna conducted it. In fact, there is no mention of a last rite of any Pandava. Surya as Karna refused to help Krishna on a point of principle. However, in another avatar he sided with

Krishna. Krishna and Arjun used Agni or fire to clear the forest for setting up Indraprastha. Krishna defeated Varuna, and he helped fuel the fire in the forest. After Dronacharya annexed half of Panchal, a humiliated Drupad returned to Panchal and performed a yagna. At this yagna, Gods blessed him with a son who would kill Dronacharya and avenge his humiliation. From the yagna's Agni emerged Dhrishtadyuma, while Draupadi arose from the container at the end of the ceremony. Dhrishtadyumna participated in the fight, which was also a Dharma Yudh. Kubera's status was given to Lakshmi. They now regard her as the goddess of Wealth. Nakul and Sahadev were the combined spirit of Soma and Surya, and they also accepted the leadership of Krishna. All the Gods of Vedic period in human embodiment accepted Krishna's leadership. They dealt with the dissidents and thus started a new era of Spiritualism or Bhakti. The concept of Bhakti requires a Bhakt or a follower. In times to come, Hindus followed Gurus or Sadhus or Spiritual Leaders. They elevated some of these leaders to the status of Vishnu Avatar.

The Epic also focuses on the values of Kula, Sanskar and Parampara. These ideas are unique to Hindu thought. Its influence defines and distinguishes each of us. Every family or Kula is known, based on their *Itihas* or history. No negativity is associated with this term as it only refers to a family. The exposure and guidance we receive from our Kula form the basis of our Sanskar. Our responses are often the outcome of our Sanskar. We need to draw guidance from precedents so our actions reflect not only our Sanskar but also our Kula; they call this approach Parampara. The word Parampara is not about tradition. It encompasses our emotional and social conduct based not just on heritage or history but also on the succession of knowledge obtained and passed on from a generation to the next. Itihas, Parampara, Kula and Sanskar are the Principal Pillars of our lives. It moulds our character, influences our thoughts, and defines us. The Epic helps us realise Dharma cannot be constant. Our behaviour is the outcome of several influences. However, we must use Dharma to make the right choice.

We must reflect on the Mahabharata as it can apply to our contemporary lives. It provides us with the basis for our actions. When we base our actions on our conviction, it is driven by our thoughts. We base them on our unique circumstances. Acting against our will or conviction, or acting in conformity with convention, can cause emotional stress. Then again, we can suffer from material stress that is caused by our needs, wants and desires. When we adopt non-conventional methods, it forces us to act against our inner voice or to accept acts against our will for the fulfilment of our wants. This can also cause stress. Conviction is the anti-dote for Stress. Meditation and prayers can only provide momentary relief.

The Mahabharata uses Dronacharya as an example. He adopts many methods to achieve his material wants, needs and desires. He takes part in the war because duty and convention bind him. He knows wars leads to death and misery. The emotional stress of learning that his son is the killed in battle overwhelms him. He drops his weapons and is killed. Mahabharata uses symbolism, emotional stress caused his death. Emotional stress is potent and can kill. Many people in the Mahabharata died in battle. It was in their Dharma, but only Dronacharya dropped his weapons out of emotional stress. He submitted himself to death out of stress.

Mahabharata deals with the principles of Dharma, the importance of Parampara, and Sanskar. It deals with the need for Satya or truth and the influence of *moh maya* or attachment and Karma in our Life. It advises us to act based on our conviction. It wants us to take the help of our Itihas, Parampara and Kula to reach our final destination. This destination is peace of mind or nirvana or moksha.

The Epic points out that as each of us are uniquely abled, it is wrong to expect the same outcome. Finally, it tells us to not desire all in life as "I, me and mine," but instead to accept reality as "I, me and that which is not mine."

❏❏❏

GARUDA PRAKASHAN BOOKS

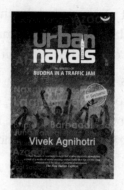

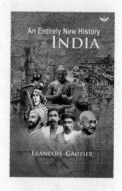

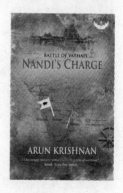

About the Author

Born in Kolkata, Bharat Thakker lives in London. In a prior career spanning over 30 years, he has led businesses in India, the UK, and the UAE. In this book, he focuses on the Mahabharata's relevance and application to contemporary thought. He brings out the Epic's invaluable messages.

For more about his work, please visit www.mahabharataseries.com